Of Foreign Build

Jackie Parry

© Copyright Jackie & Noel Parry 2024

All rights reserved.
The copyright of this book belongs to Jackie & Noel Parry.
No reproduction without permission.

ISBN: 978-0-9875515-3-5

To Noel, with love.

Contents

Preface 1
Introduction 3
MARIAH II 5
Niue Customs clearance papers ("...one female, foreign built...") 8
1. Just get me home 9
2. Responsible adults? 14
3. Crash landing 20
4. "Uhhhhm, arrrhhhhh" 27
5. The Storm 37
6. Advent of adventure 43
7. Restoring my faith in the world 58
8. Playing with orangutans 68
9. Singapore Sling 87
10. Simple food and clear water 94
11. Undies scrutinised 106
12. Lightning storm at the Nicobars 117
13. Pirates! 126
14. Egyptian sand storm 143
15. Finally ignored 172
16. Noel fulfils a life-long dream 195
17. Whale collision 205
18. Working in a brothel 226
19. Sinking in Florida 240

20. Dolphins	272
21. Man-eating crocs and muggers	281
22. Galapagos	296
23. Swimming with a whale	302
24. Absent from society, but not for long	332
25. "I hate it"	335
Time Line	342
Map of our route	348
Glossary of Nautical Terms	350
From the Author	358
Acknowledgements	359
Other reading:	360

Preface

Sailing oceans is not like a plane or car ride. Nothing is certain except a vast puddle of water and a great stretch of sky.

The days pass, measured not in hours, but in distance.

It's dynamic, fantastic, and petrifying all at the same time.

There is rarely pattern or logic; you deal with what's received, as it arrives... moment by moment.

Noel Parry

Introduction

I've written this book with Noel's help. This is my story, and it must not detract from the amount of work, ideas, resourcefulness, and responsibility Noel completed and bore during our time on *Mariah*. He was the backbone to the entire adventure.

Mariah was officially *Mariah II* – I have omitted the 'II' often, for ease of reading. I have also included a glossary of nautical terms I have used, at the back of the book.

If you'd like to view some pictures of our adventures, please visit: www.jackieparry.com and hover your mouse over books, there you can select which book and photo album you'd like to view.

MARIAH II

Mariah II was a tough but pretty boat and she felt very homely within her timber cabin. She looked after us in bad weather and taught us a lot.

Double diagonal Kauri, cutter rigged sloop with a canoe stern:

Owned us from 1998 – 2006
Length Overall: 12 metres
Deck length: 10 metres
Beam: 3.4 metres
Draft: 1.5 metres

Specifications:
- Designer: Blom
- Year of manufacture: 1985
- Similar to Colin Archer design
- Builder: Henderson
- Built in New Zealand
- Deck material: ply-epoxy
- Kauri cold moulded
- Kauri & Rimu interior
- Flush deck
- Hard dodger
- Full keel, cut away fore-foot
- Displacement: 9.5 tonnes
- S/Steel/lead keel

Engine:
- Yanmar 40hp (fitted new 2000) Model: 3JH3E

- Diesel
- Cylinders: 3
- Flexi drive shaft coupling
- 85W alternator on engine
- Dual filter fuel system
- Fresh water cooling
- Max speed: 7 knots
- Cruise speed 5.5 knots

Tanks:
- Aluminium diesel tank (225 litres)/ inspection hatch
- 260 litre water tanks (2 fibreglass, 1 bladder)

Equipment:
- 80W solar panel
- Electric auto-helm
- Aries wind vane

Mariah's set of sails

Main	Luff - 34'
	Leech – not known
	Foot – 17.9'
Yankee	Luff - 38'
	Leech – 28'
	Foot – 13.10'
Staysail	Luff – 27'
	Leech – 25'
	Foot – 9.6'
Genoa	Luff – 38'
	Leech – 38.9'
	Foot – 22.4'

Area	Main – 327 sq/ft
	Yankee – 155 sq/ft
	Staysail – 120 sq/ft
	Working area of 602 sq/ft
Genoa	425 sq/ft

From what we know Mariah was built by Henderson in Picton. The designer was Frank Blom. She was fitted out in Wellington, New Zealand.

Mariah then sailed the Pacific, with her original owners who had her for approximately ten to eleven years. They sold her to someone in Tin Can Bay, who had her approximately one to two years, with plans of sailing to England, but he met a new girl and Mariah didn't venture very far. We purchased her in 1998.

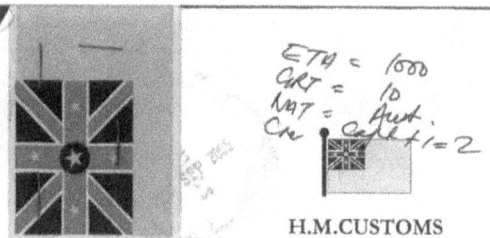

H.M.CUSTOMS

NIUE ISLAND

CERTIFICATE OF CLEARANCE

Port of *Alofi*, Niue Island.

This is to certify that, *Captain* Parry NOEL

Master or Commander of the yacht " **MARIAH II**" burthen with 10.00 gross tonnage, navigated with 1 female, foreign built, bound for ***VAVAU/TONGA*** has entered and cleared his said vessel according to the law and is hereby granted a Customs Clearance. Given under my hand at the Customs Office at the **Port of Alofi** in **Niue Island** the 22th September 2005

COLECTOR OF CUSTOMS

1

Just get me home

The grey, cool room held so much sadness that the old mismatched furniture had absorbed the heavy look of grief. The dim light, respectful of the injustices it revealed below seemed to watch the surreal story painfully unfold. Martin sat staring at nothing. His pale cheeks carried rivulets of salty tears. With faces creased in concern the nurse and counsellor looked from Martin to me. I sat looking at Martin trying to take in the awful news.

We had just spent three months in America pulling our lives back together after Martin beat leukaemia into remission. The night before we flew back home, to the UK, Martin complained about a back pain. We tried to make jokes about him pulling a muscle, but at dinner Martin just sat and silently cried into his plate. He knew. The journey home was almost unbearable, there were hours of delay which led to Martin becoming increasingly uncomfortable. This caused the stewardesses to become alarmed. They didn't want an emergency situation on board during the flight. They talked to us quietly.

'We have to know if you can make this journey,' they said. Their eyes betrayed their concern.

'Just get me home,' said Martin.

Throughout the journey, every hour the pain increased and was met with yet another passenger offering a pill. It was quite remarkable to see all the different types of medications available on board from our fellow travellers. It provided a moment of amusement within our little world of hell. I was helpless.

We arrived back into the UK and the next day I had returned to work while Martin went to hospital. Overnight, the pain relief drugs had helped. At 11 am that morning he called me. The back ache had revealed the disease's subterfuge over the months. He said, 'I have two weeks to live.'

The next minute I was in the hospital room with him, where so many people before us had lived out this awful drama. Now it was our turn to re-enact the tragic scene. But, in the tangible gloom of the winter day, all I wanted to do was hold him, protect him, and make it all go away. But I just sat there stunned, uselessly saying, 'Don't cry.' The gloomy rain tapped against the window. He looked at me, the sadness palpable. He said, 'Will you marry me before I die?'

Two days later, while I held his hand in utter disbelief, Martin left this world. Our wedding plans forever on hold. Death is so quiet.

Six months later, assaulted with a confusion of emotions in my lonely north London flat, I resigned from my job and packed my bags. I needed to get as far away as I could from the tortuous memories. To reach another land at another time in history was not possible, so Australia became my destination. I did everything my counsellor said I must not do – I ran away.

Though I had removed myself from the memories, I hadn't distanced myself from the hurt. A new relationship was not on my agenda. No one had said that the emotional pain from bereavement would actually, physically hurt. I had a pain in my stomach, and I was desperate for release, which was peculiar and in opposition with the aching barrenness. I'd watched a perfectly healthy (so we thought) man slowly die.

The vacant hurt that clung to my innards eventually gave way, but did not vanish. It was replaced with deep anger at the injustice. I wanted to blame, shout, and scream; I wanted answers. None came.

I, like millions of people before me, had to ride it out. I felt lost, detached like a leaf that was constantly pushed and spun around in the wind. My emotions buffeted me along; I could not think. I could only follow whatever force it was that led me to put one foot in front of the other.

While riding out these all too vivid emotions that left me wrung out and sometimes desperately sobbing, begging for Martin to come and get me, I met someone. Noel and I were in every way a 'rebound' couple; we were both confused by the twist of a new relationship that somehow simultaneously made no sense and perfect sense.

Sitting on my emotional roller coaster, it felt odd to feel drawn to a rather strange, true blue Aussie. I had met Noel a few days after landing on the other side of the world. What confounded me more was that he seemed to have every relationship turn-off I could think of. He was a divorcee. He had kids. There was a substantial age difference between us (sixteen years, though quite often I am the more mature), and he sported a rather thick beard. As a wandering soul, who had not quite found his place in life, Noel could not have been more different from an unworldly, shy 'English Rose.' Despite the clashing of two worlds, every wobbly particle of my being egged me on to be near him.

Meanwhile my head said, 'Whoa, rebound.'

We had met through family; actually we're related. Uncle Noel and I are intrinsically linked through marriage, not blood. Having family in Australia meant a straightforward welcome and a gentle introduction in to a new culture. It also meant a new connection for us both that would transport us into a movie-like adventure and, eventually, into an inner tranquillity I have only read about.

I spent three months in Australia, partly travelling along the east coast and partly travelling with Noel. At the end of a remarkable journey, where I fell deeply in love with one man while grieving for another, I returned to the UK for a whirlwind three weeks in Hertfordshire, where I had grown up. I had a brand new car and a rather nice apartment to deal with, and a multitude of goodbyes.

My parents had long ago accepted I was different: 'flighty,' I think is fair. In fact, I'm constantly amazed that my parents still talk to me at all after my wayward teenage years and my inability to settle – but that's another story. They weren't at all surprised when I revealed I was going back to Australia. Without a single question or thought, they offered their complete support and love.

'As long as you're happy,' they said.

They're pure gold in human form.

Not once did I question my decision. During drunken, painful farewells with friends and tearful, wrenching goodbyes with close family, I had not one doubt. Even the heart-raw farewells with my niece and nephew didn't give me pause. Their fear of a barmy aunt in the family were totally confirmed when I blubbed on their shoulders.

'Why are you going if it makes you cry?' my nephew's wide, slightly fearful eyes seemed to hold many questions, as he tried to peel off my clinging arms.

'I dunno,' I sobbed, covertly wiping my nose on his skinny shoulder. What could I say? 'There's this old, hairy man waiting for me the other side of the world, I have no idea why, but I have to be with him!'

Actually, I knew why, he made me laugh. Not just giggle or snigger from time to time, but a full, belly aching, wet knickers guffaw. On occasions, I made him laugh too, though sometimes it was a little embarrassing, as it was usually when I was trying to be serious.

2

Responsible adults?

The first major decision Noel and I had to make as a couple was how we were going to live. Not so much the financial aspect, but what to do. We were both disillusioned with life and we didn't really know what path to take to help fulfil our lives. We had some savings between us, so initially money was not an issue, however our funds would be gone before too long if we weren't a bit careful. So, we did what responsible adults should do: purchased camping gear, hopped on Noel's BMW motorbike and explored the glorious east coast of Australia. I was adamant that I was not going back into an office; Noel felt the same with his building/carpentry trade. After watching a young life stolen, I felt as though I had been given a second chance. I was not going to waste it in an office. As with all great plans, two months later we found ourselves heavily ensconced in Sydney, in an office and on a building site respectively.

During an evening stroll, amid an Australian residency discussion, Noel turned to me and smiled, 'Will you marry me?'

Although short on soft music, rose petals and champagne, the ambience was on par with its simplicity, surprise and emotion that oozed from his eyes.

'Yes,' I said, with an enormous smile on my face that made my cheeks ache.

We slipped into an innocuous little Italian restaurant at The Rocks and ate plain Spaghetti Bolognaise and drank cheap red wine. It was truly a magnificent feast filled with dreams, hopes, and huge grins. It may be that the residency dilemma had nudged the question of marriage further forward in our minds, but we both knew we wanted to be together. With a new, unexpected love, all obstacles were just minor bumps. We were married just a few weeks later. It was a private affair with close friends, family from Australia and my family from the UK, who, with little notice, dropped everything to be with us.

On a sparkling winter's day, standing on the vibrant Kiama headland in New South Wales (NSW), while looking over the deep azure ocean, we exchanged promises that would bind stronger and fiercely earnest over time.

Overlooking the ocean and its distant horizons on our special day came to mean so much more to us. Who knew we'd be seeking out those very horizons on a small boat.

Noel had grown up around sailboats and spent a considerable amount of time convincing me that buying and living on a boat was a good idea. I was keen, but I wanted to build our financial foundations first – hence the work-for-someone-else mistake. After six weeks in a dull office, I rang Noel to tell him I was resigning. I was a temp, but the boss had asked me to become permanent. Sitting behind a brown desk, hemmed within beige walls, telephones ringing, printers clacking, I could have been in any office, anywhere in the world. The word 'permanent' made the hairs on the back of my neck stand up. We decided to talk about it that evening. I struggled through the afternoon, dreaming of sailing into sunsets. It would become a common theme in our relationship: Noel would have an idea and after I'd digested it, I'd do my best to make it reality. Sometimes, this bought us both close to catastrophe and it often led us towards the most incredible adventures.

We found that our best decisions were made after several beers; the amber nectar become an excellent tonic for chewing over facts, making informed decisions, and then reaching a point where just about anything sounded like a darn good idea.

However, Noel shocked me that night.

'I'm just starting to like my job.' He was out of his depth with this new emotion. Noel's work record made a jumping bean look positively placid. It was Thursday night, and we made an executive decision that a more serious drinking session over the weekend was needed to make such a big decision. The next morning, on a gloriously sunny Friday, Noel called me at work and said, 'I've just resigned; sod this for a lark, let's go buy a boat.' And that is just what we did.

We had shed the drudgery of nine-to-five employment like a streaker relishing in the ultimate freedom, and we went searching for a boat.

'Ready to go,' was popular advertising spiel. Though in truth, stepping aboard a 'ready to go' vessel left me wondering, 'Ready to go where?' Dark, dank living quarters, creaking timbers, and nose curling smells excited me as much as navel fluff. But I didn't say much, because what did I know?

Noel would discuss beams (width of boat), LOA (length over all), and draft (depth) with the owners, and I would start to yawn. I had extracted myself from a protective cocoon of familiarity and plunged into a world where they spoke a type of English, but I had no idea what they were saying. Noel thought I was bored; I became incredibly shy. I tried to hide my ignorance and felt quite scared at being considered stupid. I was way out of my depth. It was a daunting time as I was just about the furthest I could be from home with no friends (except Noel), in a brand new relationship I was still finding my way in, and now I was immersed in the nautical world. Nobody could have conceivably looked, sounded, or felt less like a sailor than me.

Noel had an insurmountable quantity of patience, and with his calm, relaxed demeanour he started to teach me. After looking at the twentieth boat that was fit for firewood, we decided to take a break and took a trip to see family in the northern part of NSW. I was still trying to grasp what 'sailing' was all about, so before we set off on the four-hour bike ride I asked Noel, 'What's so great about sailing anyway?'

'Getting to port.'

I could feel the creases deepening on my forehead, but so as not to be put off, I asked, 'What does it all cost?' thinking about our budget plans.

'Everything we've got,' came the reply. The creases now hurt as they carved their way across my eyebrows.

I didn't talk to Noel for the rest of the day. Close together on the motorbike, we felt miles apart.

The following day, I had another go. 'Well, why the hell do it then?'

Noel grinned, 'There's always a good pub in the next port.'

'Good grief,' I replied, my conversation held no bounds.

To avoid another twenty-four hours of baffled silence, Noel added, 'Actually I can't think of a better way to live; it's the closest thing to freedom I have ever experienced.'

Now *that* worked for me.

In August 1998, three months later, we became the proud owners of *Mariah II*. A thirty-three foot cutter rigged sloop, which is a sailboat with one mast. With all the charm of timber, we immediately felt at home. Oddly enough, when we stepped on board, I was the first to say, 'I think we've just found our boat.' At this point, my sailing career consisted of climbing onto umpteen vessels at anchor, being bamboozled with boat speak, and gazing at gadgets and doodads that looked like they should live on a space rocket. I was relieved when Noel felt the same.

'We'd better have a proper look at her then.' The corners of his mouth twitched with excitement. Our idea was starting to show some promise.

I remember thinking, *look at all this space in the boat – I am never going to fill all these cupboards.* That just about sums up my ignorance at that point. As well as weeks of supplies, we would stuff the cupboards full of every conceivable spare part we could muster.

People who own sail-boats are deemed to be rich. This could not be further from the truth for most. Most people who live on their boats are financially challenged. It's been likened to putting your money in one big pile and setting it alight. As soon as you get more money, you just add it to the flames. It's not always the maintenance that's the problem; it's the fact that there are such yummy, exciting things to buy all the time. There is no end to the gadgets you can purchase. All of which can be argued to increase safety and therefore, 'We must have it!'

The freedom we acquired was mind-boggling. In the beginning, I didn't know what to do with myself. Noel was a bit perplexed when I offered to write a project plan. Old habits made me feel comfortable; listing our daily jobs, writing budget spread sheets, and organising weekly progress meetings. I really didn't have a clue about boating life. The regulated, regimented lifestyle I was used to didn't exist anymore. Now I could choose what I did and when I did it. Ironically, the problem now was what to do and when to do it!

My way of life was not just changing: my whole ethos morphed into a different world. Hair became something to pile on top of my head, clothes were comfy, and fashion was no longer in my vocabulary or on my back. I became a fan of charity shops. Our budget was as elastic as wet cardboard and just as and fragile, so these places were ideal to keep a girl happy.

Tenaciously, I hung on to something familiar: organising my life on bits of paper. Phones, computers, and faxes were replaced with boat-to-boat radios, second-hand novels, and dinghies. I had no practical experience of painting and fixing. My most technical operation achieved was hitting the stereo when the CD drawer wouldn't open, or turning the power off and on again on my laptop when it stopped working. Then there was boat-speak – it was so strange.

'Hand me the painter,' people would say. In my head this would evoke vivid images of a tall, dark Italian man with an open, cotton shirt splattered with coloured paints. Cruelly, reality brought me down with a thud when I found out that the 'painter' was the bit of rope on the bow of a dinghy. I could see I was going to struggle and withdrew further.

My discomfort was not just from the new way of life, a new husband, culture, and country to adjust to. With my new found freedom and more time on my hands, I had the opportunity to think: who am I? And, scarily, how do other people see me? The things I said, I analysed with frightening results. I had no idea who I really was.

Within this quagmire of unfamiliar emotions I notched up my tenacity. I am competitive; I don't like to be beaten. My entire faith in Noel, and the fact that I knew I'd laugh about all this one day, kept me at it. However, my ignorance evolved to new levels that approached dangerous. Just a few hours after becoming the proud owners of *Mariah*, we nearly smashed her in half.

3

Crash landing

Losing control and almost smashing up a fifty-five thousand dollar, ten tonne boat was quite exhausting. At the time, Noel and I had owned *Mariah*, our new home, for just forty-eight hours. My knowledge of sailing was on a par with my knowledge of moon landings. My first twenty-four hours at sea had been hair-raising. The thoughts of smooth seas, full sails, and clear skies were viciously blown away and replaced with a three-dimensional lurching, bumping, bucking, and gyrating hell. In an instant, I was all at once in disbelief, scared, and amazed. We had just one inch of timber between us and several miles of deep, dark, cold salty water. How *Mariah* remained in one piece astounded me.

We set off on an overnight trip to Brisbane from Tin Can Bay. Bouncing out into the ocean I sat in the corner of our small cockpit and fought the growing nausea. Looking out into the dark, threatening sky I noticed the fingers of vivid lightning sparking closer. Noel was on deck, and when he returned to the cockpit I found the energy to look up into his face just in time to watch him throw up over the side.

'Just great,' I muttered. Swallowing my fear, I was able to string a couple of words together.

'Is it always this rough?' I asked. Noel swallowed heavily.

'Actually, this isn't rough,' he said as he wiped spittle from his chin. I spent the night whimpering in the corner, thoroughly regretting the whole boat idea. Neither of us slept.

As dawn tickled the sky, we reached Brisbane River, awash with relief to be in flat, protected water. As we puttered along, watching the city slowly awaken, the flaming sun struck purple on the tall city buildings.

That wasn't so bad, I thought.

Approaching the small marina, Noel had given me clear instructions on how to handle the lines. This was my first attempt at helping to dock the boat. I leapt off and managed to hold on to both the fore and aft lines. I was rather pleased with myself. Then Noel piped up, 'I'm coming in on a bit of an angle, just chuck the ropes back on board, I'll come around again.' I shrugged and threw the lines back on the deck. *This is easy*, I thought, standing safely on a jetty. Feeling proud as punch, with a little happy-smile, I looked up to see my new boat and my new husband careering down the river, sideways. Noel stood in the cockpit reflecting the situation quite well by pulling tufts of hair out of his head. The four-knot current whisked them both away.

With a muttered expletive, I raced along with them as best I could on land while watching my home and husband teeter on the edge of disaster. The jetty I stood on was locked, and I literally dragged a half-naked man from his boat, demanding him to unlock the gate immediately. Running along the water's edge, I could see my new husband and new boat heading for a rather large concrete wall. Noel grabbed a post and managed to tie up under the watchful eyes of several cruisers and half the population of Brisbane city that stood by to watch the three-ring-circus. I had caught up with *Mariah* by then, and as Noel grabbed a post alongside the concrete wall, I took the opportunity to hop back on board. Noel nearly jumped out of his skin. He hadn't seen me get back on board and did a double take at my presence and said, 'How'd you get here?'

Suddenly, several grinning, rather hairy men appeared from other boats in an array of dinghies and offered to tow us onto the pilings; they had been watching the display of how not to go cruising.

We couldn't stay against the wall – the tide was rising rapidly. With some reluctance to hand ourselves back into the clutches of the current, we let go of our haven. Fellow cruisers valiantly tried to tow us in their rubber dinghies, but the small boats couldn't get any purchase and *Mariah's* ten tonnes pulled them back alongside us. Suddenly, we were heading side-on to a large, solidly embedded concrete piling. It felt as though it was going to go straight through the middle of our boat – which we had owned for less than two days.

'Fend off,' was screamed from somewhere, and we all did our best. The piling stopped us in our tracks, and the solid hull of double diagonal timber planks stayed in one piece, suffering superficial wounds only. With several hands scrabbling to tie us up, so we were no longer a menace within the tightly packed boats, we were finally safe. The breath I had been holding, for what felt like hours, could finally be released. On further inspection, we learned that a cush drive had sheered on the engine, which meant we had no forward or reverse propulsion. This chaos was the cause of our eleven o'clock beers that morning and my look back along the slightly frenzied winding path of my life to figure out why the hell I was there.

The purple dawn lights that stroked along the skyscrapers were now replaced by a brilliant white reflection of sun igniting glass. The Brisbane River was as calm as a koala, and after coming uncomfortably close to destroying our new boat, we were safely tied up to a piling; the adrenaline was now replaced with weary relief.

'So, how long have you been sailing?' Our saviour and newfound friend asked as we gratefully sipped a cool beer as if it contained life-saving properties.

I pointedly looked at my watch.

'Oh, nearly twenty-four hours now.' I expected sympathy and congratulations on surviving my introduction to life on board.

Instead, he smiled. 'Welcome to sailing,' he said, with not a hint of irony.

I decided to sit quietly for a while.

That summer in Brisbane, the temperature hovered around an uncomfortable thirty degrees, but the boating community was great, galloping fun. Tied between the pilings, boats from all over the world tugged against their lines while the city unfolded around us each morning. Each day the river ferries sliced past the moored boats while the botanical gardens received their regular drink from the sprinklers; the calming sights were all wrapped up in a delicious aroma of coffee from the glut of funky cafes.

Showers and laundry were part of the facilities, as was the dinghy dock. The manicured botanical gardens that stretched out along the banks were like our own, and the city was small enough to hold on to its charming character.

Kindred spirits would sit outside the brown brick shower block, on green peeling wooden benches, talking boats and gadgets. The dinghies gently rocked together and against the floating jetty. It was a quaint and peaceful existence all for about fifteen dollars (Australian) a week. Christmas came and went with an 'Orphans in the Park' party. Most people living on the river had left their family behind to break away from society or to simply take some time out to travel. We all congregated in the grassy gardens, making enough food to feed however many on each of our own boats, resulting in a huge banquet style feast. Silly presents were exchanged and daft games played. I revelled in my new life.

After just a few weeks, with the engine repairs complete, it was time to break free for a while. We enjoyed our time in Brisbane city, but the cruising community had its highs and lows. The incessant, conflicting advice became a bore. Noel had years of experience under his belt, but some cruisers would talk to us as if we were three-years-old. I was a beginner, but I didn't need to be talked to as if I was a baby. I knew diddlysquat about boats, sailing, weather, and navigation: I soon found out that there is nothing some 'old-hands' enjoy more than a new fledgling to break in.

Some days I would be lectured at and smiled at condescendingly. 'You'll have to learn how to do the dishes in cold water,' was one I remember well. *How would it be different?* I thought, *do the plates and cutlery behave differently in cold water?* Perhaps they complain.

One couple would frown at me when I said, 'She's a wooden boat.'

'Timber,' they'd say with a superior smile.

I now know that people were, in the main, trying to give me an idea of what to expect. I only saw it as them having the chance to highlight my ignorance.

Noel would placate my frustration. 'It doesn't matter if you call things orange marmalade, as long as we both call whatever it is the same name.'

Despite this, our time in Brisbane was one of our most memorable summers. We quickly made some lifelong friends and had one of the most social times of our lives.

Living on a boat is like stripping your life of several complications and adding a whole new different set. Once you've got a handle of this weird floating world, the new set of complications are exciting and rewarding. Firstly, forget any sort of luxuries. Of course, buckets of money would buy you anything you needed, but we're talking reality here. Our reality was a thirty-three foot boat, which was eleven feet wide – not much room to start with.

Below we had a galley (the kitchen), which for a small boat was quite sizeable. Squeezed in was a small oven and two burners, which ran on gas, a tiny sink, and lots of midget size cupboards. We had a navigation table big enough to lay charts on, surrounded by equipment I had yet to learn how to use. The saloon was our lounge and held a fixed-in table, two 'bunks' (settees which doubled as our beds when at sea), and a small pot belly burner, which I thought we'd never use because I was not going anywhere that cold (time would prove me wrong, of course). It was agony to try and watch anything on our small TV, as swinging three-hundred-and-sixty degrees on anchor meant that the shows were more snow, lines, and fuzz than clear pictures. There was a loo, which was called the 'head' (apparently in the time before the loo was invented the crew used to do their business at the head of the boat, over the side). A small work-bench sat opposite the head, where some of our good clothes hung above. Lastly, there was the v-berth. The v-berth is the front pointy bit, shaped like a 'v' – this is where we slept when not at sea. The engine sat under the cockpit. We call the deck our veranda for no better reason than to pretend we are wealthy enough to have such a thing.

Noel soon became my best friend and a strong supporter when he saw signs of me becoming withdrawn and shy. He'd send me off to the chandlery on my own to buy the simplest of things.

I always thought that I could step into anything new and be able to do it straight away or without much effort. That thought was fading fast, and it was a little scary. I was enjoying part of my new independence, but I hated the fact that I didn't know much about the nautical world and it would take a lot of time and effort to become proficient. I had fallen into the trap of becoming bored with the cruising life, as I didn't understand my environment. I didn't once think of enrolling in a course, or reading more on the subject. Everything was so new, so scary, so unknown, it turned me into a behavioural idiot.

Fortunately, Noel was patient with me and explained everything he was doing on the boat and why, soon he re-awakened my interest. I think I would have been a gibbering wreck in the corner, dribbling occasionally, if it wasn't for Noel's support.

4

"Uhhhhm, arrrhhhhh"

Noel and I gelled on the boat, and we started to work well together. Initially, though, the cross co-habitation of an Aussie and a Brit meant we had one or two communication problems.

'I've got a problem with my doobrie,' I said one day and had, apparently, used that word a lot.

'Okay, we'll go to the quack,' said Noel.

'What?'

'To check out ya plumbing,' he explained.

'What bloody plumbing?' In despair, I took on the Aussie vernacular, 'And what the hell's a quack?'

'Aren't you having trouble with ya doobrie?'

'I'm talking about this bowline knot doobrie you want tied.' I had become exasperated.

'Ahh, I always thought you meant girly stuff when you said doobrie,' Noel said rather sheepishly.

'Doobrie means anything,' I explained through the laughter, 'I just can't remember the right word sometimes, so I say doobrie, same as thingamajig, dooffa, whatsaname – doobrie!'

Likewise, Noel would say, 'Let's get some snags,' (sausages) and I would think, 'Will it hurt?' I soon became accustomed to the lazy Aussie language to a point where I considered myself bi-lingual, translating European English to Aussie English. I also became used to Noel referring to doctors as quacks.

We pried ourselves away from our secure haven in Brisbane and set off on an adventure into Moreton Bay. The enormous area was littered with shallows, but had the luxury of flat water, the islands offering protection from any large curling waves and the pumping ocean swell. The engine was fixed, but my nerves still twanged with tension, there was so much to learn.

In calm weather, we enjoyed some sedate sailing. *I think I'm going to like this*, I thought.

We had time to play with sails, so I learned how to haul up the mainsail and reef it down to a smaller size. I played with the foresails, furling them in and out. Time, appointments, and structure were blissfully shed and forgotten.

As the evening crept up on us, we searched the charts for a suitable anchor site. Anchoring was yet another new experience, which meant I sat back and supposedly learned, while Noel ran around like a headless chicken doing umpteen jobs on a boat he hardly knew. As we approached our selected anchor site, we silently glided past another boat that had already anchored and was lying at a rather precarious angle. The tide had lowered and the boat was aground on the sand. 'What a stupid thing to do,' we both muttered.

We found our spot. The glassy sea was mellow and Noel put *Mariah* in neutral. As she eased to a leisurely stop, he raced up to the bow to release the anchor, which fell about a metre, stopping just above the water. After much jiggling and muttering, he managed to release the chain a bit further and the anchor hit the water, only to stop running out again. More jiggling, pulling, swearing, and about ten metres came out. Finally, Noel's colourful language was enough to turn the air blue and his face red, and he managed to release enough chain for us to anchor securely.

'Deppy,' our creatively named depth sounder, was a bit reluctant to work for his new owners, but after deciphering the varying flashing numbers, we thought we had enough water beneath us. Noel checked the rest of the anchor chain below decks and found it to be in one big knot. The next two hours was spent untwisting the heavy, rusting links.

Dusk approached and the sun started her descent behind the flat seas; the soft blues and gentle yellows that are unique to Australia tinged our tired faces. The red wine and satisfaction of a successful day's sailing cloaked us comfortably. Although the bay was calm and flat, I noticed that I could still feel the boat move beneath me. I could suddenly see why boats were referred to as a living thing; in the water they are always moving, sometimes like soft breaths, hardly noticeable, but nonetheless there.

As darkness started to envelope us in our contained heaven, Noel asked, 'Does *Mariah* feel funny to you?'

With my two months experience, I tried to grasp what he was talking about.

'Erm, no not really,' I replied, a little perplexed.

Noel checked the depth sounder and then jumped up and down on deck. He ran from one side of the deck to the other.

Odd behaviour, I thought, but let him get on with it; I was in the reliable company of a rather nice red.

With an embarrassed smile, tinged with a flicker of worry, he said, 'We're aground.'

I glanced back at the other boat that we had passed earlier that was sitting at an odd angle. Now, it was even further on its side, and I realised we had done exactly the same thing. 'What happens now?' I asked, the catch in my throat revealing my fear.

Noel explained that we would keep leaning over until the tide switched and rose back up.

Not too bad, I thought.

But Noel went on to say that, hopefully there wasn't a large rock beneath us that could puncture the hull as *Mariah's* ten tonnes leant over!

We calculated another two hours of leaning further and further over, before the tide switched back and started to straighten us up. I filled a bucket of water and put it on the deck, marking the water level and watched as it changed. It was like watching the white dot on the TV after it is turned off.

Mariah leant at an awkward angle. We waited patiently in our home that felt like a quirky fairground attraction with the floor leaning at a thirty-degree angle. At last, the water level on the bucket started to change direction and we felt ourselves being taken back upright. At midnight, the sand released us, and we re-anchored in deeper water. Neptune had not awakened to witness our mistake, leaving the water calm. Noel operated the electric anchor winch while I hovered at the end of our bed where the anchor chain bucket sat, and flaked out the chain to avoid more anchoring-knot problems next time. The chain came up cleanly and we moved forward about 200 metres, into slightly deeper waters and re-anchored.

That night we slept like the dead.

The following day I had clean forgotten everything. 'I am never going to understand all of these ropes and what they do,' I groaned in frustration, 'and what's worse, what they are all called!'

'A sheet is a cotton thing you lie on!' I said exasperated. 'Oh no,' I continued sarcastically, 'it's a rope with a specific purpose, just don't ask me what!'

Who thought of all these esoteric names was what I wanted to know. However, it did start to sink in slowly. I still felt a little stupid, even with Noel's understanding and patience in teaching a complete beginner. Some days were a real struggle. But I remember my elation on reading an email Noel had written to his brother: 'Jack's becoming quite the apprentice, changing filters and oil, soldering wires, helping me fit wander (the wind vane).' It was this kind of support that kept me going.

We returned to our piling in the Brisbane River, and I started to embrace the simple way of self-sufficient life. Solar panels gave us power (with a little help from the engine). We purchased gas bottles every two to three months, we filled the water tanks via jerry cans, and sat on our little floating island away from the hassle of real life. We had no letterbox where small bits of paper with large numbers intruded into our sanctuary, sucking dry the bank account to allow landlubber luxuries. And yes, there was the odd G&T (vodka for me please) while witnessing spectacular sunsets. This was interspersed with visits out to Moreton Bay, where we would do anchor pirouettes while savouring quiet, shifting views as we would fine wine – life wasn't too bad.

We travelled ashore via our dinghy, and it took a while to get used to rowing the darn thing, especially in a powerful current. We didn't have an outboard to power us along in the little boat, so learning to control the dinghy was funnier than my hairstyle in the morning. No longer did I sweep up the car keys, turn on the engine, and drive several miles without thought. Now, I tentatively stepped down the side of the boat, trying to keep balanced on a perpetually moving eight-foot bit of fibreglass. In the current, it was like stepping onto a galloping horse. Sitting down as quickly as possible was the first trick I learned. Having the rowlocks and oars at the ready was the next, before releasing the painter. Next, I had to concentrate on my action: try too hard and the oars came out of their locks. Lastly, I had to remember to look behind: the boat maybe going forwards but I was sitting backwards.

The dinghy dock in the town was always chock-full. To tie up, we would part the sea of small boats to reach the dock, then unload our gear (rubbish, items that needed fixing, shoes, shower gear etc), tie up on a lengthy painter, and push the dinghy back out. It was here that I noticed a strange phenomenon: most cruisers tied their dinghy up strangle hold, that is, with about one foot length. It was senseless and rather infuriating when trying to get ashore. Courtesy dictates that a decent length of painter (a couple of metres) be used so everyone can easily push the dinghies aside in order to reach the jetty. Still, it added to the daily events for half the city occupants who were fascinated with the comings and goings of the sea gypsies.

One morning, I made my way ashore alone for a job interview (this strange phase did eventually dissipate). In a small bag, I carried my smart gear to dress suitably after a shower. While getting dressed, I realised I had forgotten my bra. This was not a good look under a white blouse, although it may have given me a better chance at getting the job. Short of time, I had to row against the strong current, about 200 metres back to *Mariah*.

With lack of skill, due to lack of practice, I couldn't row away from the clutch of dinghies. The current kept me pinned to the other dinghies that were tied up, preventing my oars from getting a clean stroke. I was scared of pushing too far away from all the dinghies; I had visions of a rescue boat and news cameras coming to find me up the river and everyone seeing my face on the six o'clock news that night, all because of my lack of underwear! The crowds grew quickly, watching my ridiculous efforts with amusement. My face turned redder. Finally, a fellow cruiser took my painter and towed me out. He didn't use an outboard (small dinghy engine), he was rowing too! There was tittering amongst the hordes, their voyeuristic expectations duly met. Utterly engulfed in livid embarrassment, I was determined to avoid a repeat performance of this little episode. (I actually got the temp job – it was a good job, but I promptly left when I realised employment wasn't what I actually desired!)

Noel wasn't at all taken aback by my job-hunting-then-leaving ideas and he never made me feel inadequate in my abilities. My faith in him was growing rapidly, and I admired his abilities. Each day he would repair, replace, and adjust something that was totally alien to me. I was fascinated in his capability in knowing what he was doing. But this fascination would quickly turn to boredom. I needed something to do; I needed my own challenge. I was learning to cook on a tiny stove, becoming creative with food, as there was no fridge on board. I started to read boating magazines, but my knowledge was still so poor, I could hardly understand the articles and soon went back to my faithful novels. The boat was tidy, laundry, letters, and paperwork all up to date. I couldn't figure out what to do with myself.

I was brave enough, however, to admit that my ignorance was not going to change much until we had put some miles under our belts. I was looking forward to moving, learning, and settling in to the watery way of life properly. I learned best by doing.

From Brisbane, we sailed south to a small town in northern NSW called Iluka. Currents, wind changes, and shallows make the Australian east coast a fickle, difficult stretch of water to traverse. It seems to enjoy taking boats between its teeth of wind and waves, tossing them relentlessly. I don't remember sea-sickness or boredom, just the freedom and enjoyment of excitement and fear in setting sail.

Iluka sits on the northern side of the mouth of the Clarence River; the town of Yamba sits on the south side. Noel's brother, Colin, and Colin's wife, Brenda, lived there and gave us a hearty, warm welcome. It was a relief to be with family and have something familiar back in my life. They generously opened up their home to us and we relished the simple treats of a hot shower and comfy armchairs that didn't move.

Mariah was anchored in a small, protected bay. We still lived aboard and rowed ashore each day and jumped on our pushies (bicycles) for half a mile to their house. Iluka is a small, easygoing town, and we enjoyed the friendliness of Colin's golf club where most of the locals got together. Socialising with non-cruisers was a welcomed break. We completed many jobs on board, and my learning curve lost just a little of its steepness. We lifted *Mariah* out of the water for the second time in Iluka. The first time was when we purchased her and a surveyor had checked out her bottom. At that time, I had disappeared with the vendor's wife to have a girly chat!

This time, I was in charge of anti-fouling the underwater part of *Mariah's* bottom. I learned about preparing the surface for re-painting and claimed this job as my own. It was exhilarating to understand and be able to get on with a large, important job without supervision. Colin and Noel thought I was a little odd, as it is not a pleasant task. Mostly I was bent in half trying to reach the underside with paint that was highly toxic. The two brothers worked hard on the clever stuff; steering gear, propellers, and engines. But, if there had been a competition for the most inventive idea, I would have taken first prize. I had opened a tin of anti-foul paint. At that time, five litres of this noxious stuff cost about one-hundred-and-fifty Australian dollars. On top of the paint were a few drops of rainwater.

'Uuhhm,' and 'arrrhhh,' were all Colin and Noel could come up with as they stood over the paint tin.

Meanwhile, I'd been rummaging in the boat and I strode up behind them.

'Step aside,' I said with authority, holding a tampon aloft.

'Arrhhh,' and 'uuhhm,' was repeated by the two brothers.

'There, that takes care of that,' I grinned. I had gently placed the tampon on the offending water and it had sucked it all up, leaving the expensive paint untainted.

'Arhh, uhhm, well done,' said Noel, and everyone went back to work.

I realised then that perhaps a new perspective on board was a good thing.

Brenda played her part in this busy time. After a long day with the three of us working many hours so *Mariah* was out of the water for less time (the longer out the more we pay), we trudged back to Iluka Lodge and ate a delicious meal that Brenda had put together. All in all, the four of us made a good team. This was the first time I felt completely relaxed and happy with the direction of my life. Colin and Brenda played an enormous part in assisting me with fitting in and finding my place in this new watery world and warm, relaxed country.

My confidence was building, but in one fell swoop it could be knocked back to infancy. I was standing back to admire my paintwork on the undersides and a local came up and stood beside me; he was looking over *Mariah*. On her white hull were tyre marks from a fender used while tied to a wharf. The guy looked at me and said 'I bet *you* were steering when that happened.' *Charming*, I thought, but I didn't say anything. *Bugger off* – was my second thought, which I may have said out loud! I went back to work with the hump. Sadly, it was often I would come up against these narrow-minded comments. I had to learn to take them with a grain of salt.

Although my days were starting to fill up with boat tasks and I finally forgot the idea of project plans, I still needed a challenge, something to stretch the grey matter.

I helped with the maintenance, but this wasn't enough. Amid the mayhem of working on the boat, completing my UK and Australian tax returns (where mutterings of bazooking the whole UK government could be heard), I studied and achieved a diploma in travel writing and photography. It was a correspondence course with plenty of support from a tutor. During the course work, my first piece was published in a local paper. This gave me the motivation to build my knowledge and write more.

'You'll have plenty of material to write boat articles,' commented Noel. This thought horrified me; I would never know enough to write about sailing and boats.

I mixed my studies with boat maintenance and just loved painting the v-berth (the bow end of the boat, where we slept). Tackling a job where the end result looked better than the beginning was so rewarding; I had never done anything like it before. The deep furrows working across my forehead were finally starting to relax.

The time came for us to leave Iluka. I had changed so much, finding that life was less of a struggle. However, Murphy and his law must have been lurking at this time and realised that I had not been challenged enough. He took his opportunity to test our fortitude to its limits on our trip from Coffs Harbour to Fiji. The excitement bubbled around my stomach like fizzy champagne. To think we could sail all the way to another country!

The journey would take about two-and-a-half weeks, but we both felt ready. By now, we had been working on *Mariah* for almost a year: getting to know her, replacing, and updating equipment. The trip south to Coffs Harbour was not a good start. A quick moving low pressure weather system crossed our path and I suffered my worst bout of sea-sickness; I couldn't get out of bed. Noel sailed most of the way on his own, while I moaned and groaned from the bunk below, fervently praying for the relief of death. I questioned our lifestyle again, but I had become so attached to our new home that I resolved to buy heaps of sea-sick tablets and get on with it. But I didn't know that this bout of sea-sickness was a walk in the park compared to what was about to happen.

5

―――

The Storm

The organisation for the long trip to Fiji was incredible. How to stow food for two weeks without a fridge; how to survive without constantly being plugged into the mains? Dried and tinned foods were our staples: potatoes, onions, garlic, and cabbage kept a long time, if they were kept in a ventilated area and out of the sun. Meat was relinquished. As a hearty carnivore, this was hard in the beginning, but over the years I became so smart at food management that three to four weeks or more at sea was easily catered for with delicious concoctions of one-pot repasts.

The small space we lived in moved three dimensionally twenty-four hours a day. The land, trees, and shops were replaced with sea, birds, and sky. Then, like a switch, it all changed; a gale was brewing, the sea washed black and was kicked into a chop by the building wind. The gale gathered momentum and became a storm. It grasped us firmly in its tumultuous fist. It scattered the birds, turned the sky an angry black, and the sea frothy white. We had left Coffs Harbour with a four-day weather forecast that was excellent; it was on the fifth day that it turned on us. For five days, we were held in the jaws of the wind that was building to sixty knots, and five-metre seas. We were buffeted and tossed relentlessly. Keeping watch for other traffic was a waste of time, because the climbing walls of water hid any view. The force in which the waves smashed against *Mariah* was terrifying. Neptune was angry, his fist pummelled into her hull, as if trying to break through. I could hear the rumble of waves gathering their skirts, lifting higher, and rushing to meet *Mariah's* hull. The enormous smash as the green water fought to break-in, caused *Mariah* to lurch, churn, and cork-screw. Meanwhile, my stomach did the same. Cleaning teeth became a major exercise. Going to the toilet was a battle with layers of clothes, and sea-sickness. Which would win first? Peeing in a bucket in the open cockpit became a viable option, but it could become tricky with sliding feet. I could cook food, but then I'd reach my limit of being below decks. I couldn't eat, and at times even water would not settle in my stomach. I realised how easy it was to become seriously dehydrated. Day after day and, night after night we rolled, bashed, and vomited. With nail splitting effort, we pulled down the mainsail and hauled up the strong storm sail, the veins in our hands swelled as if yelling out in effort. My hair escaped its elastic and whipped drenched strands against my red cheeks. It's at the most inopportune times you think about a short hair cut. It was relentless. There were no breaks, just endless walls of water and *Mariah* dancing her way up and down, side to side. Everything in our home continually slid, bashed, clinked, and clunked.

Our navigation chart was folded in half to fit onto our navigation table. No matter how hard we tried, we could not sail past the crease in the chart! We reached one-third of the way to Fiji and were considering going north to Vanuatu.

'This is Mariah II,' Noel gasped on the HF radio as he tried to hang on and talk with other boats north of us, 'we have fifty-five to sixty knot winds and are turning north to Vanuatu.'

Our radios worked very well and we received a response immediately.

'Don't come this way,' gasped another voice, its owner clearly struggling too, 'we have sixty to sixty-five knots up here!'

'That's it!' Noel roared, 'we're turning-tail and going with it. Dig out the drogue!'

We turned for home.

With the drogue out behind us we took back control of *Mariah*. We stopped surfing down the mountainous waves. I realised how good it was to have a canoe stern boat, she didn't attempt to broach once.

Now we had the storm jib sheeted amidships, the wind fine on the quarter, the drogue steadying our course, and we entered a period of comparative tranquillity.

Gradually, the motion softened as the storm slowly eased. The seas, having been stirred up so vigorously for so long, took their time in calming.

As we approached land, the mobile phone sprang to life.

'Hi, guys, this is Mum, just checking how things are with you.'

This was one of about eighteen voicemail messages from my mum in the UK. Once or twice a day, every day, she had called to leave a message. This made me realise that the unknown world I had immersed myself into was scarier for my parents than it was for me. I had grown up with horses, manure, and competitions; an amazing outdoor life that was a stark difference to the water world. Boats and their unique ways were equally as alien to my family as they were to me.

We arrived safely into a comfortable, friendly town called Mooloolaba in Queensland, grateful that all three of us were unharmed: battered and immensely tired, but relatively okay. Noel and I had both lost a lot of weight, but it's not a diet regime I'd recommend. My respect for nature was growing, as was my knowledge.

As we settled into a safe, secure berth Noel said, 'What were you thinking during that storm?'

I was silent for a while.

Noel revealed his thoughts first, 'I was thinking that I was going to step off the boat onto land and never step back on board again!' His blood-shot eyes told the extent of his exhaustion. He'd got us back safely to land, and I was grateful.

'I was wondering how, if we had made it to Fiji, you were going to sail the boat back on your own.' I said, with a small smile.

'What do you mean?' he asked. He was struggling mentally and physically with the deep exhaustion.

'I wasn't going to sail back, I was going to fly home!'

We both smiled. We could reveal our feelings without incurring judgement.

'What now? I asked as I looked around at the mess. Mariah looked like a giant had picked her up and shaken her vigorously, and we didn't look much better.

'Food,' said Noel.

Over coffee and several hamburgers, Noel fell asleep in the café chair. After stealing what food and coffee I could from him, I woke him to take him home. He climbed over the rubbish tip that was our home and collapsed into bed. My nerves were still jangling, so I tidied the boat and rang family to tell them we were still alive. Noel slept for thirty-six hours without moving; I kept going in and checking he was still breathing! I had managed to grab some sleep at times during the storm. Noel had not, so he was exhausted. With Noel clearly taking all the responsibility on his shoulders, I still didn't realise the enormity of the phrase 'ignorance is bliss' until much later on during another adventure.

Noel vowed to never leave Australian shores again, but I was ready to mount back up and have another go. I utilised the skills I'd gained from horse riding, climb back on when you've been thrown-off, and before long I was ready to take to the sea once more. First, we decided to take some time out and head south to Sydney for the summer, while we figured out what we should do.

With our tails between our legs, we slowly sailed down the coast to Sydney, where we sought work.

This gave us time to get over the traumas and accumulate some funds. We thought we had failed. We later learned that a successful voyage is about getting into port unharmed. We hadn't failed; we had made good decisions and survived.

Going back to the working world seemed to calm us. We didn't have the energy to think about what-next and what-ifs. Taking on a routine we didn't like, but knew, gave us time to regroup. We were moored at the International Anchorage in Sydney harbour. I could walk to work and nearby trains. A tap in the park made water collection easy, and the grass verge was a good car park for the dinghy. In the evening, the privacy and tranquillity on board helped shed the city drudge.

Eventually, we started to discuss our next adventure. After six months, we headed north to see where the wind would take us. We signed up for the Coxswains course, which gave us both tickets to captain boats up to twelve metres. After completing the course, which was male-dominated and held people of varying degrees of experience, I realised I had learned quite a bit on board *Mariah*. We were both gaining more confidence to have another go.

As we puttered north one day along the coast, with the old Volvo engine ticking over, the rhythm of the motor changed, chugged, and stopped. We looked at each other and tried to contain the panic.

During the storm, we had been thrown about so much that our fuel tank had stirred up all the crap that gathers at the bottom and this had clogged the diesel lines and filters. After one or two hairy moments with the engine cutting out, I became a dab hand at changing filters quickly in rolling seas, and it was done in world-record time, any racetrack engineer would've been impressed. I was really chuffed to be doing this. In fact, I would volunteer, compounding Noel's thoughts that I was a bit loopy. But learning to be capable within our floating home was starting to become a reality and not just a dream.

Our first wedding anniversary came and went without gifts of flowers and chocolates, but with a new hammer, tool bag, and a book called *The 12 Volt Bible*. I started to make an admirable effort to learn.

We went back to Brisbane and decided to plunge more money into the boat before having another attempt at some serious miles. A new engine, water tanks, fuel tanks, new steering gear, and endless weeks of tireless work meant we had no excuses – it was time to leave Australia. We did all this work ourselves; I was Noel's apprentice and made a big adjustment from a beginner to a person tottering on the brink of becoming a little wiser.

That was my first two years in Australia: our relationship and living on board *Mariah*. We had survived the roller-coaster ride where the tracks of our lives had spiralled into new directions. As we clinked glasses, remembering the events of the last twenty-four months, we giggled, bit our lips, and softly swore.

We both wondered aloud, 'What will next year hold?'

6
___

Advent of adventure

In August 2000, we left the city harbour under our own fanfare of celebration. We deliberately sailed out on a weekday, so we could wave farewell to everyone that was scurrying to and from work.

I revelled in the freedom. We had spent six months as one of those uniformed faceless people, scuttling around the city. The only way we had coped was to look forward to our departure – not just a salary at the end of a long, pointless month. Pursuing a mortgage and pension was no longer one of our goals in life. We wanted our own career within a life we relished and controlled. Our ticket to freedom was swinging happily on anchor, just waiting to be released into the oceans.

We could wait no longer. In my head, I held dreams of venturing to new countries, but Noel still wasn't sure. The responsibility of handling the boat and navigating us safely back to Australia in the storm still clouded his dreams. We slowly made our way around to Darwin with gentle winds stroking the sails. Following the seasons, we were sucked into the vortex of travellers heading the same way and just kept going. Arriving in Darwin, I hardly dared hope that we would leave Australia.

On reaching Darwin, we hauled down the sails and packed up for port. We were staying in a marina, a rare luxury for us. Continuous marina fees were prohibitive, besides we usually enjoyed the privacy and ever-changing views of swinging on anchor. The small sail on the foredeck, the staysail, was usually neatly folded and stowed below decks at the end of a trip. I carefully placed it into its yellow canvas bag, then started to haul it below decks when Noel said, 'Leave the staysail out for when we leave.' The magnitude of his statement made my heart flip-flop: he meant another country. I stared out across the horizon that held no beginning or end.

We'll be going out there, I thought, and a slow trickle of fear mixed with anticipation started to skip along my spine.

They were shooting Christians in Bali – or so we thought. However, within the world of boating where jungle drums are continuously beating, we learned that the country was safe due to the flood of money from tourism. The new idea of heading to Bali started to percolate in our busy minds and brewed into a new plan. This change of direction was bubbling in our heads just two nights before leaving for South Africa. Still unsure and feeling the burden of decision maker on board, Noel rang a cruiser friend in Brisbane who said, 'You're too late and too slow for South Africa; you'll get caught in a hurricane.' And just like that, instead of leaving for Africa the following day we purchased charts for Bali and altered our headspace to a different direction and country.

Suddenly propelled into the flowing currents of departing Australia, we pointed *Mariah* west, heading for the horizon. The waves of excitement swept over me. When I was a headstrong teenager and constantly arguing with my dad, I had shouted with crushing frustration, 'I just wanna be free!' I clearly remember feeling mortified when my dad had retaliated with anger and sadness, 'No one is ever free.' But I now had the sweet taste of possibilities and travel was gnawing at my vitals.

Watching Australia shrink behind us on the horizon filled me with a refreshing sense of relief. It was time to see other places together, experience new cultures and challenges. Somehow, we had worked through the first year of storms and crash landings and a second year of hard graft in an alien world. To a degree, we had shaken off our pasts and leaving Australia felt like a new beginning. Slowly, I was becoming more confident and competent. With two years living on board under our belts, I was getting into the swing of the sea gypsy lifestyle. I had found my place in the world, an unsettling feeling as it created some comfort that felt, all at once, peaceful and peculiarly unfamiliar.

At this point, I wasn't aware of, or chose to ignore, Noel's responsibilities. With his prior boating experience, his decisions were imperative. I could add ideas, feelings, and a little knowledge to the team, but Noel carried the full brunt of our decisions firmly on his shoulders. As our journey continued, I realised just how much weight that was. But it wasn't until our next adventure, many years later, while trekking in the bush with five horses (my forte) and a tent, that I would come to realise the anxiety and responsibility Noel bore during this time.

Many sailors have a love-hate relationship with offshore sailing with the requirement of getting from one port to the next. It is better than coastal sailing in one respect, as there are far fewer things to hit. Once you have the sails set for the wind (which can shift constantly), all that is required are hourly checks of the bilge, heading (course), position, and sea conditions and then a good book. Of course, we kept watch twenty-four hours a day for other traffic. It was like a tag-team match, with one of us always awake. Large ships have a limited crew: their radar should detect small boats like ours, but they often don't. Stories of a larger ship returning to port with a sailing boat's mast caught on its bow sent shivers down my spine. On our watches, we were vigilant. Close to sleep deprivation, we persuaded our bodies to become accustomed to four hours on, four hours off.

When all was settled and *Mariah* was gliding to her mission, I became drenched by memories that had no regard for place or circumstance; some thoughts were enough to make me blush into the night. Recollections of those I had hurt made me squirm. I cradled my own hurts in time with the rocking motion of the boat. I recalled forgotten good times as a kid, and card games with my family by candle light during frequent power cuts. It made me smile, and I realised that even happy memories can make you sad. Those moments were gone. With no pattern or logic, I thought of things I should have done with my life. When the sailing charmed me, I realised there was still time. It was like a switch flipping: good sailing thawed morose thoughts.

Boredom played no part. There was clearing up to do, receiving weather, radio Scheds, power monitoring, fixing/maintaining, reading, checking the lines, rigging, resting, and sail changes, too! We navigated with paper charts, joining the dots, creating a highway that proved we were moving, drawing a line we seemed to follow. I day-dreamed of sweet grass and grand trees, succulent roast chicken, and gooey ice-cream. We kept moving; our thoughts did too, drifting away like clouds.

When I heard Noel "galley squirreling" I anticipated the smells. Tea meant it was my time to stand watch. Coffee meant I could close my eyes as he was making a mid-watch eyelid boost. Efforts of sleeping were linked with conditions – the gentle motion like a swaying train, or the vicious rolling in a malevolent and restless ocean where your insides jostled within your skin.

In tune with the vessel, new sounds were more obvious to me; "Hasty Tasties" (tin cans) could wriggle loose and create a drumbeat with a thriving echo. Snuggled in a comfy bunk listening to the patter of rain on deck, the ocean rushing alongside and creaking lines comforted me.

It was no fun being woken up at three o'clock in the morning and stumbling around in a vessel that was moving three dimensionally. Dressing in the dark in order to maintain night vision, while trying to keep balanced, was a great recipe for sea-sickness. Staggering into the cockpit, I'd clip my safety harness on and rapidly search the horizon, trying to grasp my bearings. At this point, Noel would hand me a cup of steaming tea and provide me with a run down on what had happened during his watch. At times it was so dark that the sea and the sky became one. Across the horizon, boats that were just pinpricks matched the pinprick stars in the black sky. Sleep bartering became a way of life, with Oscar-winning yawns to try to entice sympathy and maybe a minute or two longer in a warm bunk.

Ashmore Reef is a clear-water lagoon, a mid-point between Darwin and Bali, and a welcomed rest stop. The Australian Customs catamaran, *Wauri*, was posted here. As we approached the lagoon, the radio crackled into life.

'If you're coming in here, hang fire guys, I'll come out and show you the way in.' Doug, second in command of *Wauri*, armed with a huge grin, sped towards us in his RIB (Rigid Inflatable Boat) and gallantly revealed the route into the protected lagoon. We could stop for a few days and were delighted to have the knowledgeable guidance into the winding channel. We had had two gentle days at sea, but welcomed the opportunity of a break. By luck, we had timed it perfectly.

'It's quiet for us at the moment, so we'll show you around.' The customs men and women seemed glad to have some new company. Ordinarily, the team on board the huge vessel *Wauri* picked up Indonesians that had paid their life savings to be dropped, literally, into Australian waters. The refugees hoped to be arrested by customs and taken into the land of gold. The current hiatus enabled Australia's defence team to spend some time with us, so the next three days were like a pre-paid, all inclusive, once in a lifetime tour. The customs vessel housed up-to-the-minute equipment. Noel, myself and a couple of other cruisers also en route to Bali felt as though we were in a candy store for boats. After a gadget-go-round, we were offered freshly baked chocolate cake and coffee. Next we discussed the afternoon's activities, which involved snorkelling.

'Don't mind the sea snakes,' Doug said with a sly grin.

'Sea snakes!?' I mouthed silently at Noel, trying not to panic and test my walk-on-water skills.

'They're harmless,' announced Doug, 'just a bit inquisitive; their mouths are so small that they can only bite between your fingers or your ears.'

In the clear, cool sparkling water, we swam with gliding turtles, teeming fish, and glowing coral. The snakes didn't stand a chance with me. I swam with my fingers together, firmly covering my ears.

At the end of an incredible day, the customs team said, 'Tomorrow, we'll take you for a spin on our speed machine. In the meantime, here's some videos to watch and if you want to do some laundry, just bring it aboard tomorrow. Sleep well.' And with that and a smiling wave, Doug dropped us off at home on *Mariah* and motored off back to his base on *Wauri*.

'I don't want to leave,' I said to Noel. They had won me with the chocolate cake. Right at that moment, all the effort and heart-stopping happenings during our two years on board, plus the work and study, all faded into insignificance.

'Whaaarrrrhhhheeeeeeeeeee,' this was yelled from someone, probably me, as we hurtled around the lagoon strapped into a six-seater, James Bond style speedboat. The g-force crushed my cheeks and gave me a wicked smile as the air was forced into my mouth. The team from *Wauri* were showing off their boat-handling skills. Hooning alongside turtles, spinning impossible doughnuts, speeding fast enough to distort our faces, I felt free. At last, we were starting to reap the rewards by having fun. But after two days of rest, raucous exuberance, and wine filled evenings, we reluctantly bade farewell and pointed *Mariah* towards Bali.

Seven days of endless water stretched out from the bow. Never had we felt this ready for a voyage. Within the nautical group at Ashmore Reef, I had held my own. I understood the watery conversations and enjoyed the array of nautical nuances. Even better, I was starting to handle the boat on my own. During my first watch en route to Bali, staring out across the endless carpet of water, I pondered that for a bit. The thought, that I was completely in charge when Noel was sleeping, felt daunting. I was in control of a ten tonne beast. This really only occurred to me now as we were doing longer voyages. I *had* to ensure that Noel had a good rest between shifts. I was resting well. So when I was on watch I had to take responsibility and be in charge. All at once, I felt powerful and completely petrified.

The uneventful sail to Bali was filled with days of clear skies and smooth seas, warm nights and the purring Yanmar propelling *Mariah* due to the lack of wind. Occasionally, I woke Noel to help me manoeuvre past a large ship. Night watches could be hard work with my body nagging for sleep. Engulfed by deep darkness, spotting the loom of a ship from miles away was easy, leaving plenty of time to monitor its direction and adjust our course if necessary. The red and green navigation lights helped decipher the direction of the other traffic. It felt a bit odd to rely on lights for a vessel's heading, but all this was happening at only seven miles per hour. However, coupled with the three dimensional movement, at times it became near impossible to guess what was happening. I could become entranced with other boats and stared at them for hours as they were slowly swallowed up in the spangled black. I just didn't feel comfortable averting my eyes. I had no idea why. It could take hours for a boat to pass, so it was pointless to keep watching the silent silhouette until it eventually became indistinguishable. At three in the morning, tiredness stabbed at my eyes and mental ability; I found it easy to let my imagination run away with me. I would imagine the ship coming sideways towards us! Eventually, my fears would gather momentum and hold hands with my inexperience and I would wake Noel from his slumber. He would rarely need to take any action, because I had already altered course as necessary, but sometimes I needed him just to be with me in the cockpit. It was at these times I was starkly reminded just how much of a novice I still was.

Noel never complained about being woken up. We both agreed that being completely sure of the situation was better than the unthinkable. A dalliance with a 200,000 tonne steel ship was going to do more than step on our toes. We did, on occasion, find ourselves on a converging course. Learning to use a hand-bearing compass to note and log the other vessel's angle from us was important. If the bearing didn't change (after taking two to four bearings, every few minutes), you knew you were heading for the same patch of water and you had to do something about it. Collision Regulations (Col Regs) are the international rules of the waterways. Sometimes, we had right of way. But if there was an enormous vessel heading straight for us at twenty-six knots, we made sure we got out of the way. The navigation lights on these mountainous ships seemed the same size as our own navigation lights and were hard to distinguish, especially if they had other cabin lights on. Even with all the equipment, common sense, and checking, I still managed, at times, to get into a bit of a pickle. The heavy tiredness, the fear of being hit, and the odd sensation of being awake at 3 am night after night could reduce me to tears. The thick cloak of darkness coupled with my total lack of night-time experience could mix up to create a great dollop of doubt. We had met people that had been sailing for years and still claimed they were learning.

Surely there is an ending to learning at some point? I thought, foolishly. I found this highly daunting, but I had come this far and was determined to continue climbing the almost impossible heap of knowledge. It was fortunate that I could let Noel into my mind to take a look at my perspective. This provided him a semblance of understanding the tapestry of my life and how my thoughts led to the fears that I tried so hard to swallow.

By our fifth day at sea, we had settled into a comfortable routine and cast grateful glances at the sea, sky, and clouds to thank Mother Nature for being kind. At dawn on the ninth day, after leaving Darwin, Bali crept slowly over the horizon to meet us. We furled the sails and puttered across the smooth water, untouched by any breeze, into Benoa harbour. Unwrapping the gleeful smiles that were stuck on our faces, we looked like a couple of silly fools – we had sailed to another country.

As the land became clearer, we spotted a small speedboat heading straight for us. A brown, wrinkly man manically waved while trying to steer a straight line, I wondered what we'd done wrong. Impressively, he was hand delivering our mail. The day before leaving Darwin, we had organised our Indonesian visa (most people organise these a week or two before leaving). I had selected a date we would arrive in Bali. The sun-dried Balinesean postman had been looking out for us continually on the day I said we *may* reach their shores, and he promptly delivered our Indonesian visa before we stepped onshore. Mail and communications were a completely new ball game now; we had so much to learn. Giving our families the address for the harbour in Benoa, we thought they would have plenty of time to send on mail. They duly sent lots of updates, which did not reach Bali until a few weeks after we had left. Another sailboat carried our letters all the way to Thailand until they caught up with us. We soon learned that the Internet and phones would be our only communication from now on.

Benoa harbour was a colourful, esoteric feast for eyes. Awash with peeling paint, top-heavy fishing boats languidly wallowed side-to-side, curiously in dead calm waters. Armies of tiny, brown men scurried around the drunken blue and red decks. Large motors roared *boom, boom, boom* as they cruised by with black smoke spiralling aft. Locals zoomed by closely, trying to peek inside our alien-looking yacht.

Anchored amidst the cavernous bay, the row to shore was about a kilometre long; we had not purchased an outboard for our dinghy, so we relied on oars and our rowing ability. Fortunately, my ability had improved since Brisbane. While getting ready to leave Australia, we were both fed up with endlessly emptying our pockets of cash for gear for the boat. The outboard was a long way down the list and never materialised. Going cruising is all about learning when to stop writing more lists, getting to the end of your current list, and just going.

Now faced with the long row in a busy harbour, we understood our mistake. We became the locals' entertainment whilst rowing across the busy, commercial harbour. We dodged charter, local, and fishing boats with nothing more than two oars, a torch, and plywood. People pointed while we wobbled up and down in huge wakes perched on our small timber dinghy (we had managed to swap our fibreglass dinghy for a lovely timber sailing-dinghy). David and Petrea, our friends on board *Dolphin Breeze* (an Australian couple whom we had met at Ashmore Reef), took pity on us and lent us their spare outboard with a warning of its temperament. Out of practice and with an amused Balinese audience, Noel started up the motor and we slammed, bumped, wriggled, and giggled out of the body of dinghies tied at the jetty. The small marina was chock full of other international sailors. But the borrowed motor soon showed its dislike for water and work. Inspired to own an outboard of our own and a more civilised way of getting ashore, we toured Bali for the best deal. Spending a whole day negotiating, drinking tea, and telling stories to the only place on the island that sold the motor we wanted, we finally became the proud owners of a little two horse power outboard.

Typhoid fever claimed two fellow cruisers as hosts. The couple had spent over eight hundred Australian dollars on jabs before leaving Australia, whereas we had injected no more than coffee. Our guardian angel must have been on his or her toes. Initially, I had envied Petrea and David. *Dolphin Breeze* was a beautiful fifty-foot sailing boat, and they were paid to take it around the world, the owner joining them at certain locations. An amazing job, I thought. However, when Petrea became ill, she cried, 'I just want to go home.' I realised then that Noel and I *were* at home; *Mariah II* was our home wherever we were. Suddenly, their attractive career had lost its sheen for me.

Benoa's expensive marina was held together with string. The added attraction of rats and festering heat along the packed jetties left us dumbfounded as to why sailboats were vying for a space within the marina. On anchor, the fun didn't stop.

THUD, 'What on earth was that?' Noel called out.

I was already half-way out of the boat, 'oh dear, a ship has just drifted into us.'

This made Noel spring-up from our bed.

'It's okay,' I continued, 'no harm done, it sounded worse than it was.'

In the dead of a peaceful night, a rather large, rusty tanker drifted into *Mariah*. The Balinese vessel had swung too close and had given us a noisy nudge. Apart from the fact it sounded like they were coming through our hull, we suffered no damage and like ants spotting a yummy snack, the crew frantically scurried into clearer water.

The next day, armed with cans of Cola and small toy koalas as a thank you gesture for moving away from us straight away, we puttered up to the long, elderly tanker.

'Hello, hellooooo,' we called out as we tried to hold on to the rusting ship. As we approached, the crew became nervous and avoided eye contact; their covert scurrying seemed a little odd. Eventually, a serious looking man leaned over the corroding decks towards us, clearly thinking we had come to complain. His white eyes pierced out from his sun-baked skin and thick, dark hair.

'Hello, we've bought you some gifts,' we unholstered big smiles. 'Thanks so much for moving so quickly last night, we really appreciated it.'

Our friendly behaviour channelled around the battle-scarred boat, and the crew started to appear. Pure delight smothered their lined faces and toothless grins, and they all came out of hiding when we lifted aloft our small gifts. Their wide, bright smiles were priceless. Cola, it seemed, was a useful currency.

So much had happened in such a short time. New friends, cultures, and experiences were a daily event. All my life, blinkered in an office, I had never known this alternative world existed. I had broken away from the shackled drudgery of the norm. My second life had only just begun at twenty-seven. After a heart-breaking time in England, I began to see some truth in the saying, 'Every cloud has a silver lining.' Later though, I would be surprised how those hard times in the UK would come back and devastate me all over again.

The watery way of life soon revealed itself as being extremely social. I was intrigued about why other people were sailing and not going to 'work.' 'Work' is where I previously believed everyone belonged.

Some people were following a dream, others were escaping or just didn't know what else to do. We were all the same in the fact that we had taken a leap of faith and given up the home, car, and mortgage – the normal way of life and the regimented nine-to-five. In fact, I came to realise that making this change was a brave step, not a cop-out. My judgements and beliefs were starting to change. Landlubbers talked about breaking free from society, but when it actually comes to the crunch, it isn't that simple. Friends at home said, 'You are so lucky.' I agreed that we were lucky to have our health and wits (mostly) about us. But we had *made* this decision. We had got up off our backsides and made this happen for us – it wasn't a gift. And there were certainly compromises that came hand-in-hand with this life. No running hot water, constant shifts at sea, distance between friends and family, and sometimes terrifying moments where death seemed inevitable or even wished for. We were on a constant budget, because there was no income. We watched every single penny.

Ageism was something that raised its ugly head once or twice when Noel and I had met landlubbers in a pub.

'You obviously married Noel for his money,' someone once said to me. It didn't help that in my late twenties I had looked about eighteen, but I was conscious of what other people thought. Noel is sixteen years older than me. I was, therefore, surprised that ageism didn't exist in sailing folk. We would all get together with a vast range of cultures and ages, and there was never a barrier between us; we were kindred spirits with a desire for freedom and adventure. It was like a breath of fresh air.

In Bali, the days raced by with frequent trips into town. Just getting ashore was a project in itself. It was too far to return if we had forgotten an item.

Each time we went ashore at Benoa harbour we'd first check that we had all our necessary items: shoes, bag, money, laundry, water containers, shopping list, sun-cream, passport, ad infinitum. We'd balance all our gear and ourselves in the dinghy and find a space to sit. Next we'd play dodgems with all the other vessels (no 'rules of the road' exist in Bali). It was necessary to frantically bail-out the dinghy and keep a three-hundred-and-sixty degree look-out while holding aloft all possessions to keep them dry. When we reached the marina we'd tie up cursing those who tied their painter too short! Then to complete the trip ashore we'd traverse umpteen dinghies of varying stability to reach land.

There was never a dull moment.

'Oh crap, I've forgotten my sandals.' We had almost reached the jetty.

'What do you want to do?' Noel asked, clearly not happy about returning to the boat.

'Oh, sod it,' I grinned, 'I'll buy some sandals in town.' I went into town shoeless and purchased a pair of cheap sandals. My feet were embarrassingly filthy by the time we reached the shops. Bare feet were not considered unusual in Indonesia, but with our western world of dressing, I felt partly naked without shoes.

Road travel in Bali was yet another challenge; in fact, it was a real battle of nerves. Viewing the traffic and behaviour, their road transport rules must read:
1. Don't stop for *anything*.
2. Do not remove your hand from the horn – *ever*.
3. Precariously balance as many family members as possible on one scooter to terrify all the tourists.

Scooters were the locals' choice for transport, and they thought nothing of loading up the entire family. Mum, Dad, three kids, and gran all piled together onto the machine! In town, skinny children washed in a filthy stream, while further up-stream a mother washed her family's well-worn clothes; further along, a man used the stream as a toilet. We were not on a package holiday, shielded from the real life by a modern hotel. We witnessed how the locals really lived.

The two weeks in Bali were spent re-stocking (food, fuel, and water), hand-washing clothes, boat maintenance, officialdom (customs, immigration, police, marine officials including open baksheesh/bribery), making new friends, and some sightseeing. Folks at home imagined us sitting on the aft deck watching sunsets with our G&T (vodka for me still). This did happen on occasion, but most of our time was spent sourcing supplies, making repairs, and organising both *Mariah* and ourselves for the next leg. There was no car to hop into, just our own propulsion and the odd taxi. Sightseeing consisted of fighting off tactile locals who wanted to sell us their fake wares; this daily battle came to tarnish the beautiful mountains, lush green paddy fields, and clean air.

With many new friends and promises of a reunite in Thailand, we finally packed our last fresh items on board and hauled anchor.

At this time, computers didn't figure hugely in our day-to-day travelling, I tapped away on our old laptop to keep a diary, but that was all. Little did I know that soon I would have a whole wealth of heart-stopping information I would want to record.

7

Restoring my faith in the world

Grooming each morning to make myself appropriately respectful for the office used to be a way of life. In my sailing days, my well-worn tweezers had become as effective as chopsticks. But it didn't really matter, my eyebrow shape morphed monthly. September I looked surprised, October continually perplexed. My fashion became fifteen-year-old Levi's that were holding up quite well. My style was chameleonic after a DIY attack at the long, brown mop atop my head. The make-up I owned, at its third birthday, had congealed into a honey-like substance. I still used a dab of mascara, once every year or two. The bizarre thing was, I enjoyed this state of being. My friends who still did battle in the 'real' world thought I was quite odd, and they were probably right. But, I had found the liberty I craved. No longer did I have to speak the corporate speak and dress correctly. Those blinkers I had been wearing all my life were gone. My senses craved more and were not let down by the feast that was about to be bestowed upon them.

It was the little things that meant more, like good food, wine, and a good time with lots of laughs. Of course, I had these things before, but life on board was different. The laughing was hearty, the enjoyment complete; for the first time ever I was being me and not dressing-up myself or personality to fit in. Being free to go where the wind took me had restored my faith in the world.

Before freeing myself from land life, I had started to think that maybe I was actually living in hell. Not too long ago, I had walked through Hades, holding hands with someone who was to leave the torture, to go into a better world – not hell and not earth. This part of my life would haunt me for some years. Later in my watery world, as I learned to relax during the lonely night-time watches, the acute stab of loss would, again, twist in my gut.

As well as all the personal changes, natural changes, like weather, were a major factor in our agenda. There were the "trades" (the trade winds) that dictated all of our departures, the length of time at sea, and the quality of journey. As we headed north towards the equator, squalls became a main event. A thick, black cigar shaped cloud would spiral towards us, like an evil hand ready to give us a shove. Within the wink of an eye, a severe wind would blast down from the tumultuous cloud and slam down on us hard. Thick curtains of rain would surround us and make any sort of lookout impossible. During the day, we had time to reef down the sails in preparation. At night, bruised clouds carrying squalls sneaked up on us under the camouflage of dark. Without warning, the clouds would intensify, and we would be suddenly thrust out of control, speeding towards an unfamiliar coast at break-neck speed. This all added to the excitement of unknown waters. Indeed, we often experienced our best ever sail and our worst ever sail in a matter of a few hours.

I had read a theory somewhere that each human has the same number of heartbeats in a lifetime. It didn't take long for me to realise that life on the water reduced my quota rapidly on a regular basis.

After leaving Bali and settling the boat to match conditions, Noel took a nap while I did the first watch-keeping shift. *Mariah* was clipping along, the water relatively flat. Mother Nature provided enough wind to propel us smoothly along. Tucked in the cockpit, I was contemplating such things like why men were gifted with a multi-directional tube to pee from. Every time I wanted to pee, I had to go below to the loo, which was fine most of the time. But in wet weather gear, the performance could take ten minutes. Trying to balance in a confined space, smashing soft bodily parts on thoughtlessly placed metal handles, could put me in a real pickle. Either way, trying to hang on, muscles taut to stop moving, yet relaxing those important ones in order to fulfil the need, became quite an interesting exercise. It's a bit like trying to act cool on a roller coaster ride.

After trying, unsuccessfully, to invent an appendage to allow me to easily pee over the side, I settled down to the escape of a novel. I would try to read four pages before looking around the horizon, scanning for other traffic. Being a bit twitchy, if I read two pages before looking up, I felt quite proud of myself.

All was well with the world. There were no boats to worry about, and we were sailing smoothly along with everything under control. All of a sudden a violent gust of wind grabbed hold of our sails. Boats do funny things when there's a blast of unexpected wind, and too much sail aloft, and they can dramatically veer toward the direction the wind is coming from. This is known as rounding up. On this particular occasion, it meant that *Mariah* headed, full pelt, straight for the land.

'YIKES, I may need some help up here!' The boat lurched and Noel jumped up.

'I'll get the boat back on track and ease the sheets, can you pull the main-sail down?' Noel yelled. The noise of the wind pummelling the boat swallowed our words.

Noel manhandled the tiller (we had gadgets to steer the boat which freaked out, like us, when the wind became overpowering), he coaxed our ten tonne boat to point away from land. He eased the sheets while I hauled down the main sail, my fingers clawing the unforgiving fabric, my nails vainly hanging on to their anchor of skin.

As my toenails tried to dig into the tilting deck, I flicked time-wasting glances at the approaching land, then back to Noel to see if he was winning his battle. Carried on the wind, I am sure I heard Neptune giggling. Gasping with effort, inch-by-inch I lowered the sail. As the sail area decreased, Noel was able to resume a sensible course that avoided any hard stuff, such as land. It was all over in about three minutes, but seemed like a century of nausea. With mixed feelings of exhaustion and satisfaction, we settled back into our respective corners: Noel to snooze, while I read or invented useful appendages.

Our teamwork was becoming naturally automatic. With little communication, Noel took his position and I took mine. I knew which rope ("line" for the purists) did which job, where it should be, and how tight. I had morphed from the total ignorant novice to the start of a knowledgeable sailor. With still a lot to learn, I could finally see and put to good use what I had learned already. The first two years of living on board now seemed like a breeze, I quickly forgot the agony of ignorance. The boating way of living was a real tonic for my life weary soul. I couldn't wait to reach email and telephones again to tell my friends all about my new life and how it was panning out. Unfortunately, I would be disappointed in their reactions.

About two days out of Bali, we anchored at an island named Kangean. The idea was to stay for one night, for a rest; we stayed for three. Leaping from one plan to another and altering schedules now felt normal. For a long time, I had hung onto to project plans and timelines. Now, I finally released these daft notions and embraced the gypsy life. There was only ourselves to please; so what if we stayed longer, who's going to know? Who's going to care? I found, with a sense of relief, that I didn't.

Even though we had anchored next to a verdant, uninhabited island, we felt no desire to venture ashore. The foreshore with its thick coating of flora was not inviting. Instead, we took advantage of the crystal clear water that sparkled like diamonds and a completely private anchorage with not a soul to be seen. Was it time to romantically skinny dip? Well, not quite... armed with stiff brushes, plastic scrapers, snorkels, and cotton wool firmly pressed into our ears, we dived in. Our skin tightened and tingled, the refreshing surge of chill propelled us on to the job at hand – scraping the hull clean. This became an on-going job at every port where we weren't anchored in soup. Tenacious, alien-like barnacles clung to the hull, "fouling" the normally smooth paint; ultimately, this reduced our speed. The tough, conical shells housed tiny crab-like sea creatures that seemed to live within goo not dissimilar to the slime used in the movie *Ghost Busters*.

It was always good to see the under-water part of *Mariah* and check that nothing hideous was happening to the only barrier we had between endless depths and a dry living area. When possible, we dived in to check that the anchor hadn't hooked onto a loose rock. Jumping in, I took a while to relax and slow the heartbeats that are amplified in water, through my body to my ears. As usual, my mind started playing the theme tune to *Jaws*. It's funny that if you *know* the water you are swimming in, you become more relaxed. In unknown waters, you never know what creatures are lurking – as if creatures in another country would be any different from your home waters!

Clouting the barnacles with plastic scrapers is like throwing a punch with your arm in treacle, the water's resistance makes it heavy work. As the barnacles lose the battle, thousands of tiny sea creatures stir in the water. Bigger sea creatures come and eat them, in turn bigger sea creatures arrive and eat those and so on until, well, one doesn't like to think about it too hard. Holding our breath became an art form, and we walked a fine line between lucid and losing it. As my lungs were threatening to explode, I tried to reach a few more tenacious shells. My heart was now screaming in my ears. Flexing my feet hard, thirsty for air, I powered towards the surface and smashed my head on the hull. While rubbing my head and cursing, Noel popped up beside me and we took a companionable breather, deciding on what was left to do. The bright sun made us squint, our chests heaved with effort. Clinging together on to the boarding ladder with the water lapping around our pink shoulders, one of my cotton balls fell from my ear and floated off, bobbing in the ripples. I stared at the white, saturated blob and giggled furiously. I could not stop.

'Out you get,' said Noel, 'You've had enough.'

Scraping the hull brings new meaning to having crabs. Climbing out of the cool water, we were covered in tiny, skittering critters; they made for the belly button and inside our swimwear. They did not hurt, but the thought ...eughh. We swiped them off while trying not to scream and dance around like two-year-olds seeing their first boogieman.

Within our watery world on the sea's horizon, we did not see many sailboats but they were out there doing the same thing that we were. At a rough guess, a couple of hundred boats must follow the seasons each year. Some people sail alone, what we call single-handers. Most are couples like us, but there are some families with one or several kids growing up on the water. The nicest kids we met on our travels were boat kids. My lack of maternal skills was never tested too hard around boat kids. My normal attitude to ankle-biters was that of taking pain killers – take two and keep away from children. With boat kids, the lack of materialistic luggage and ability to take on serious responsibilities seemed to create common sense, a lust for learning, and just damn nice kids. It's an ideal place to learn. My own geographical knowledge had vastly improved. Experiencing new cultures and meeting different races had to be a good education. Sailing into diverse countries together meant you knew exactly where they were located.

As we munched through the miles, the HF radio was really starting to earn its keep. It's a long-range radio and while in port with other cruisers, we would choose a frequency and time to speak whilst traversing the seas (ensuring we were on the same time zone). We soon latched on to these organised Scheds or Nets, which ran through a programme typically like:

'Good morning, this is the Indian Ocean Net, this is Jackie and Noel on board sailing vessel Mariah II on (date).'
'Firstly, are there any emergencies or priority calls?' Thirty seconds of silence – hopefully.
'Nothing heard, does anyone have weather details they can share with the Net?' With any luck, someone would know something, if not we would try to translate our Weatherfax.
'Now, I'll run through boat call.' We had a list of boats that had already joined the net.
'Frodo, Frodo, this is Mariah II, please come now with your report.' Frodo, and all yachts in turn, list their position, wind strength and speed, course, boat speed, barometer, weather for their location, and if all was well on board.
The Net controller runs through the entire list.
'Are there any other boats who would like to join the Net?'
'Any news for the Net?' This could be funny, informative, anything! *'I'll close the Net now and open up this frequency for boat-to-boat traffic.'* Boats could then call buddies on other boats and pick another channel to go chat on.

These Nets served several purposes; most importantly, if someone went missing the Net Controller had their last known position. If there were problems, there maybe someone nearby to assist.
There were other positives to having a good radio and joining a Net. With a time set to chat to others, it broke up the day

and gave us someone else to talk with other than each other. We heard stories of a sea-eagle catching fish, taking its kill to a particular boat and ripping its catch to shreds on the deck, the crew on board were all vegetarians. Vivid yarns of the head (toilet) breaking loose whilst in use were a welcomed, short reprieve from endless blue sky, blue water, and the odd cloud or bird scudding past. Best of all, when we arrived in a port, we had already spoken to some of the cruisers that had already anchored there. It was like opening a jar of coffee – instant friends.

Our first experience of the Net had a huge influence on our journey and thus created remarkable memories. We were en route to Batam (Indonesia, near Singapore) from Bali. After the official Net, we listened in to other cruisers chatting. This was a great way to glean useful information. We heard others talking about the fantastic time they were having in Borneo. Questions were asked, details absorbed, charts checked; we were now bound for Borneo.

Two days later, blessed with an easy trip of peaceful waters and a glorious full moon, we arrived into a huge bay some thirty miles away from the mouth of the river that housed Kumai, our destination. We anchored for the night in order to leave early the next day for the trip up the river. There was no wind and as the sun was quenched, we both turned in.

Sleeping in calm waters sometimes felt like we were sleeping on land. The salty air and fresh breezes were a good bet for a deep sleep. Well rested, just before the sun broke over the horizon, we hauled anchor. The bay was as smooth as glass, not a breath of wind ruffled the surface. The tangy smell of the salt laden breeze was diluted by the fresh river water and moist foliage. Relying on our faithful Yanmar engine, by lunchtime we arrived at the mouth of the Kumai River. Usually we would have charts or Pilot books, but due to our unplanned diversion, we were ill equipped (or so we thought). Using our VHF radio (short range), we tried to call up another boat already anchored near the town of Kumai. Cindy and Faith, two American cruisers on board *Carmen Miranda* answered our call and relayed all the information we needed to wind our way up the river to the anchorage. Moving through the water dragging a one-and-a-half metre keel below us and running aground is severely dull and can be dangerous to crew and boat alike, so knowledge is imperative. The Kumai River was like puttering through beef soup.

'Does anything live in here?' I wondered aloud. The rainforest on our starboard was a stunning lush green; on our port was sand, palm trees, and grass huts. 'Blimey we're sailing into Borneo!'

Noel laughed at my British accent coming to the fore through my wonder.

Navigating up a river is quite different to traversing an ocean. To start, there are more things to hit. The traffic was thick with many small boats towing what seemed like mile-long lengths of naked trees that were barely visible above the water. There were leads (two markers at different heights; once aligned you are on the right course) to help. We both had to be alert to check our position and depth; we worked like a well-lubricated team and safely worked our way up the snaking, dirty river. Reaching the other boats that were already comfortably anchored, we slowed down to search for a space. Theoretically, on anchor, all boats should swing the same way, but you still have to leave enough room for different shaped boats that might react slightly different in a breeze or tidal stream. We agreed on a spot, and Noel deftly turned *Mariah* as I stepped up to the bow to organise the anchor ready for deploying.

As we did this, a catamaran came racing up from behind, turned in front of *Mariah's* bow, and dropped his anchor in the spot we had chosen. Now, there is a certain anchoring-etiquette. Clearly, common courtesy dictates that we were there first, however, the space wasn't that great, so we just shrugged our shoulders and puttered on down to the next available space. Later, as we relaxed, swinging on anchor amongst twelve or so other boats, we revelled in our self-satisfaction of anchoring properly and enjoyed watching the catamaran having to re-anchor – he was too close to other boats.

I had become the expert anchor person. Handling the heavy loads and forces of the equipment is a skill. Arranging the equipment for a smooth anchor became my forte.

As our minds relaxed, we tried to absorb the fascinating scenery and sounds of small thatched huts, jungle and concealed screeching from within. As we unwound, we remembered that we did in fact have Pilot details for the river stored on a floppy disk! We chinked our glasses and with big grins said, 'Cheers.'

This was typical of us. It wasn't that we were a bit forgetful, though we were, but we found humour in our foibles. Noel had shown me how to enjoy laughing at myself. Not having to perform expertly all the time, or wonder if I was viewed as stupid when I did something a bit daft was a blessed relief. It felt like a lead weight had been lifted. I felt lucky to have found someone so lacking in judgmental traits and seemed to love me more as I let myself just be me. At school I had been shy. I had thought that I was not very smart and this shredded any confidence I may have had. Given the freedom to be me, completely, revealed my clever side.

8

Playing with orangutans

There was so much to see at Kumai, such as Tanjung Puting, an orangutan rehabilitation centre. Dr Birute Galdikas had, for twenty years, been reintroducing orangutans to their natural habitat and rescuing them from captivity. The animals were taught how to live wild within the forest of Borneo. The Tanjung Puting National Park was one of the few protected tropical jungles. It was unique in its diversity of ecological zones: wetlands, lowlands, swamp forest, hardwood rain forest, and mature tropical heath. The park had been the site of the longest running studies of orangutan behaviour. The animals that were at the rehabilitation centre were confiscated pets destined for the lucrative black market. We were told that nowhere else on earth could we see so many orangutans in their natural habitat.

The humidity in Borneo was exhausting, but after a good night's sleep, we ventured ashore. True to form, we left half of the relevant paperwork we needed to check-in back on the boat (passports, boat papers, crew lists). Although we were still in Indonesia, we had to check in and check out with the officials at each port. The pain could be taken out of the rigmarole if you hired an agent, but this was expensive. You could complete all the paperwork yourself by visiting all the authorities one-by-one. In this part of the world, in order to "smooth" the pathway-of-paperwork, the officials regularly asked for bribes. It was cheaper to deal with the bribes ourselves than to hire an agent.

Taking our first steps on Kalimantan, we were assailed with the usual sounds and smells of a developing country. The faint odour of sewage, dust, and spices mixed with the noise of umpteen motorbikes and mopeds, ridden with a serious absence of road rules.

The small town of Kumai was delightfully lacking in the normal tourist trade. The locals were exceedingly friendly, and foreigners were the centre of attention. Feeling a bit like Hollywood stars, by the time we reached the end of the dusty street our faces ached with smiles and greetings. The grubby, barefoot kids flashed white smiles at us and continuously shouted 'Hallooo Meeeeses; Hallooo Meeester.' There was no hassling from the street peddlers selling their fake trade and invading our space. In fact, despite the obvious lack of money, Kumai was rather pleasant. It seemed that the town had found its own structure. It was littered with small retail shops, a few tailors, a market, and other such small establishments, where the locals generated their own income. The majority of Kumai was residential. The houses were mainly large sheds that were basic, unpainted, a bit dull and sad, but coloured by the remarkably bright, happy smiling locals. Instantly, we could sense that the locals were content with their lot in life.

The Indonesians were generally small in build, which made us feel cumbersome and clumsy. Many of the girls tried all sorts of tinctures and lotions to lighten their attractive dark skin. They all sported inordinately shiny, black hair. The women were slim and even though they were small, they mostly had model figures. We didn't see many of the familiar pear-shapes prevalent in the first world. It's here I found out a secret to the perfect bust: enormously padded bra's (which are as attractive as two buckets and bailing twine). These industrial sized items were rife in South East Asia, but obesity here was not a problem; Asians eat rice like the Brits drink tea.

The town felt comfortable, like wearing your favourite jumper. Kumai's main street had about four interconnecting side streets. Wandering around trying to find the officials' office, we spotted what looked like an alfresco restaurant, with dancing and singing, all amid a brimming rainbow of colour. We should have been checking in, but we were ashore now and wanted some lunch. We meandered past, trying to covertly spy on the party.

Wafting from the stage, there was funky Arabian music played by a ragamuffin band sitting cross-legged, with homemade drums, violins, and guitars. On the other side of the stage were young men dressed in strangely plain, but beautiful, long Dish-Dashers (tunics), dancing and singing. Around the tables were the usual family members that gathered for a wedding. We were invited in. Well, not so much invited, but physically dragged in. I had worn a long sarong and a shirt with long sleeves in respect for the officials we would meet when checking in (some Indonesians are not used to seeing women's bare legs and arms). Other cruisers passed by and were not invited in, because they were wearing shorts – Indonesians can find this offensive. At first, we were reluctant and I felt shy. We had been reading about the way of Indonesians, their culture and do's and don'ts. I was terrified of making a huge faux pas. Taking a proffered plate, we were manhandled around the buffet, Mum and Dad ensuring that we sampled everything. It's actually rude to turn down an invitation, or pretty much anything offered by an Indonesian, so we just went with the flow.

Our unbidden hosts tossed out a local family from the best seats near the stage and indicated that this was where we must sit, as honoured guests.

'Everyone is watching us,' I said to Noel with a broad smile, hiding my embarrassment.

Noel and I sat and took the first tentative steps of trying the unidentifiable food. Noel smiled at me reassuringly.

'I know,' he said, 'my goodness, try some of this, it's delicious.'

It wasn't long before we were spooning it in with gusto. The flavours were incredible. New spices assaulted our taste buds, sending them into a frenzy of wanting more. All washed down with the sweetest lychees and plenty of water.

Eventually, the performers on the stage insisted that we joined them for a dance. We put them off for a while by slowing our eating and resisting eye contact, but it was inevitable. Still nervous of doing the wrong thing in this fresh experience and novel culture, we tentatively stepped onto the makeshift stage. The groovy music pumped around the band, vibrating the stage; we sedately boogied on down, trying to mimic our hosts' dance moves. I didn't feel like dancing like a westerner, because I wasn't sure how hip swinging would be received and all the guests were watching our every move. The laughter was infectious: from the pleasure of their guests dancing and enjoying themselves, from the men who could tell I was nervous, from the jokes at our expense from the stunningly dressed girls; there was no stopping it.

Fine fabrics in an array of different colours beaded with sparkling rainbows, flitted around the party, pointing and staring at the plainly dressed visitors.

After a couple of songs, we were thanked profusely and settled back into our prime seats. Several guests joined us to talk. We didn't understand a word anyone said! It was enormous fun speaking in our own, unprofessional, sign language.

Noel and I were both handed a gold painted, heart-shaped photo frame as a gift, and we thought it might be appropriate to present one in return to the bride and groom. I always carried a few handfuls of sweets for kids and some small koala bear figurines that donned cork hats and 'I Love Australia' t-shirts – a bit tacky maybe, but it was all we had, and we liked to think it was the thought that counted. Once our hosts realised what we wanted to do we were promptly pulled up and gently shoved to where a photo session was taking place. We were reluctant to interrupt, but were literally pushed over to the supposedly happy couple and made to stand with the rather stiff and sombre bride and groom – the photo session merrily continued. Some years later they must have wondered who on earth these strange people were in their wedding photos, handing over koala toys!

Sadly, bureaucracy nipped at our conscience, as we had to get our entry paperwork photocopied before the shops closed, so we took our leave. The families didn't want us to go; handshakes were long and firm, and we had to wrench our hands free from theirs. We received requests for our return and thanks from everyone around us. Far more attention had been lavished on us than the bride and groom. We would learn that these unique opportunities just happened. Events that were spontaneous and unplanned were the cherished moments we could never repeat.

Eventually, we headed back to the dinghies and found other cruisers ashore.

'We need another couple to make up numbers,' a smooth Irish tone emanated from the huddled group, 'why don't you join us?'

'That'd be great,' Noel and I answered together. 'Where're we going?'

'We're hopefully going to see the orangutans in the jungle,' another cruiser from New Zealand explained, 'pack a lunch.'

The tour guide's office was a timber shack that sported more holes than timber. On the pitted desk, up to the minute stereo, TV and DVDs lay incongruously. Some of the gear was so new we had never heard of it, let alone seen it before. The array of cruising foreigners congregated within the mishmash of old and new surroundings, and we all cast fearful glances at the drum in the corner of the office. As our guides organised the rabble, they chain-smoked. I became mesmerised by the blue whorl of smoke that spiralled into the gaps in the rafters. In the corner, just an arms stretch away from the stained fingers holding the cigarette, quietly sat an enormous drum of diesel. We all knew it was diesel for the drum had no lid. It didn't seem to worry our guides at all, but the cruisers from every corner of the world, all felt uncomfortable with the potential bomb just a few feet away.

So far the assembly of boat people consisted of Americans, Swedes, Kiwis, French, Irish, Brits, Hungarians, and Aussies. This, to me, was what life was all about: not luxury hotels (although sometimes it would have been nice to have had running hot water), but rather mixing with the locals; stuff that just wouldn't happen on package tours. I was having the time of my life.

The next day we were collected by our chauffeured speedboat from our yacht at 6 am, and we soon felt like extras in a James Bond movie. Speeding up narrow creeks, caged in by thick, tangled jungle. After sailing for thousands of miles at five knots it was great to feel the wind in our hair at a supersonic thirty knots.

The resplendent green forest was bewitching, the smooth mirror-like river, cool, flat, and inviting. Indolent fresh water crocodiles peered over the horizon of water waiting for their prey; small monkeys swung aerobically from tree to tree, unaware of the splendid tableau that was their beautifully menacing home. We visually devoured the terrain, one of Mother Nature's truly remarkable gifts, absurdly protected by humans, from humans. It was magnificent.

The Park was one of the few protected areas of tropical jungle. We arrived at the first camp, covered in extra strong bug repellent and sun cream, armed with hats, sunnies, socks, long pants, long-sleeved shirts, and enough lunch for about sixteen people!

Walking along the jetty, we met Michael, a small, long-tailed monkey. I was stunned as I offered him my hand and he took it. His hand was narrow, but long and unbelievably soft. Noel took his other hand, and we swung him back and forth like a child. We made our way along the sturdy, timber jetty with Michael between us; soon he let go and skipped along at our heels, his long arms held drunkenly awry and his shorter legs peddling fast. He grabbed Noel's rucksack strap and up he went, sitting parrot fashion on his shoulder. I felt jealous, but giddily happy, at being so close with this little creature, and perhaps a little relieved that Michael's bare bum was not on my shoulder. Our furry friend left us and went to play with his other cousins that were clomping along the jetty.

After reading and dreaming about different places and happenings, we were finally in the middle of those places, doing the things we'd thought were fantasy. We trekked through the dense jungle with the guides puffing out their chests and expelling extraordinarily loud, deep bellows to summon the orangutans.

As we hiked under the blanket of heat and trees, we made friends with an Irish family that were travelling together on two sailboats a similar size to *Mariah*. Bob and Christine with their youngest son, Jamie, were on *Breakaway* and Kirstie (Bob and Christine's daughter) was on *Chinook* with her British husband, Andy. It was an easy chat, all of us grateful for the pauses in conversation to catch our breaths in the airless heat. They were all on the home straight, having left Ireland some years before. They had already traversed the Atlantic Ocean, played in the Caribbean, piloted through the Panama Canal, and conquered the Pacific Ocean. We were beginners in comparison.

'You'll love the Pacific Ocean and its islands,' they said. 'You're doing the hard bit now; the Pacific is easy, all downhill.'

I thought most of the sailing was pretty easy so far but this opinion would rapidly change. And I couldn't come anywhere near to imagining that we would make it across the Atlantic and over the breadth of the almighty Pacific Ocean. Noel and I had an agreement to take the trip one destination at a time. Ultimately (and privately), our goal was to reach England, but we never really spoke about it. Thinking of the distance and lands between England and us was far too daunting. The next port, in whichever country, was our immediate goal that we focussed on – baby steps.

Eventually, accompanied with a layer of sweat, we reached the orangutan feeding site. On a square, wooden platform sat a bucket of milk and several enormous bunches of ripe bananas, their bright yellow skin contrasted to the vivid green surrounds.

The orangutans weren't in any hurry, because the forest was teeming with their natural food. As the small group of humans gazed around and enjoyed the peace, an orangutan suddenly appeared. Cleverly making his way about fifteen metres up in the trees, he grasped small branches and bent them so he could clasp the trunk with his huge hands and feet. The contortionism performance left us with cricks in our necks and mouths hanging limp. Their limbs bent in every direction and stretched out to seemingly impossible lengths. After large, vocal gulps of milk from the bucket, he grasped several dozen bananas, it seemed his favourite eating position was upside down. Two or three other orangutans appeared and happily sat and ate with thirty intent eyes watching. These hairy creatures listened to umpteen cameras clicking with apparent apathy.

The antics of one great character kept us amused. He swung from a vine high up, launching himself off the platform, playing human skittles with his spectators. He then hung upside down on a flexible small tree, taking pleasure in showing us his half-regurgitated banana, then letting the tree flip up. This cheeky character proceeded to steal anything we had left on the bench. Then he grabbed Noel's shirt and fully inspected his chest. The hairy orangutan and the hairy man with their heads just millimetres apart, a kindred spirit, was a priceless moment in time. Before he took his leave, he lay down amongst us, letting us all inspect him fully, his tummy, feet, nails, hands and head. These beautiful orangutans had long red, patchy coats. They had gentle, unassuming faces, tyre-rubber lips, and innocently round, brown eyes. Their long, slim hands and feet were identical, both with effective prehensile digits, which were incredibly soft. They were powerful, gentle creatures. He held my hand; he was so strong.

I had a vast appetite, so we ate lunch at 10:30 am, all the walking and oppressive heat making us hungry. With a new spring in our step we set off for the next camp, where we could apparently swim. As the group gathered, we peeled away t-shirts that felt like wool-blankets. The black-tea coloured river ambled along next to us between dramatic emeralds of jungle plants that hid the hooting birds. On the grassy banks, a small, dark woman crouched, scrubbing her laundry. With a wry smile she offered us her soap; a communal wash ensued (in swimming gear I might add). It is not usually a habit of mine to bathe with so many men. Many of the women did not want to venture into the dark water where crocodiles lurked. The cool, fresh water washed the sweat and jungle off our tired bodies. There were no showers at our anchorage. Water could only be purchased in small bottles; it was expensive and scarce. We washed clothes and ourselves in the dubious, soup like river and prayed that we would not catch some diabolical disease. We had to conserve our precious drinking water. This surplus of tannin-stained but clean water, with the added bonus of soap, was a much appreciated treat.

Without towels, we dressed while wet. Within minutes, our clothes were completely dry. We arrived early at the next feeding site, so a guide took us for a trek further into the jungle. At this camp, we were warned that the king was nearby (the male orangutan leader) and some decidedly aggressive females that could, and would, bite if in the mood. It was extremely hot, but the plethora of information on the vivid flora and fauna from our guide held all our interest. Stepping over toe-sized ants and concentrating on avoiding wet leaves to dodge the alien like leeches, the group suddenly came to a halt. Saucer-eyed, we all watched in horror as our guide turned on his heels and sprinted back past us! With somewhat puzzled and worried faces, it didn't take us too long to follow; comically, we all politely kept our order in the queue. The king was coming in our direction along the same path. After catching up with our guide and convincing him to stop for a moment, we suggested that maybe we could stand aside, off the track, and let him pass. Our guide was horrified and made it clear he thought that we were complete imbeciles. He then showed us his scars from previous attacks.

We followed the guide's advice; he knew the orangutans and the terrain, and he was clearly worried. We soon saw why. From around the corner, he appeared. The king presented himself to an awestruck audience. He paused and stared at the clutter of pale aliens that stared back at him. The air disappeared as we all collectively gasped. He turned left to look at Princess, his current mate, who was close by. Another female lurked nearby carrying a baby, and she was reportedly aggressive. Air became available as a few of us let out a breath; the king had been diverted. Forgetting our fear and the odd predicament we were in, tentatively and rather stupidly, in a tiny cartoon like huddle, we all scuttled closer peering through the trees to have a good look. The king was enormous with tremendously long, thick, strong arms. We did *not* want to mess with this guy; we were in his territory, on his terrain – this was *his* home. We were all in fearful reverence of this magnificent creature.

The king stood at about one-and-a-half metres tall, but that was with his legs bent; with his arms and legs out-stretched, he would easily be twice as tall. He weighed 150 kilograms and was about thirty-four years old. He was one of the first to arrive at the camp at the tender age of four. His head was at least three times the size of a human's head, and his arms were almost twice as long as his legs. He could scratch his bottom from reaching over the top his shoulder. He was simply amazing.

We edged forward in our comic human cluster. The king must have smelt the fear and intrigue. We paused and watched; the king moved and we all turned and ran. This little skit occurred several times, when suddenly he bellowed an eardrum-rattling cry. Rather startled, we soon learned that it was his mating call, and us girls hoped he wasn't calling to us (there were plenty of horror stories along those lines). We bravely hid in the bush and watched this almighty male and a female copulate; it was an incredible sight, and the group was somewhat relieved that his mind was on other things aside from us.

On the walk back, we were all glad to have been completely ignored by our hairy cousins. The usual jokes were told after seeing something sexual, but it didn't take away, from any of us, the honour we all felt to witness such a unique sight. The king only appears every few weeks for just a couple of days, we'd seen him at his most personal – even the guides were astonished.

At feeding time in the afternoon, we were blessed with seeing youngsters cradled by their mums and the mighty king again. He nimbly climbed onto the platform and viewed his spectators with their clicking cameras and flashing lights. He could reach any one of us in a split second, so we were content in the knowledge that he was quite used to watching clumsy humans. Even so, we all kept quiet and tried not to attract personal attention. Unlike the other feeding sites, none of the orangutans initiated contact. We were glad, as none of us wanted to be dragged over to the platform to be introduced to the king. The orangutans seemed to be different in the king's group; they were less willing to cross the border and make contact.

Dusk was falling and the mozzies were singing their incessant chorus, so after one more quick dip, we headed back home to the boats. Near the river, Noel climbed a decrepit tower to gain a better view for one last picture of this unique day. He stepped up to the first platform, and a shy, but aggressive, female orangutan took this opportunity to follow Noel and his tantalising, swinging camera, up the tower. With gasps and exclamations of, 'Boy, he's in big trouble,' Noel did a quick recce of his prison for an escape route: either up the rickety tower, where he might be followed or straight down to hopefully hit the water. With breaths held, at the last minute the orangutan jumped off of the ladder onto the side of the tower. Noel took his moment, and with lightning speed that I had never witnessed before, he shot down the ladder to the safety of his fellow humans.

Visiting our cousins in the wild was exhilarating. To have their trust – a trust in a race that is persistently trying to destroy their race and their natural habitat – was something I will never forget. To hold hands with an animal from which we descend, to study their soft palms, experience their powerful grip, their human nails, and their clandestine power was a privilege. The memories of those beautiful beasts, our relatives will never leave me. We may never get the chance to meet again.

The next day, we caught a Bemo (local taxi-bus) to the main town. The Bemo had seating for a maximum of eight. At last count before we left, there were fourteen of us crammed in, in thirty-degree heat and ninety-nine percent humidity. Astonishingly, some of the passengers were wearing jeans and jumpers! Once we managed to ignore the uncomfortable feeling of sweat literally pouring out of every single pore of our bodies and pooling around our thighs, we could enjoy the surroundings. There was no air conditioning in the Bemo, in fact, there was no anything; it was the most basic transport (and I use that term lightly) you could find. I was sitting next to and on top of a girl who was mute, she signed that she could hear but could not speak. All in all, I had one of the best conversations with this girl than any other non-English speaking Indonesian.

In town, we were pleasantly surprised with the lack of tourism. I relish in the fresh feeling a new town holds, the weird smells, alien language, unidentifiable foods, and new customs.

Once again, we were the stars of the town: strange white people with brown hair with colourful, relatively scant clothing that caused quite a stir. We needed to find a bank and located young locals with some basic English to help. Once they realised what we wanted, they whistled to a couple of passing motorbikes. The bikes stopped next to us with two young lads sitting astride. We were motioned to hop on board. I sat side-saddle, as I'd seen the local woman and girls doing it this way. The journey was only five minutes, but everyone in town jeered, shouted, and waved as we sped past. My driver explained that I should have gone astride the seat, which was impossible in a long sarong. I think it had something to do with riding that way if the driver was your partner! We had learned to take the constant attention with a smile and laugh. Though, sometimes it was exhausting, we were gaining a small insight of what being in the limelight meant.

The main town was dirty, busy, and hot. We preferred smaller villages, so we quickly purchased some supplies and made our way back to where the Bemo had dropped us off. We had become the butt of many a joke from the locals hanging around. After a good laugh, it wore a bit thin, especially when about ten people climbed in the Bemo before us. Being a Brit, I'm a big fan of queues. Not really in the mood to play human sandwich, Noel and I decided to hitchhike our way back to *Mariah*.

We took shelter under a large, shady tree and it was not long before we were negotiating with a couple of local guys on two motorbikes for a ride home. I re-fixed my sarong and jumped astride on to my ride.

'See you in hospital,' Noel laughed as he sped off on the back of his ride. It was then I realised what we had got ourselves into. A huge grin appeared on my face and I hung onto the complete stranger, trusting that he was not having ideas of a kidnapping-ransom scenario. A passing thought was given to my dad, who would have had a pink fit seeing me without a helmet.

The rules of the road here were similar to Bali, but fortunately there was far less traffic. The cool breeze tugging at my cheeks heightened the sense of freedom. The riders kept overtaking each other, and Noel and I found it amusing to pretend to beat our respective steeds with a whip!

Back on board *Mariah*, on anchor, we appreciated the calm stillness and soft sea breeze that found its way into our home. While trying to keep up with my diary on the laptop, the battery power had become low. On board, we received power via two battery banks: one for house batteries (lights, TV, GPS) and one solely for the engine. We had a solar panel, which kept our batteries charged quite well. However, if dull days persisted, we needed to run the engine to charge up. We were both busy below, preparing the boat for departure. After a week on anchor, household items were left out and had to be stowed safely away. I also wanted to charge the laptop, so I decided to run the engine for a while, during which we both continued preparing the boat down below. After ten minutes or so, we heard voices calling and knocking on the hull. Noel stuck his head out to be met by a fellow cruiser.

'I say, old chap, do you realise you are running around in circles?' Much to my embarrassment, I had left the throttle in gear and we were driving around our anchor. Fortunately, we didn't sideswipe any of our neighbours, as we were far enough away from other yachts and our anchor held fast! Phew! We got away with that one.

Back home, the support for our unusual lifestyle was unsurpassed. My mum and dad, who lived in Hertfordshire, thought us a little mad and worried a lot, however, they couldn't do enough for us – handling our UK mails. Colin and Brenda did all they could for us in Australia. You can never fully escape if you want a bank account. Mail, taxes, and credit cards have to be looked after. We could not have our mail chase us around the world and messages on the Internet from our families were our sole correspondence.

We missed friends and family deeply, but rapidly made more friends. The Irish family on *Breakaway* and *Chinook* became close to us. Other cruisers would comment that they thought Noel and I were part of the Irish family. In one sense, we were. Having friends of similar ages and interests was something we had missed a little. I especially needed a girlfriend, and Kirstie and I became friendly. We were both learning about boats and the cruising lifestyle as we went, although she had dealt with the change in life onto water a lot better than me.

We met people from every corner of the world. I was delighted with my life and the freedom I had claimed. My relationship with Noel was growing into a deep friendship, and I was starting to handle myself in this world. I was incessantly grinning and happy to chat to everyone about anything, my energy never waned.

In any situation, whether you are satisfied in your life or not, you still have to live with yourself. I believe that we all have our demons, or downsides. Sometimes, we simply get depressed, or in a bad mood for no reason at all. I was learning a new way of life, but witnessing more about humans and their eccentricities and that included me. I had everything a girl could want but there would be days when I had a mood swing and became grumpy. A tiny thing could set me off, and Noel was the same. The ability for Noel and I to talk about this after the mood had finally waned, was like a good medicine. I was extremely argumentative, and if I felt like having a good ding-dong of a row, I would do my best to get one. Noel wouldn't argue, and this would infuriate me. But after, when he had given me ample time to calm down (safer then), he'd point out the pathetic reason I was moody and explain that arguing back would cause us both to lose our cool and say things we would only regret. We were by no means perfect, our well thought out ideas and rules for moods didn't always work, and we did have our arguments, but it was something to work on. Soon I caught onto the idea (and even though it was nearly impossible for me), I bit my tongue and was amazed at the results.

I tried to live graciously, but it didn't always work. I'm not sure what these times were linked with, leaving one life for another, missing folk back home, or taking the time to dwell on unhappy events in the past. Just because life was an incredible adventure, I still had to live with myself, and sometimes I just didn't like me very much.

Emotions were given a freer rein, or it was simply that I had more time to think. With just the company of my own thoughts, night watches could be a cauldron of tearful memories. During these lonely, dark times I had time to reflect on where I had come from, how I had got there, and where I was heading – to Malaysia, on a ten-metre boat!

This would lead me back to the events in my life in the UK. Martin had been my fiancé. A handsome, fit, fine man, he had had a routine doctor's appointment and blood test, resulting in the knowledge of his leukaemia. We vowed to beat it, and I just knew with my positive thinking and strong will that we would beat it together. For six months of hideous chemotherapy, he lived in the hospital; I lived there too, in a chair. I left at 5 am to go shower and then go to work. I'd try to work all day and return straight to the hospital and my chair. Only to comfort a man who spent most of the time in incredible pain and fear, wasting away each day as the almighty cocktail of drugs would not share his body with food. I recalled with too much clarity his final days, his sorrow, his pain. Every expression, every line on his face etched in my mind. I knew his face would never fade from memory.

Martin had asked me to marry him before he died. As I organised our wedding, my dad had pulled me aside. I waited for the down-to-earth lecture, with only my best interest at his heart, about how I was going to be a widow, and to think about things - instead, he said, 'Anything you want, anything at all, you've got it, just ask.' I was speechless and so emotional that I couldn't even thank my dad, his whole body urged me to believe he meant anything, if I had wanted the moon he would have gone and got it himself. But what I wanted wasn't going to be possible.

Two days after the two-week diagnoses, Martin passed away in my arms. The cold world suddenly became too harsh, too bright, too loud. I wanted the world to whisper, to dull and be still. I had wanted to die.

On *Mariah*, absorbed in guilt during the night watches I would think about this; some nights I would cry so hard I would make myself sick. With the fires of hesitation extinguished, just six months after losing Martin I had run away and met Noel. I certainly didn't give myself enough time to grieve properly. My night watches became my grieving time, which worked for us both. Noel was supportive and I could talk about my feelings and worries, but he didn't need to see my crying and witness my tangible sadness. It was all mine, I just had to get through it. I didn't cry for me, or a love I wanted back. I wished Martin had his life back. I grieved for a life lost, a good person, taken for no reason, for the senselessness of it all.

I had thought my life was over, and at times I still became sad and had trouble understanding. I still felt the anger at the injustice. At times, I wondered if I would have left work and gone to Australia and met Noel had this not had happened. I'm not saying I'm glad I had something to spur me on to wringing everything out of my life I could, but it did give me the shove to go out there and find what else goes on in this world. Life has a strange way of guiding you on to another path. The nightmares continued, but Noel was an amazing listener and a patient comforter. It was through this time he truly became my best friend; we created an incredible bond that would never break.

In my new life, Noel kept me in check. I tell him my dreams, he knows all about my vivid nightmares. I dream of things I wouldn't tell anyone but Noel. He gently wakes me from my sad whimpering and draws me away from my nightly horrors. Noel has saved my life in more ways than one.

Sometimes nights were filled with horrors, but conversely my mind seemed to be two-timing me. I also had a few dreams of great happiness, where I'd laugh so hard I'd wake myself up, still laughing. I think I was a little unstitched at this point in my life.

It is said that time is a great healer. I don't entirely agree with this sentiment – you don't heal, rather over time you simply get used to carrying the indescribable pain; the grief matures into a settled sorrow.

At this point, my relationship with Noel was still building. I missed everyone back home so much. They had carried me through my darkest days. I'm sure I scared Noel a little by telling him that he wasn't only my husband, but my friend, girlfriend, mum, and sister! I just meant I could talk to him about anything and he understood.

With all these thoughts, we were still preparing to leave Borneo. Carrying water via jerry cans in the oppressive heat created a need for a cool wash, which also meant that we had to carry more water. Finding food we could identify to stock up with became a challenge we could do without; finding more space on board evoked dreams of a larger boat. The memories of the wedding and orangutans kept me positive. I wondered if our adventures could get any better. They did.

9
___

Singapore Sling

I felt like a bit like Alice in Wonderland, as the journey became curiouser and curiouser. On 23 October 2000 at 3:20 am, we crossed the invisible equator. Noel had a wee nip of a thick, warming liquid, with a good measure offered to Neptune. Two days later, we arrived safely at Batam, Nongsa Point in Indonesia.

I can tell you that this part of the world keeps you on your toes. The day before we arrived, I was on the graveyard watch. On board our bobbing world, we were surrounded by hundreds of dancing lights of various shapes and sizes.

'Is that a large boat far away or a small boat up close?' I asked aloud, trying to dispel my fears. It seemed that in this part of the world marine regulations were as popular as tax revenue. Navigation lights were regulated through the choice of the locals' favourite colours.

On boats the night-time lights are red for port side (left) and green for starboard side (right), a white light at the stern, and, if motoring (and not sailing) a white steaming light at the front. This helps to identify which way the vessel is moving. The locals favoured green; a good start you would think, a nice bright starboard light. However, the green would be an all-round light, on its own, which made it a trifle hard to work out what the beejeezus was going on.

The night was as thick as soup and as black as a mine. Our three-dimensional movement created quite the challenge in working out other traffic's courses. Only a few months before I would have made Noel stay up with me all night to weave between the walls of surrounding traffic; now I was handling the boat, figuring out and understanding other vessels' movements, and controlling my fears.

I was alone and managing to control the ship, this thought boosted my confidence, which was sadly about to be dashed.

At first, I was a bit dismayed with the odd and indistinct navigation lights, but as the night went on my dismay morphed into unmitigated gratification for any visible navigation lights at all. At about 3:30 am, I became tired and my feet were sore. I had been standing up for the entire time on watch. Noel and I had worked up to doing about six hours on, six off, so we could get better sleep. With over twenty boats around us at any one time, I was constantly taking bearings with the hand bearing compass, frantically jotting these down and noting direction of every vessel. Suddenly, I heard another putt-putt engine, but I couldn't see another boat. I checked our motor and it was making the same dull noise (there was not enough wind for sailing); the new noise I heard was different. Out of the darkness, a man appeared, then another. They were on a fishing boat skimming around our stern, and they had not one light on. I still, to this day, have no idea how they missed us. I grabbed the spotlight, which threw a solid white beam into their eyes. I sliced up the air with angry words; they understood how angry I was even though they didn't understand my language. I used one or two of those words that *everyone* can identify. This really shook me up. They were so close that I could have shaken their hands, although I felt like punching them on the nose. Eventually, their engine faded into the night, and the gentle lapping of waves reclaimed their rhythm on the night.

Soon after Noel woke, he said that he hadn't heard a thing. I was just glad to go hide under the covers, knowing I was in Noel's safe hands. Dawn was brightening the horizon, and we would be in a safe harbour tomorrow.

Good, I thought, I could do with a quiet, boring day for a change.

'Here we are in Singapore,' I said. It seemed that verbal acknowledgement was needed to make it real. We had sailed to Singapore! Actually, we were in Batam, Indonesia, at a place called Nongsa Point. We could see Singapore from the marina, just across the water.

It was muggy and sticky; the cloying atmosphere had hung around for weeks. Every day, a thick cloak of cloud sat over us, blocking the flow of air. I learned a hard lesson that the clouds did *not* block the sun. I burnt. Feeling perpetually sticky and continually sweating was no fun and caused tempers to shorten.

With *Mariah* safely tied in the marina, we caught the ferry for a short ride to Singapore. I was like an excited five-year-old, with another county to explore that I had always wanted to visit. But the hot air took its toll on Noel and worked its way through his thin layer of patience. Growing up in the strong sun-rays in Australia had made him far less tolerant of the heat, he'd had enough of it. In the midday heat in the middle of bustling Singapore, we stubbornly almost went our separate ways, like two-five-year olds sulking. I wanted to explore, and Noel wanted to find somewhere – anywhere – cool. Before the situation became completely out of hand, I remembered my tried and tested remedy to keep us all happy. My skills for boat handling were not the only skills I had developed: husband handling was becoming my other profession.

'Come on, follow me, I have something to cure all your ills,' I said. Noel looked at me and wasn't quite convinced, so I went on to explain, 'I'm taking you to Raffles for a Singapore Sling.' A smirk played on his lips, and he followed like a good puppy wanting to please, knowing he would receive a reward. I'm sure if he had had a tail it would have been wagging.

This plan worked well. The famous Raffles Hotel is unassuming and easy to stroll past without noticing it. On the outside it appeared colonial and small, but step behind the facade and it is immense, gorgeous and opulent. It houses history museums, every kind of shop you can imagine, umpteen cafes, restaurants, and bars. They served Singapore Slings in the Long Bar, which opened at 11:30 am. We were the first through the doors, not quite, but almost, drooling.

'Singapore Sling, sir? Madam?' They can spot a tourist a mile away. I felt like I wanted to explain that we were not tourists, we were sailors. Didn't they know we had sailed here on our own? The drinks were already made up and were served in a tall glass, vibrantly red and suitably exquisite. The Slings were a combination of gin and, well it seems to be a bit of a secret, but they were scrumptious. Unfortunately, so was the price at thirty five American dollars for two drinks. We savoured every mouthful.

After enjoying a heavy dose of alcohol, a cool breeze, and a couple of cigarettes, Noel was ready to hit the town. 'Bring it on,' he said with his cheeky grin, only a flicker of self-deprecation played on his lips.

We ventured around China Town, weaving our way between colourful stalls, weird and wonderful food, pirate videos, and CDs. Dodgy blokes behind combed moustaches offered us pretty much anything we could desire. Animated characters scattered throughout the markets called to the punters as they strolled by. Noel spotted vibrant Chinese silk dresses; they looked beautiful on the hangers, but on me they were stifling, badly cut, and frumpy.

The night in our cheap, and not-so-cheerful, hostel was a long one. Doors crashing, women screaming, and men shouting could be heard at alarming regularity. I kept my left eye propped open all night, convinced that somebody was about to crash through our paper-thin door. I was never so happy to bid farewell to the dark side of dawn. With only the cockroaches in the bathroom to contend with, we then bid a hasty retreat.

That afternoon, we headed back to *Mariah*. Our budget could not accommodate us to stay in the hostel any longer, besides I needed some sleep. We failed miserably in buying supplies for the boat. We were so wrapped up in the feast of smells, sights, and sounds that we forgot we needed bread! We were a good team on board, but the normal living logistics left our minds when we ventured into new cultures. Waiting for the return ferry, we bumped into our New Zealand friends, Judy and Barry, from their yacht *Theta*. They had been in Singapore for the day shopping, sensibly, for food. They kindly donated a loaf of bread to us. I felt embarrassed and unorganised (and, of course, grateful!)

We didn't have a fridge on board, so our shopping was pretty simple. We used powdered milk and olive oil instead of butter. Over the years we had learned which vegetables and fruit lasts the longest and how best to keep them. Fruit with a thick peel keeps for a long time, along with cabbages, potatoes, carrots, garlic, and ginger. So there was plenty of time to cross an ocean before needing to reach shops to replenish.

Our simple diet had erased the weight I had gained during the first flush of marriage. No fridge meant no meat. Constant sailing meant constant exercise. Humidity stole my appetite. I was svelte, fit, free of office stress lines, and I felt great.

After the trudge of sightseeing and shopping, it was a relief to get home to *Mariah*. The marina at Nongsa Point was a bit of a coup for all cruisers. The marina itself was just eight American dollars a day and within a hotel complex complete with a swimming pool, hot showers, and cheap, yummy food. The hotel was mainly used by locals and holidaymakers from Singapore. As it was out of season, we had the run of the place. Sea gypsies lazed daily by the pool, talking about the jobs that had yet to be done on board.

'I'll do it tomorrow,' could be heard wafting over the sparkling water. The most physical exercise was done while raising our arms to summon a waiter for, 'Another club sarnie, if you please!' We decided it was time for a holiday. Swimming, shady trees, and waiters filled our days. The covert luxury of lunch 'added to our bill' made us feel like millionaires.

It may sound odd that we were exploring different countries and now we wanted a holiday. However, the fact that we had to basically keep our own mini city running (what with the engine, fuel, rigging, sails, etc) and maintenance and repairs, meant that we received little down time. We had to work constantly to maintain a safe boat and therefore safe passage.

We were now within a good group of boats, *Breakaway* and *Chinook*. We had all left for Nongsa Point around about the same time, but as we did not have radar on board *Mariah*, we had battled straight through the middle of the numerous squalls that were prevalent in this area. Other boats had tried to go around them, using valuable fuel and time. Ultimately we all were hit by squalls, but we arrived at Batam two days before everyone else. Reefing the sails at night, clipping onto lifelines, and braving the elements had served us well. We now fully trusted *Mariah*. She was a strong, seaworthy boat that could handle nature's elements better than we could.

With all boats now safely in harbour, a party was on the cards within our small holiday haven, and one evening an impromptu celebration started on board *Mariah*. At one point, I counted eleven bodies squished into our small cockpit. Cruisers are used to making do within small spaces and utilising sparse cushions. We all settled into the normal rowdy cruisers party scene. Most people travelling on boats are on a fairly strict budget. It is an unwritten rule that when visiting other boats you take what you wish to drink with you and contribute to snacks or dinner.

On board, as usual, there were at least six different conversations occurring at once. Some people told stories that made you laugh so hard your stomach ached. After the boat started spinning, I retreated to one of the bunks under a fan while the party continued. Noel checked on me, tucked me in, and resumed partying. A while later, after slipping in and out of consciousness, I woke up to Noel staggering into the v-berth to join me in oblivion; meanwhile, not eight feet away, the party continued.

The next day was a write-off. Venue: poolside with plenty of greasy food, water, and dips in the refreshing pool. A couple of cruisers wanted to go water-skiing and tried to rope me in to drum up the numbers. I considered going, but realised that I was having trouble walking, let alone hanging onto a piece of twine, balancing on two planks of wood on water. I sensibly declined. I was realising that I didn't have to please everyone in order to make and keep friends. My wants and needs should be just as important to me as someone else's; that's something I hadn't given much thought to before. I was changing from a Corporate Girl into a Sea Gypsy Woman.

Eventually, we thought that we really ought to continue on our voyage. We stocked up and prepared *Mariah* for the next phase of our trip. Quite a few of our friends were taking their yachts to Singapore, but we had already been there via ferry. So, we left Indonesia and headed into Malaysia. Our next stop was a place called Port Dickson, but first we had to cross the Malacca Straits.

It seemed normal now to rest a few days at one place, sightsee, work hard at replenishing the boat, purchase and fit spare parts, and then head off once again. There was just no wind in this part of the world. We were motoring 95% of the time. Diesel was an incredible six cents per litre, and the seas were smooth and inviting.

10

Simple food and clear water

Great sailing is when you put your cup of tea down and it stays put. But the Malacca Straits had other ideas for us. We could indeed put our cup of tea down, because the movement was not the problem, but rather the fog. We motored across, filled with dread. The soupy water seemed to thicken the fog that hung limply above, camouflaging other vessels. Huge monolithic ships continually glided silently up and down the busy, narrow stretch. To add to the fun, a strong current pushed us along sideways. Imagine sliding on your bottom on ice. You might be facing left, but your body is going forwards. In a strong current this is how boats behave. It is rather disconcerting when you are weaving between enormous ships that are moving at twenty-six knots. Our maximum speed, under motor, was about six-and-a-half knots. We put a lot of faith in our equipment on board, as well as our ability.

We arrived at Port Dickson in the beginning of November 2000. So much had happened already; we had only left Australia in September. I felt like we had been sailing away from Australia for years.

Port Dickson was oppressively hot. The marina, surrounded by tall buildings, prevented any breeze from reaching us. However, it was clean and well equipped with a pool. By now, we had seen a few pools and nice marinas, but that wasn't what our travelling was about. However, we were grateful for the refreshing plunge.

Port Dickson is a funky town in more ways than one. It contains almost everything you could desire except good bread and most western supermarket food, which was exactly what we needed. Checking in was dramatic – customs was difficult, and I don't think my mindless wardrobe helped. I had forgotten to cover up and exposed arms and legs were a big no no; after much grovelling, they stamped our passports and sombrely let us go. The bus station was nearby, so without thought or plan, we jumped on a bus to Kuala Lumpur. The ride provided a welcome reprieve from walking in the heat. For two hours, with air conditioning blasting on our damp skin, we sat back and soaked up the scenery.

Kuala Lumpur was buzzing, so it didn't take us long to find the markets and barter for items that we just did not need. There were no clothing bargains to be had, as they were expensive, fake branded gear with very *real* prices.

We walked through the town seeking an Information Bureau. We found it in an unremarkable basement, hidden, with no indication of its existence. Organised tours were ridiculously expensive, so we stole some ideas from the shelved brochures and set off on our own tour. We bumped into a German couple that were also sight-seeing; they gave us some other must-see ideas.

Armed with knowledge, we first thought it prudent to check the departure time of the last bus – 9:30 pm – plenty of time to play the tourist. We booked a Chinese buffet restaurant for dinner and a show and then hot-footed it to the Telecom Tower, which offered a staggering view of the city. Bustling with dozens of other tourists, we viewed the magnificent sights of Kuala Lumpur. We paid one ringgit (about thirty-three Australian cents) to use the telescope and found we had to fight to keep it. Malaysians had no idea of queuing and even less idea about paying. At first I thought they were ignorant, then I realised that they were actually quite smart.

Soon we were heading back to the restaurant for the show and dinner. Of course we picked a night there was a school outing and we were accompanied with about one-hundred-and-fifty kids! Just as we were about to avail ourselves to the buffet, a secret signal was given and one-hundred-and-fifty kids stood up en-mass and charged towards the feast. The swarm of locusts eventually cleared, and we went up to pick at the remains.

The show consisted of Asian dancing. The girls looked bored and only one of the guys knew what he was doing. Still, it was colourful. We finished our scraps and all too soon we were on our way back to the bus station from hell.

The bus station was underground within an enormous concrete coffin. Since building the airless tomb, newer buses had been built, which meant bigger buses. Unfortunately, the concrete coffin had no way of expanding. The engines grunted and groaned as they were slammed backwards and forwards, trying to edge their way into the tiny bays. It took a surprisingly short time for the basement to become thick with lung clogging fumes. No vents or windows meant the fetid air had no escape. The black exhaust fumes smeared walls and covered any lighting that may have been there and our lungs disintegrated with every breath.

Our bus, the last bus, had broken down. We waited an hour for a replacement. Even though there was a language barrier, the ticket-selling attendant managed to indicate that we should buy tickets when we stepped on the bus. It was getting later and later; we were becoming a mite sceptical of getting home. Spending far too much time in the deadly basement of buses, we awaited eagerly for our transport home. Finally, it arrived. The trip was once again pleasant: comfy seats, cool air, and thought of our cherished home waiting for us. I dozed and Noel chatted to a friendly Indian man, who subsequently gave us a lift back to the marina from the final bus stop (with wife and two children in one car). We were to experience endless helpful gestures such as these in every country we visited.

We arrived late back to the marina, and all the gates were locked. No security guards were to be seen. Our Indian friend helped us break into the kitchens that were part of the restaurant (causing no damage), where we could make our way back, through deserted buildings, to the sanctuary of *Mariah*.

The next night we opted for a quieter option. Barry and Judy on *Theta* were coming over to *Mariah* for a quiet dinner. First, they were having cocktails on *Fraden*. Early in the evening, after our swim, Noel and I strolled past *Fraden*.

'Come on board,' Francina and Denny called out, 'we have made some punch we'd like you to try.'

'Oh, okay only a quick one,' we said – famous last words. Two hours later, after meeting new cruisers and sharing unique, strange, and mostly hysterical stories with the added ingredient of plenty of punch, we were ready to hit the town. A group of about ten international sailors set off in three taxis to a highly recommended Indian restaurant. The group consisted of Australians, French, Americans, New Zealanders, and English; needless to say, the joviality continued, as did the flow of beer. The food was delicious and the company great. My shyness had all but evaporated, I wasn't sure anymore if it was my confidence, knowledge gained, or that I was simply quite drunk most of the time in this particular port!

The clock was ticking and it was time for us and our knackered kidneys to leave. We travelled from Port Dickson in a convoy with two American yachts. All of us reluctantly steered over fishing nets, as there were too many to avoid. The worry of what might happen at these times was exhausting. Fouling a propeller in an ocean meant someone would have to dive overboard (with a snorkel) to fight the waves and rolling boat in order to untangle the tenacious fishing line, all the while hoping the boat didn't sail off into the sunset without leaving him or her. Of course, being tied on with a rope and having a competent partner on board should allay these fears – but it was still a concern. Fortunately, we did not have to contend with this drama.

It was now 9 November, and we made an overnight trip to Lumut. The night stint contained the normal hair-raising fishing boats with indecipherable lights speeding around us in all directions. We made it through the night safely, and at dawn we were almost there. We had chosen this destination to take the opportunity to head up into the hills. We wanted to see the tea plantations and longed for some cooler air. With *Mariah* safely tied up on her own in a small marina, we arranged to catch a bus the next day into the hills.

Cameron Highlands tea plantations looked like a green velvet carpet, and the air was cool, clean, and crisp. It catered for tourists, but it wasn't over-run with the travelling breed. The taxi driver recommended to us accommodation that a friend of his owned. Our room for two nights was clean and cheap: a double room with a bathroom down the hall to share, all at 30 ringgit per night (about ten Australian dollars – a great bargain). We even asked for extra blankets that night! It was so refreshing to be cool again.

The next morning, we organised a half-day tour. Honey bee farms, markets, butterfly farms, and best of all, a tea plantation. BOH plantations were the biggest in Malaysia and carried the most tantalising smells. Tea comes from the original wild plant, *Camellia Sinensis*. The leaves are fermented, dried, and rolled differently to give each tea its particular flavour. A nice pot of tea and a bun was the perfect end to a touring day.

The second night we stayed in our accommodation and watched a complimentary movie. Continuous sightseeing could become tiring. Noel and I enjoyed meeting the locals in their environment and other travellers/visitors that had their own goals in life. We didn't need to keep seeing the latest tourist attraction – sharing a home with different people of new cultures was just as thrilling.

Most off-putting was the ridiculously loud music that was blaring from two enormous speakers, which swamped the town, and prevented any ideas of having a conversation. This was quite common in Malaysia, and we never found out exactly why this occurred; it presumably held some religious connotation. We just settled back in our own egotistical summation that large speakers were the worst objects to arrive in Malaysia.

Arriving too early at the bus station for the journey home the next day, we started a conversation with a couple: he German, she Thai. They were heading for KL, so we could share a taxi part way together. Racing down a steep, winding hill in a bus that would have been lucky to have had a service in the last fifty years, was not a prospect we were relishing. We were all glad to share the cost of a private car. We stopped at the waterfall again on the way down. Noel and I wanted a blowgun (we had had a practice with one in a shop in the Highlands, blowing small darts through the tube – not poisoned projectiles though!). We found an authentic Malaysian gun, which we proudly mounted on one of *Mariah's* bulkheads. I wondered what future customs officials would make of it.

Arriving home was, as always, a great joy. Although tired from travelling, we both had this continual need to move, and so that afternoon we prepared *Mariah* and left the following morning at dawn.

Twenty-four hours of motoring later, we arrived in Langkawi. This was our last stop in Malaysia. Our next stop was Thailand then, unbelievably, Sri Lanka. Were we really going to sail all the way to Sri Lanka? I asked myself in my disturbingly regular soliloquies. It would seem so.

My parents booked a flight to visit us. We had a few weeks up our sleeves before they arrived on 21 December. There was painting and varnishing to be done, and we were only permitted to stay one month in Thailand. We decided to anchor in Langkawi and set to work. Noel was becoming more accustomed to my strange ways – my soliloquies one of many oddities. There were times when I would say something to him and he would ignore me. I could be quite snobbish and get really offended, finding this behaviour rude. However, it would seem that I often chatted to myself more frequently than I realised. Noel had tried to talk to me when I was talking to myself. I, apparently would tell him off quite sharply, saying, 'I'm talking to myself, not you!' Quite rightly, thereafter, he was never quite sure who I was talking to, him or myself!

Before anchoring in Kuah, Langkawi, we anchored near the entrance, between a couple of islands inhabited only by wildlife. Anchored between sheer cliff faces without neighbours was heavenly. The water was, at last, much clearer. It was still slightly a green-pea colour, but certainly cleaner than it had been for some time. We spent two days watching the wild monkeys trapeze in the trees before dipping in the water; the wild pigs tentatively rummaged on the small beach, and the graceful eagles glided and swooped for their dinner. The anchorage was tranquil, still, and a calming balm for our moving souls. Thick, green jungle gave relief to our eyes; the clear and crisp azure skies with white birds cutting a gliding arc consolidated the serenity.

Langkawi had two marinas, both of which required taxi rides to reach town. One marina meant a lengthy taxi ride and was expensive. The other marina was a lot closer to town, but continually buffeted by the wakes from the constant ferries. Anchoring was easy, safe, and free. It also had a cooler breeze, and we liked the price. We liked Langkawi.

To get ashore we took our dinghy into a small lagoon, tied it up, and climbed up a bank into the town. We had heard through the grapevine that there was a bar here called Jimmy's, which was popular with the cruising folk. The town was not huge, so on our arrival we walked around the dusty streets trying to locate Jimmy's.

We stumbled upon a hotel, and seeing as how we had plans to call home, using the hotel's phone, we decided to have a quick beer. The hotel beer was incredibly expensive; this was certainly not Jimmy's!

The cold beer had become our ritual on arrival to a new port. Making a safe landing in a new place was an achievement, the beer the reward. We never drank at sea.

Refreshed, sated, and thoroughly skint, after letting our families know we were safe, we had another look around town. We noticed that there was plenty of duty-free alcohol, so this was where we would stock up for Christmas. We also found where we could buy bacon and cheese. Asking for the bacon was done in a whisper, once you had found the right shop; it was illegal to sell it in a Muslim village. It was excellent and made a great change from noodles, which had been our main diet.

Food was simple on board; we didn't have a fridge so it had to be. Pasta and rice were our main diet. We kept vegetables in the cupboards below the water line where they kept cool. Cabbage was peeled, not sliced, and would last weeks and weeks. Eggs were turned daily. Tomatoes kept in egg cartons, separate and unable to roll around and bruise. Buying supplies became a bit of an art. Not only did we search for the freshest items, but the quantity of bruising and general all-over condition was important, too. Of course, green bananas and tomatoes helped – any fruit or vegetable that could ripen along the way was useful. Bananas give off a natural gas called ethylene, which speeds up ripening. So we spread the bananas around to other places within the boat. If we were lucky to find a big bunch of green bananas, we would lash them under the solar panel, out of the sun. Each day we would pick one or two and put them in the sun for ripening. It all became incredibly easy and life was simple. It was surprising how little we needed. *Mariah* was a simple boat all round: having fewer gadgets meant fewer things broke down and needed maintenance. We were always a little smug when hearing about cruisers searching for parts for their fridge, water-maker, radar, and so on.

The next day, we found Jimmy's. We had had a preconceived image of leather chairs, green palms, and revolving fans. Jimmy's was simple, though. It had plastic chairs and tables and basic decorations, but produced the most wonderful, cheap Chinese food. We found out why all the travelling boats all thought of it as a cruisers' bar. There were no waiters or waitresses; you simply helped yourself to the beer from the fridge. A plastic menu was available, and at the end of your evening Jimmy counted the number of empty beer cans and plates and presented the bill – simple, just as we like it. We always felt we had been under charged.

One evening while sitting back in Jimmy's enjoying company from around the world, a sunset laid out bruised purples, vivid blues, startling pinks, and hot orange in a hundred layered shades right outside the door, reflecting off the still, silvery water. The traffic stopped, people came out of their shops and stood on the side of the road. Momentarily, the world turned into a kaleidoscope of colour. A hush spread throughout the town in reverence of nature's splendid show. The scene is forever etched into my mind. This was the first and last time I didn't carry our camera.

Noel and I knuckled down to preparing *Mariah* for my parents' visit and some timely maintenance. Three weeks of sanding, painting, and varnishing the interior and we had transformed *Mariah*. It was sweaty work in the still air and heavy heat, though the small fans had helped. The eighty-watt solar panel provided our power. Every day the skies were clear in Langkawi and therefore our batteries were constantly topped up. The local food was so cheap, we ate takeaways most nights. Besides, the entire interior of our home was covered in the fine dust from sanding. We also found a great video shop and for very little we could rent current movies. Shutting ourselves off from the world, in our little home, at night was a great way to wind down. We easily forgot where we were, but best of all, we were always at home.

We left Langkawi on 8 December 2000. At the end of a long day sail, we watched Ko Rok Nok slowly creep over the horizon. It was funny how some day sails felt more exhausting than a longer passage. After two to three days at sea, our bodies settled into a routine and became accustomed to the constant movement. On a day sail we couldn't rest properly, as we were near land and it just seemed to make us more tired. It was nice, however, to have a sail without thinking about the long night ahead.

Ko Rok Nok was comprised of two deserted islands between which you can anchor. They offer protection from the weather and are encompassed by beautiful, clear water. A few other yachts were already anchored, and they passed along advice that many boats had dragged their anchor as holding was poor, meaning anchors could not get a good enough grip to hold the boat. Noel and I had our anchor routine down pat. Noel would usually steer the boat into position in a place we both agreed on, and I would operate the anchor, releasing it as the boat stopped and started drifting back with the wind or current. I would let go of enough chain for the anchor to sit on the bottom and then control the speed in which I released the chain, so it didn't fall in one big heap. We developed straightforward hand signals, which allowed a simple, silent, and slick operation. We were always a little amused (and a bit smug) when we witnessed couples yelling at each other during anchoring. We both thought it prudent to swap roles regularly, so we could both operate every aspect of the boat. Serious injuries can occur on board; if one of us was hurt, that left a crew of one. It was imperative that we both became competent on every aspect on board, and for me it made living on board far more interesting.

Noel taught me how the engine worked and how to keep up the necessary maintenance. Electrics weren't my strong point, but I learned the basics. Navigation was now second nature and manoeuvring *Mariah* was a skill we both worked on. We understood the effect of the wind and currents on *Mariah's* hull, but as these were constantly changing, our abilities were constantly tested. With her long keel, applying reverse was a lottery as to which direction she would go – unless there was a stiff breeze, in which case she'd always feather into the breeze – eventually.

In Ko Rok Nok, anchoring was a delight. Once we had found a good position to drop the pick in sand, I let the anchor go and watched it drop ten metres to the bottom in beautiful, clear water. With the anchor settled and dug in, we donned the snorkelling gear and jumped right in. Since leaving Ashmore Reef the water had not been clear, but now it was like swimming in a large fish tank. Between having fun with nosey fish, we scraped the barnacles from the hull. The anti-foul paint kept most critters at bay, but there were always some tenacious barnacles that needed knocking off. A smooth hull meant *Mariah* slipped through the water quicker, and therefore we made the next port quicker. Having an understanding of the necessity of regular maintenance and care on board provided some routine into our lives. This work was for *us*, to improve *our* life on board – that's what I really liked about it.

We spent a few serene, peaceful nights at Ko Rok Nok. On the small, deserted beach, we anti-fouled the dinghy and gave the invisible sand flies a banquet feast, spending the following days in itching agony. Later, we had our own potluck banquet on the beach with a dozen other cruisers. Everyone took a dish and we all shared. It turned into a delicious and diverse feast.

Between the fun times, day-to-day maintenance kept us busy. We changed the engine oil and re-arranged the galley supplies, moving forward foods that had wriggled their way to the back of cupboards. We also made lists of spare parts and necessary food, a job so ordinary it made me feel right at home in these foreign lands. The rest of the days were filled with cruisers from other boats popping over to say 'hi'; the kettle was always on. If a boat had a particularly tricky problem, it would become a joint effort of knowledge, tools, and spare parts, followed by a debrief in the evening as we all watched the sunset. Life was good.

11

Undies scrutinised

Pee Pee Don in Thailand, more commonly known by tourists as Phi Phi Don (pronounced Fee Fee), was our next stop. It was now 12 December 2000, and I was looking forward to seeing my folks. They hadn't seen *Mariah* yet and had met Noel only the once when we were married. I'm lucky enough to consider my mum and dad as friends and couldn't wait to show off my new life and catch up with them properly.

Clear, calm water carried us into a busy anchorage, where vast rocks reached up high into the sky, the clouds tearing across their peaks. The deep water allowed us to anchor close to the shore and near a magnificent cliff face. There were about ten other boats already there, none of which we had met before, but there was plenty of room to share.

'We've sailed into Thailand,' I said to myself again. We were blessed with beautiful beaches and clear water, our own private swimming pool surrounding the boat.

Ashore we found a maze of alleyways with a plethora of cafes, restaurants, knick-knack shops, men who were money changers, and bars. Tourists, young and old, well-worn and new, mingled with excitable locals. No cars interrupted the hubbub of bodies, pedestrians, tourists, travellers, cruisers, dropouts, locals, and general riff raff. The place was buzzing.

'I like it here,' said Noel, grinning, absorbing the kicking atmosphere, which was in stark contrast to the peaceful anchorages we'd experienced so far. As a rule, we generally tried to avoid touristy areas, but Phi Phi Don was unique. The place was heaving with like-minded people, more traveller types than tourists.

The following day, cruiser friends from *China Dolphin* and *Obsession*, caught up with us after being a few weeks apart, and an impromptu lunch was arranged. Overlooking the beach we waited for our food, while different conversations fought for domination; we all had stories of adventures in reaching this point on the globe. Steering our own vessels into foreign countries and figuring out how to tackle it all was part of everyday life now. Sourcing supplies, new friends, parts for the boat and good times for ourselves was just how we lived. It all felt right, as if I had the zest and bite of my entire life wrapped up in travel. The emotional years of my hormone-fuelled teens, and the devastation of losing a loved one was moving farther into the past. I had also survived a brush with a frightening illness that others hadn't been so lucky with. It all led me here, carving out a new space for where I fit. (I had had a brief dalliance with an illness myself just a few years before running away to Australia. I was told I was one step away from treatment being too late. Fortunately, I had treatment just in the nick of time, with success. I was lucky and that's all I want to say about that).

While *Mariah* swung on anchor, exploring in our tiny dinghy transported Noel and I back to being kids, we puttered alongside a huge rock face, which hid caves begging to be explored. Stalagmites and stalactites and tiny bays hidden by rock curtains were waiting to be discovered. With an uncontrollable urge to always see what's around the next corner, we found ourselves in a coal black cave, cloaked in darkness, with no torch. It was quiet and creepy, cool and striking. Our two horse-power outboard, purchased in Bali, ran like a dream. The soft purring of the engine bounced off the vertical stone. We were alone and enjoyed the solitude of the secret place we found.

Finding light, we made landfall on small deserted beach only small dinghies, like ours, could access. Simple moments such as these gave us time to reflect on our achievements, and gave us a brief moment to revel in feeling just a tad proud.

As usual, focussing on supplies took second place to fun, and the galley cupboards quickly became too spacious. With just a short hop to the next port, we were not too concerned. With time moving on and the appearance of my parents looming, we upped anchor; we were ready to see other parts of Thailand. We arrived at Ao Chalong on 5 December. There was no marina here, and there was quite a few boats at varying stages of their sailing adventures, all swinging in unison within the tightly packed boat park at anchor. Choices of anchoring nearby to shore were limited; our little timber dinghy just had to cope with the one-kilometre journey to the beach.

Zigging and zagging between destinations with the other boats was how we lived; at some ports we would know lots of other cruisers, at others we would make new friends. Ao Chalong was a popular spot, and we were delighted to catch up with our Irish friends on board *Chinook* and *Breakaway*.

The dinghy ride to shore was about ten minutes and in protected waters. Andy, Kirstie, Jamie, Christine, and their new guest from Ireland, Neil (Jamie's and Kirstie's brother), were having a beer ashore. Neil was visiting for two weeks and the Irish family was together for Christmas. They'd been elephant riding and were still on a high. The evening was spent drinking vast amounts of beer and trying to string adult sentences together. In true cruiser sense we arranged to share a large taxi together the following day and find the best supermarket/local markets to stock up. It was exciting, at these times, to find such a shop: a proper supermarket. For the past few months, we hadn't seen much more than small shops crammed with items covered in dust and cobwebs. To identify each item we had to wipe off the grime and try to see how far out of date it had become!

The next day, after a good shop, on the return journey to the boat, the wind had strengthened and the anchorage had become choppy. We all hopped into our dinghies that were loaded down with shopping. Noel steered, as I was constantly bailing out as the waves were plopping over the sides, while balancing the shopping in the air to try to keep it dry.

Noel and Andy decided to race back to the boats. Well, Andy did as he had a much more powerful outboard. However, we knew all the tricks to gaining speed, being often one of the slowest.

'You're on!' Noel grinned at Andy.

'Come on, come on!' Andy yelled at his motor, which should have left us behind.

'I need to get closer to his wake,' Noel explained, 'with no water to push aside we'll glide effortlessly.'

We were soon on Andy's his tail. The wake from Andy's dinghy smoothed the water for us. We actually overtook him, as he had to bash into the waves, which slowed him down. We won the race! I still don't think Andy has forgiven us.

With food re-stocking ticked off the list, next on the agenda was spare parts. Bouncing around in the oceans stirs up the diesel tanks and sometimes the filters need to be changed more regularly than usual. So, the next day we ventured into town again to track down spare parts, mostly fuel filters for the engine. The spare part shops were dark, dusty places that looked like they hadn't seen a customer for twenty years. Language was a huge barrier, not many tourists are looking for oil and diesel filters for a Yanmar, and the translation was not something that was listed in the average phrase book. By now, Noel had become adept at sketching out our requirements. After several attempts, coupled with engine noises and air driving, a light seemed to appear in the owner's eyes and his small, brown, wrinkly body disappeared into the bowels of the shop. We followed him along the crowded tunnel of boxes and under four inches of several centuries of dirt, he slid out a box. The small container had certainly not seen the light of day in some decades, but after rubbing off the dust he pointed the box in our direction, accompanied by a large toothless grin. It was the exact type of filter we needed. The price was staggeringly low and we soon emptied his shop of fuel filters! The owner was delighted; he must have given up all hope of ever selling them. We must have been his biggest sale for years.

Back on anchor, Neil had brought out some videos from Ireland, so the guys off *Chinook*, came over to watch *Chicken Run* on our video player. Most of the boating community either didn't have televisions, or watched them infrequently. Power was premium, and there were lots more inspiring things to do than to stare at the box. However, every so often, when a good movie was available, we all became excited to dip our toes back into what used to be so available. Even with our fun lifestyles, we all still needed to mentally escape occasionally. I think it had something to do with being content. We all seemed to have found the most satisfying way to live, however, we still had to live with ourselves and to just forget about everything for a couple of hours was good. We all settled down to become absorbed in another world. However, we missed most of the film, as we had far more important stuff to talk about, like where to find the best Thai beer.

We decided to head to Yacht Haven, which is in the northeast side of Phuket Island and much nearer to the airport. There was little in the way of shops at Yacht Haven. However, there were three restaurants, shower facilities (whoopee hot showers!), and the marina.

Satisfyingly stocked with spare parts, food, and water, we were soon on our way to Phuket. We left Ao Chalong on 19 December; my parents were due to arrive in two days.

Ao Chalong to the marina was a one-day journey. The usual checking in procedure was easy enough, with the customary tutting and rolling of eyes from the officials who filled in all our blanks on the forms. At times, the paperwork held such odd questions. Typically, the forms were used for the arrival of cruise or cargo ships and were creatively adapted to cruisers such as us. Therefore, when asked the volume of our cargo hold, we tended to leave the space blank. We signed a declaration stating that we would pay 600% of *Mariah's* value if we stayed in Thailand longer than the allotted one month, and took careful note of our required leaving date.

Noel and I spent some time trying to find Mum and Dad accommodation. *Mariah* had spare beds, but it would mean that they would be sleeping in the saloon with just the toilet separating us all. I was concerned that they would be arriving in the dark and stepping onto a boat, an odd world when you are not accustomed to it.

'Let them get on with it,' came the advice from Bob (on board *Breakaway*), whose dulcet Irish tones had become a voice of reason to Noel and I over the months we'd known him. He made us think harder about what my parents may want and cope with. As per Bob's advice, we decided to just give it a go. We were in the marina, which was one concession already. Anchoring was our preference, as we enjoyed the breeze and free rent. Admittedly, from time to time it is rather nice to have the luxury of a marina, my parents provided us with a good excuse to indulge!

It was Noel's birthday on 21 December, so we had organised a small party the day before. After a few drinks on *Mariah*, we went to the Yacht Club where a few good friends joined us for a happy dinner and lively conversation. Between us we had organised a cake, candles, and a rather rough verse of "Happy Birthday" – a pleasant birthday in Thailand for Noel.

By this time, we were fully acquainted with the area. To get into town, we needed a car. It was incredible to have a Tesco's to shop in and hot showers to stand under for as long as I wanted. I used to take these things for granted. Now they were a real treat. Materialistic things are something I no longer craved; happiness, freedom, and the odd hot shower (and supermarket) was all I wanted.

The marina office arranged our car hire, laundry, and taxi. There were three restaurants: Yacht Club, Anchorage and Omar's. A ten-minute stroll from the office led to the smart, clean Yacht Club with reasonable food and drink and showers. Next door was The Anchorage, a restaurant with calming ambiance and thatched hut roofs that teetered over the tables directly on the golden sand, a perfect view looking over the water. The Anchorage was slightly more relaxed and of better value than the Yacht Club. Omar's was next door to The Anchorage and was our favourite. The 'restaurant' was a hut perched on a small jetty. The jetty floor boards had had a serious falling out with each other, so you could view the water beneath; household junk and weird and wonderful bits and pieces clung to the walls, acting as decor. They served meals with chilli, the type of stuff you could use to force confessions. But, Omar's was the place to relax, you helped yourself to the fridge and opened your own bottles. The food was delicious, hot, and ridiculously cheap. So much so that we were nearly always querying the bill, as it seemed we were undercharged. However, with the language barrier between us, it often led to Omar believing we thought we were charged too much. Understandably so, because who in their right mind complains about a cheap meal? A dinner for four, including a couple of beers each cost around 300 baht, which was about three Australian dollars each! By the time we had gone shopping, paid for the food, and used our gas to cook it, it was probably cheaper to eat out. And so we did.

On the 21st, Mum and Dad arrived at the airport around 7 pm. They looked more than happy to be back on land after the plane ride. They were pale, but well. Mum was her usual emotional self, which of course, set me off. Noel and I had hired a rickety old car and we packed in the parents and luggage for the ten-minute drive back to the marina. My folks were seeing *Mariah* for the first time in the dark, they coped with the alien environment admirably.

We spent four good weeks with Mum and Dad, cramped within *Mariah's* thirty-three feet, but everyone coped pretty well. With little space and hot sweaty weather, it made for a couple of sharp words, the main culprit being me. I have never been a patient person; fortunately Mum, Dad and Noel were quite accustomed to this and were forgiving. Mum and Dad spent a fair bit of time travelling Phuket Island in a hire car; at times when Noel and I had to work on the boat, my parents saw more of Thailand than we did. Everything had to be just right for our voyage on the Indian Ocean to Sri Lanka, because once we were on our way, we only had what we had.

At times, we roped Mum and Dad in to help, too. Mum and I hauled out our rusty anchor chain onto the jetty to unwind it, as swinging on anchor can cause the links to twist up. Noel and Dad took off in the car to source spare parts. My folks enjoyed this, as it gave them an insight to our lives. If the cruising world still felt new to me, it was a completely unknown lifestyle for Mum and Dad. They thought we were always on our own, when in reality we always had many friends around us, which helped set their minds at rest.

Amid the raucous fun, Christmas flew by. My birthday (the big thirty!) on Boxing Day was, presumably, going to be a quiet affair after a big day on the 25th. But in the true spirit of fun and an excuse to celebrate, a huge table of friends and family, lots of presents, good food, and music came together for one of my best birthdays ever.

Quirky creativity is synonymous with cruisers. I received all sorts of wonderful (and unexpected) gifts for my birthday. My favourite? A jar of salad cream. Away from regular supermarkets, finding treats we usually took for granted was sometimes impossible. A good brand of a favourite item made a wonderful present.

New Year's Eve was a great deal of fun with a jetty party – all the cruisers tried to save money by avoiding the bar, having dinner before the party, and bringing along our own alcohol. Fancy dress was the order of the evening, with Hollywood as the theme. Noel went as Hannibal the Cannibal, only because he had a bike mask that looked identical to the one in the film; the rest was easy with his shirt sleeves stuffed and sewn around his back like a straight jacket. On reflection it wasn't such a good idea, as he couldn't pick up his drink or get to his mouth even if he could find a way to raise the alcohol to his lips. I was Suzi Quatro: leather pants, tie, dark eyebrows complete with a guitar. Mum and Dad were definitely the best. For one night only we had Dame Edna Everage and her alter ego Les Patterson together. Mum and I made some wild additions to a pair of glasses frames. We put bright orange and yellow bows on a black skirt and made a boa from tinsel, a perfect Dame Edna. Dad had yellow plastic teeth (made by Mum, who insisted on umpteen fittings whilst Dad and I were in the dinghy painting part of *Mariah*), a cushion up his jumper, brown sauce on a yellow tie, and greasy hair. None of us could look at him without becoming hysterical. It was bedlam on board. Four of us in a thirty- three foot yacht, trying to do make-up, hair, clothes, and each of us vying for a glimpse of ourselves in our one and only six-inch-by- four-inch mirror.

The fun theme carried through to the last week of my parents' visit. We freed *Mariah* from her lines and put the Yanmar to good use. There was no wind, which was fine, as this meant no waves. Stunning scenery fit for a movie set, glided by. Anchoring near James Bond Island and caves, one by one we clambered into our tiny timber dinghy. A worried silence descended upon the little boat and its four occupants. With barely enough room to take a deep breath, Noel started the dinghy and with great precision steered us to the small beach near the caves. As our feet touched the sand, the chatter commenced while we swam and explored hidden parts of the caves, with not another soul to share it with. Our little dinghy was really made for two. With four on board it had sunk within inches of completely submerging; a slight tip and we all would have been swimming! Fortunately, the water was as still and smooth as ice. As we prepared to return to *Mariah*, Noel said, 'I'll take one at a time,' which was met with much agreement and relief.

I had managed to spend some quality time with Mum and Dad separately and together. We found chatting easy and even restful, but it was my conversation with my mum that made me chuckle and Noel feel guilty.

'Are these your knickers, or are they rags?' Mum frowned.

'Erm, well, I haven't had time...'

Mum held up a rather threadbare pair of knickers, while we were sorting the laundry, and said, 'Right, we're going shopping.' Later on she cornered Noel. 'I'm not having my daughter go around the world with underwear like that, I'm taking her out to buy some more!'

Poor Noel tried to explain that he always encouraged me to spend money on myself. I just found too many other, important and fun things to do. I was quite adept at putting myself last, the boat was the most important item to keep up-to-date. From that point on, whenever my mum visited, or we went to the UK, Noel always asked, 'Do you need new knickers?'

The time flew by, and soon we were back at the airport saying goodbye. Fortunately, the farewell was quick as we were late. (Long story about shopping and mixed up times). So, it was fairly painless, with no time for tears.

After spending 10,000 baht (about 420 Australian dollars) on supplies we were ready for the next leg.

12
———

Lightning storm at the Nicobars

Weather is fundamental to sailors. We used Weatherfax. Through our SSB (HF) radio (long range) at certain times of the day and night, we could dial up a frequency, link the laptop to the radio, and receive synoptic charts. Simple software that we downloaded from the Internet decoded the signal. Receiving free twelve, twenty-four, thirty-six, forty-eight and seventy-two hour weather reports, while on board and, in the middle of the ocean was simply marvellous. There were stations all over the world that transmitted these weather reports regularly, covering every inch of ocean.

Receiving Weatherfaxes was a daily task and was usually in direct association with my internal weather system. When we were tossed and buffeted, I felt beaten. As the weather improved, I shifted from thoughts of selling the boat to designing a new vegetable rack. Viewing the complete picture on synoptic charts, we were sometimes anxious, but always ready.

En route to Sri Lanka, we passed through The Nicobars. The Nicobars were a collection of reefs and islands approximately one day's sail out of Thailand. Regular navigation was imperative at these times. Underwater islands agitated the waters, odd currents swirled and larger waves could be found traversing these peculiarities of the sea. The underwater terrain made barriers for the ocean to churn around and flow over. In the middle of this area, a lightning storm scratched the sky, bringing sheets of rain as thick as ice.

At midnight, my shift was coming to an end, just as the rain and lightning gathered full momentum. The pleasure of peeling off my wet weather gear and snuggling below in our warm, cosy, dry boat was short-lived. Just before I slipped into a warm-body-heated bunk, I looked out at Noel, double-checking that he was clipped on to the lifelines. We always wore our lifejackets and harness when in the cockpit or on deck. At that moment, the lightning cracked with an ear-splitting crescendo and the rain stepped up its onslaught. Noel sat in the cockpit, cloaked in full wet weather gear, arms folded, head down, plainly miserable. CRACK, another shot of lightning almost hit us.

'Do you want me to stay up for a while?'

'That'd be nice,' Noel replied gratefully. Although I was desperate to sleep and hide from the storm's onslaught, I knew I wouldn't want to be left alone in these conditions.

We sat up together all night under the deluge of rain, huddling in a corner of the open cockpit with wet weather gear and Wellingtons our only protection. Thankfully, the wind did not kick up too much, but the walls of rain made a lookout pointless. Hanging tightly together, the lightning consistently cracked and crashed around *Mariah*, toying with us. The boat's outline was seared onto our retinas beneath our closed eyelids. We witnessed the fingers of electricity strike the water an arm's length away from where we sat.

A lightning strike would be devastating. We could navigate with our sextant, but that was not easy. We liked our GPS; it made life simple. During the storm, our radios and GPSs had been disconnected and placed in the oven – our temporary Faraday's cage. Our electronic steering gear was in use. We'd just have to hope the lightning didn't find our mast. We felt like sitting ducks, teasing Mother Nature by waving a tantalising finger, our mast, in the air.

In our little huddle of fear, we thought, *well, we're either going to wake up or we're not!* After a long night, as we peeled open our soggy eyes and tried to un-glue our bodies that had clung tightly together, we awoke to what felt like a movie set. Blue skies stretched into infinity, birds soared swiftly across the bow and the sea sparkled diamonds under the sun. Wrung-out with lack of sleep and hours of tense fear, we still managed to grin; we had survived!

It was necessary to reduce sail and slow down as we approached Sri Lanka. The winds had lifted their game and a favourable current had opted to give us a hand. That's a real oddity about sailing: you can go too fast or too slow. Some harbours and ports need to be entered during the day. It is not always safe to enter in the dark, navigation lights and aids are often not kept up to date, or present at all! This mean, at times, that we had to try to speed up or slow down to ensure we reached the port in daylight.

Another peculiarity is that you can slow down in good winds and favourable currents, only to find that the current and winds turn against you and suddenly you need to speed up. In our case, after slowing down the wind had then died, so we had to run the motor. Two days out of Sri Lanka, our fuel was low. We were probably going to be okay, but didn't want to take any risks; fortunately for us, we had caught up with our friends on *Breakaway* as they had been happy to travel around two knots and sail most of the way. Therefore, they had ample fuel. In the middle of the Indian Ocean we did a fuel/beer exchange. We manoeuvred *Mariah* alongside *Breakaway*, keeping about twenty feet apart to allow for the boats' movements. Jamie threw over a rope, attached were two drums of fuel and some yummy homemade scones. We hauled in the line and attached half a dozen beers in a bag for them. Visiting islands meant trading at times; this was our first mid-ocean trade, though. Typically, after we took on this fuel, we sailed the rest of the way and were able to give them back their entire fuel supply in port!

The last few nights in to Sri Lanka were dark, the moon working her way up from a slither. I preferred full moon nights, but the dark nights held their own magic. The sequin-sewn carpet of black was breathtaking. Endless shooting stars helped me offload some of my wishes. Sighting satellites was easy. They're like slow moving stars, a remarkable feat of human ingenuity that astounded me every time I thought about it.

During most trips, dolphins became part of our journey. At night, nearing Sri Lanka, we couldn't see the dolphins themselves, but their outline in the green phosphorescence that ran off their backs and around their sides. So dark was the night and so bright the phosphorescence, that the dolphins appeared as shooting comets as they slipped through *Mariah's* wake. The green, breathing torpedoes accompanied us for some time, relieving the monotony of the dark, lonely night.

While sailing, we usually slept in the single bunks in the saloon. This is the centre of the boat and therefore a bit more stable than either end. In feisty weather, single bunks are better. A lee-cloth is used, which creates a cot, so you can't fall out. When it's really calm we can sleep in the v-berth, which is a double bed at the forepeak.

I was about to climb into the v-berth for a snooze when my nose curled at a really strong fish smell. Flying fish have wings, which give them flight to escape a predator. With the v-berth hatch open, a flying fish had flown into our bed and died. Fortunately, it was still fresh and I was tired, so I just threw it out the hatch and plopped into bed. I briefly wondered how many people thought nothing of finding a dead fish in their bed.

Flying fish are incredible creatures. In the dead of night, all of a sudden you'd hear a thump, a brief pause then a rapid flap- flap- flap. Quite often the fishy smell would then assault your nostrils. I tried to find the source of the flap as soon as possible. I couldn't bear the thought of a little fish fighting for breath. Noel would catch them, cook them, and eat them.

The strong olfactory confirmation that a flying fish had landed on the deck was in the good company of many other smells: the tangy brew of percolating coffee and the salty damp. Onions sizzling in the pan became a near daily event on board, meal creativity started here. Sun-dried canvas evoked memories of summer holidays in our youth; the damp cotton cockpit cushions, penetrated by salt, never quite dried. The contrasting whiff of exhaust encouraged sea-sickness, the sweet smell of freshly baked bread inspired hunger.

While travelling, we trolled a fishing line. This had been one hundred percent unsuccessful so far on the voyage, but apparently as we approached the Red Sea fishing became better. The countries there are so busy fighting each other they had no time for fishing.

We heard it was expensive to stop here, but we would never be sailing by again, plus we needed fuel. The northeast trade winds were supposed to be clipping us along by now, but there was no sign of them.

At 7:45 am we were sailing into Sri Lanka. It was cloudy and drizzling, just like good old English weather. The dawn was beginning to break and the peacefulness was calming. I sat on the bow of the boat, watching the land grow bigger. I could smell grass, one of my favourite smells. Land has a distinctly sweet and welcoming smell; Sri Lanka's scent was strong, replacing the salt that had tickled our noses for the last nine days. I knew I was going to like it here. This was our first successful long ocean passage, and we were ecstatic.

At last, we were anchored safely in Gaulle harbour. Combating the heat and weariness after a journey, we organised all of the relevant paperwork to check in. This took a whole day. The police, marine police, customs, immigration, and health were all armed and all unsmiling. The boat was searched, although not too thoroughly, but it irritated me when they checked through personal letters, as if I'd hide a person in them. As usual, there was a fee for checking in plus taxes for this and that, which ran into hundreds of American dollars.

At this time, the Tamil Tigers were causing grief on the northern part of the island, which we were not permitted to visit. Due to the problems, every two hours throughout the night, bombs were let off in the anchorage. This was to prevent underwater attacks. We couldn't help but jump when some sounded far too close for comfort. We did manage to sleep though; curled up in our v-berth with the satisfaction of arriving safely into a new port.

At times, it was hard to comprehend that we had sailed into another country. The absurdity of our popping in to different countries on a regular basis and meeting people from all over the world was condensed in this extract of a letter by Noel, to his brother Colin, in Australia:

I'm sitting on a Kiwi built yacht, Mariah II, with a Pommie wife, next door to our new friends (we met in Borneo) who are Irish, in a harbour of Sri-Lankans. Jack's playing a learn-to-speak-French tape while doing the dishes and repeating all these avoirs and merci's etc. I tell you it's enough to make me feel a little strange and disorientated. But most of the time I'm maintaining a balance of these absurdities, and with the help of the GPS I know where I am at, even if I can't remember how I got here.

By some miracle, we are both still alive and not in hospital or lying in the side of the road or in jail for strangling our driver and beating him to a slow, fearful death. These guys are maniacs, our pleas of, 'Slow down for chrissakes,' went unheeded as they drove pedal to the metal, dodging pushbikes buses, ox towed carts, cows, elephants, and meandering pedestrians.

In between being scared to a frazzle, we saw an assortment of ruins from ancient periods in Ceylon's past. When kings were kings and the people seemed to have only one passion in life: to stack bricks and stones in a pattern to their masters' liking. All of course in the belief that, having been good little slaves, they would be re-born into a better life. Well, two thousand years later the majority of these workers are eating rice with their fingers and generally following tourists around. They are picking tea-leaves, cleaning ruins, making carvings for tourists, living in hovels, crapping in holes in the ground and trying to sell something to a tourist. They don't eat with the left hand as that hand has a specific use – there is no toilet paper (only a bucket of water if you're lucky). Not exactly the Promised Land, but hey, if they keep building temples and putting money in the donation boxes along the sides of the road (outside the temples), and if they don't actually rob a tourist with a gun, well then they'll definitely come back a better person and richer, no doubt, one day. Well you've got to believe in something as you dig mud, plant rice, and by and large Buddhism seems a little kinder and peace loving than most other religions.

Mostly, the countryside is lush and beautiful. Swaying coconut palms amid light seeking tropical vegetation provided the spectator a vision of soft greens, romantic rice fields, and oxen images. All of which camouflaged the blind beggars and open drains.

The majority of the population seemed healthy enough, bright eyes flashing, white teeth, and lean muscled bodies, putting us fat puffing whities to shame. Then there's the elephants; there's flocks of them, a positive gaggle of elephants. The elephant orphanage, free to the local public, foreigners pay 150 rupee (about five Australian dollars and fifty cents) to enter and view the animals. The orphanage was set up to accommodate any elephant that decided to start stomping on a few heads. Apparently, they tend to start head stomping when the said heads chop and burn down their forest homes. Elephants like foliage, mobs of it; elephants also like water, lakes of it. Little heads, supported on spindly legs tend to clear the forest foliage and plant gardens and rice. They clear (drain) the lakes and plant rice.

The elephants think, 'Okay, we'll eat the gardens and wallow in the rice paddies.' The little heads start yelling, shooting and poking the elephants with sticks. The elephants think, 'Okay, I'm going to stomp on your little head.' The little heads talk to all the other little heads and gather even more little heads with guns and trucks and herd the remaining surviving elephants into the compounds. They feed them palm leaves, chain them to the ground for photos, charge the white heads admission, and sell carvings of the elephants. The white heads pay for the carvings. The timber comes from the cleared forests. The elephants are still thinking about this, but a general plan involving considerable head stomping is being formulated. Elephants think for a long time...

On our trips to and from shore in the bombed anchorage, the waters were littered with rusted, sinking, abandoned boats. After tying our dinghy to a make-shift jetty, we weaved our way through starving dogs, revered fatted cows, and skinny brown workers, who are masters in doing a lot of standing about. The guards, in heavily starched uniforms, hold big, black, ugly guns, which they nurse in their finger-twitching hands while demanding to see our shore passes. Without fail, they tried to boost their salaries with our belongings. Usually this was done on friendly terms, admiring a hat, a bag, or simply asking for a smoke. However, one day I was asked by one of the guards with a particularly big gun if he could try on my sun-glasses.

'Sure,' I squinted as I handed them over. He put them on and turned his back to me.

'Excuse me, we are going now; could I have my sunnies back, please?'

'No, I will keep these,' he said, as a statement, with a severely serious face. I swallowed, glanced at the gun and the other eyes of the guards turning to watch the situation brewing. Noel had tactically moved away, and I literally witnessed his loyalty take flight.

'No,' I said as firmly as my shaking voice would let me, 'they are my glasses and I need them.' We both stood our ground, I held out my hand and after an interminable time, he took them off and handed them back. I shook for a few hours after berating Noel.

The local transport around town was via Tuktuks. Tuktuks were three-wheeled vehicles that were a cross between a car and motorbike. They had the stability of a unicycle and the equivalent safety of a doll's pram on a motorway. The driver, who sat in the open, out front, on the single wheel, had total and complete disregard for anyone else and did not move his hand from the horn, or his eyes from anything but the road. In the back, we huddled on a bench under the shade, which was constructed entirely with rust. We viewed glimpses of fields, cattle, and petrified people mirroring our faces.

Too soon it was time to leave. We could stay longer, but the winds were blowing and our friends were leaving. The England Cricketers were coming over to play Sri Lanka in the stadium a short walking distance from our boat. However, we were only allowed to stay for a few weeks, and our visas were close to expiring. On 10 February 2001, we left Sri Lanka, bound for the Maldives.

13

Pirates!

'Look darling I've brought you to the Maldives for Valentine's Day!'

'Yeah, right,' I replied.

My Valentine's gift hadn't been Noel's idea; it hadn't even entered his brain. I had spent the previous night, on my watch, making Noel a Valentine's card. Creativity on board was not all about making vegetables last longer. However, it wasn't me who jolted Noel's failing memory. As we approached the serene island in the Maldives, we called up our friends Ed and Dwayne, an American pair on board *Dream On*, to gain information on the anchorage.

'By the way Noel,' said Dwayne, 'wish Jackie Happy Valentine's day from us.'

'You bugger!' said Noel, 'you got in first!' Noel had totally forgotten. I then presented him with the card I had laboured over during the night, which made me feel rather superior and made Noel feel even worse. I then, rather stupidly, offered him a get-out clause.

'Well you got me to the Maldives.'

It took but a second for Noel to turn the tables. 'That's right dear, look,' Noel's arm swept along the vista of pure golden sand, clear water, and palm trees that bent at exotic angles, 'Happy Valentine's day!' To this day, Noel still claims that it took a lot of effort to arrive at the Maldives on Valentine's Day in the year 2001 and that Dwayne had spoilt the surprise!

In the northwest Indian Ocean, Uligamu (or Uligan) is one of the inhabited islands in the Maldives. It was a good rest stop for cruisers between Thailand and the Red Sea.

Malé is the capital of the Maldives. Uligamu was further north and a more convenient stop for us. Tourists were not allowed here, and concessions for transient boats had been made. The government had a defined policy on tourism, which it stuck to. It had recognised the benefits of tourism and the income it generated, but it was also determined to preserve the local culture. Therefore, some Maldivian islands were open to tourists and some were not.

It was a privilege to be there. The streets were swept daily, and because they were merely sandy paths, shoes were oftentimes unnecessary. Chocolate skinned children played tag and were overjoyed when we joined in, their startling white teeth glowing beneath the sun. Crystal clear water buoyed our boats and beckoned us in for a swim. There was not a car insight, not an engine to be heard, a vivid contrast to Sri Lanka. The thrill of sailing into a bustling city of Sri Lanka was matched here, with the excitement of landing in paradise.

Uligamu was a small Muslim village and not long after anchoring we were boarded by local officers who cleared us in and briefed us on the dos and don'ts. We ventured into town in search of a shower and supplies. The town had one tiny shop, which stocked a few exorbitantly priced tins of food and some staples of rice and pasta. Eggs, bread, fruit and vegetables were what we were seeking. We were promised every day that bread would be, 'Here tomorrow.' It never did materialise, but that didn't matter; the islanders made flat bread, which was different, but good.

At the back of the shop sat a freshwater well. This became the gathering place for the cruisers. There were about eight boats on anchor. We would sit cross-legged on the clean, grey sand with buckets and bowls and hand wash our laundry. Thereafter, we'd strip off into swimwear and shower. We knew most of the boats there, but some we only said 'hi' to. It still felt perfectly normal to wash our clothes together, then shower together, sharing the bucket.

The shop owner was glad of our business and free use of the well was thrown in. Uligamu, a tiny slice of heaven within an atoll on a tiny land of paradise; no pollution, dirt, or crime existed here.

It was therefore a shock when we went snorkelling. The coral was dying. Expecting to see bright colours, vivid fish, and tangles of growth, we were disappointed with dull greys, few fish, and a stark landscape. I thought that there were pockets which still lived. Viewing the world from deck level was shocking; the cover of beauty this island offered hid the underlying fact of nature dying.

That first evening, beneath the flickering stars that crowded the magical night sky, we were invited on board *Dream On*, where Ed and Dwayne became our hosts and organised an impromptu party.

Couples from four boats crammed into the cockpit. We all contributed to the bar and kitchen. In Sri Lanka, Noel had bought some cigars, to try and cut down smoking cigarettes – there was some sort of theory there somewhere. So, with great amusement, we all started smoking these cigars – even the girls. As the still night wore on and the Thai marijuana appeared, our tongues loosened with our new friends. We then cooled off in the sparkling moonlit water. Dripping bodies, slurring tongues, and fantastic stories, all wrapped in the curling, pungent smoke of cigars made one of our best party nights. I was glad not to witness the hosts' cockpit in the morning.

The next day, a refreshing swim sharpened all muzzy heads. Shampoo lathers in salt water (soap does not), and we rinsed most of the bubbles back into the sea; after a quick rinse with fresh water, we were ready to play tag with the kids on the beach and see if the bread had been delivered.

After five days, we said farewell to this a coral fringed isle, where the paths were lined with coral walls, ensuring just enough privacy for the occupants. Coconut palms swayed a farewell in the breeze. The azure water, looking just like the pictures in a travel brochure, carried us away. Paradise was finally found, only to be left behind.

We crossed the second half of the Indian Ocean in about nine days, arriving in Oman on 3 March 2001. As memory automatically deletes any horrible stuff, it remains only to be said that we either had fair winds or none at all, which of course suited us just fine. The radio Net, which we maintained twice a day with six other yachts en route with us, was a good break from routine and made the ocean seem not as empty or frightening.

All was well with the world until about two days out from Oman. Someone on the Net had heard a report that a yacht had been attacked by pirates. Automatic rifle fired through the rigging, knife at the wife's throat, ransacked boat, but fortunately no casualties. Noel stepped on deck after hearing this report. There was a fishing boat on the horizon, which now took on sinister tones. Instead of the usual wave or quiet contemplation, they received the finger salute and the view of *Mariah's* stern. Our poor Yanmar engine had to adjust itself to the owners' request for full speed ahead. It took two hours to leave the fishing boat on the horizon. It felt like two days. We still had 400 miles to the area of attack, so we thought we'd better calm down and reduce the revs from the red line on the tachometer.

We continued our radio Nets and information was gathered on where the attacks had been occurring. We plotted the area on the chart. It was all happening off the coast of Yemen. From Oman we had to pass the coast of Yemen in order to reach the Red Sea. Cape Town was sounding like a good place by this stage. Nerves were fraught. A meeting was planned for us all for when we arrived in Salalah, Oman. In the meantime, we spent our solitary hours mentally designing grenade launchers, camouflage nets, and dummy infantry to stand on deck. Where was the Royal Navy when you really needed them?

The meeting was arranged to take place at the local ex-pats' clubhouse and was to be chaired by one of the more apparently knowledgeable cruisers. He's American and our friend, who goes by the name of George. George has served time as a marine, or so the whispers went. There were various ideas put forward, such as, 'Can the French Navy form an escort?' Apparently they were sympathetic to this ongoing problem, but they couldn't help; all private vessels entered these waters at their own risk. There were, however, some radio distress frequencies we could use. These were for the US Navy, the French Navy, and the Yemen Maritime rescue services. However, none of these stations guaranteed a response and, if they did, it was unlikely that they could reach us in time to be of any assistance during an attack.

'Bloody brilliant,' we all murmured, 'if the cavalry arrives, they can help sift through the wreckage!' Those with guns on board had been discussing whether to open fire on sight or only if they had to. Most of the Yanks wanted to start firing as soon as they left port. Then, presumably, not to stop firing until they reached New York, and that was only to re-load.

The trouble with guns is that you need bloody good ones. The reports we'd received said that the pirates had automatics and approached the boats firing into the rigging. Do you open fire in return to save your radio and hidden American dollars? By this time, Noel was wondering where we could buy a Navy Bofur, find a place to mount the critter, and join the Yanks heading to New York. The pirates, we were informed, travelled in high-powered speedboats and carried radio monitoring equipment. Using this gear was apparently how they had located yachts that talk between themselves on VHF.

Personally, we thought that George, who can't drink because he gets a bit mean under the influence, should have been given a carton of rum, armed with a few Uzi machine guns, and let loose. Our ideas weren't appreciated, mainly because this chap had been known to be indiscriminate in his rages.

The final plan was for everyone to maintain close quarters to each other under sail, which was interesting as there were not two boats the same; we also agreed to maintain strict VHF silence and only use the HF radios (with too many frequencies to detect) on set contact frequencies that were not divulged to anyone else. Was this the great plan?

'What happens if a boat is boarded?' Noel asked. 'Do we ram the culprits, if it's a matter of someone's life at stake?'

This was greeted with silence as everyone, including myself, pondered the reality of such a scene. Do we ram or observe? Or head for the horizon, blocking out the sounds of mayhem behind us? Noel and I privately thought we may stop to help the girls on *Carmen Miranda*, but a certain unnamed American could get it up the backside, for all we cared. He really was a prick and didn't want us to join the convoy, as he thought we'd be too slow. (Fear, a forty horse power Yanmar, and the ability to put up every square inch of sail we possessed later proved him wrong). The meeting ended. I was stunned with real and imagined horrors. We adjourned to the bar.

'I'll have a triple whiskey and ice and my wife will have a large gin and tonic,' said Noel, a glazed look in his eye.

'That will cost you a pretty penny,' said the guy next to me.

'Mate,' Noel responded, 'sometimes money just doesn't come into it. As a matter of fact, barman, just give me the bottle.'

Salalah was a hot, dry desert. Despite the turmoil of real life pirates, we tried to enjoy the stark lands, as we were certainly not planning a return trip. The town was about ten kilometres away from the anchorage. The best way to get into town was hitchhiking, which goes against everything I was taught by my parents. The locals were a helpful, friendly bunch and only after an hour or two of wilting in the excessive heat, with not a tree in sight, we were picked up. Usually, the guy that offered us a lift spoke little English, drove like a lunatic, and it took the whole four-minute ride to explain where we wanted to go. Words such as phone, spare parts, and, supermarket were not understood. However, we quickly learned that Pizza Hut, McDonalds, and all artery-hardening restaurants was a worldwide language and their location bound to be in the centre of town. We were dropped off outside Pizza Hut, which was rather convenient as we were starving and had been eating lentils, chickpeas, rice, and pasta for far too long.

In town, we were armed with the perpetual list, money, and determination to complete all of our tasks and a belly full of the yummiest pizza ever. By now, we'd been out of touch with family for some time. Many boats had Internet on board and satellite phones: a luxury we could not afford nor wanted. If we had a satellite phone, I knew my mum would have called at an inopportune time when we were changing sails or hauling in a large fish and she'd wonder why, when a phone rings on a small boat, it wasn't answered. Her imagination would run riot, causing her even more sleepless nights. On board, we'd then have serious debates whether to spend five pounds per minute calling back to say all was okay, and our little watery sanctuary would be shattered. With modern day communications it was impossible to escape communications on land – at sea we could. To avoid world news, home news, and all other news was a sweet, peaceful gift that we enjoyed.

You would think buying a phone card and calling home a simple task anywhere in the world. Let me tell you, it is not. Firstly, the town was stretched out over five kilometres and was extraordinary in that all the jewellery shops were together, all the fabric shops together, and so on.

'Where's the phone card section?' I asked through sweat and sand-caked lips, grimacing as another painful crack opened on my bottom lip.

After an hour of traipsing around in circles, wide-eyed and rubbernecking, all the shops suddenly shut down. It was remarkable, wherever we were in the world, we always just reached town to have lunch and watch all shops close down for a few hours.

We found solitude in a small café where the owner felt sorry for us, and we drank warm sodas. Miraculously, we spotted phone cards hanging on their wall. Finding a phone was the next obstacle. After a tour of smashed phones and empty phone-boxes, we found a phone that worked. Under the direct heat of the sun, in a heat-generating plastic box we inserted the card. Before we had a chance to dial, the phone whirred and beeped.

'That sounds like it has just wiped our card,' I said. Bless it, it had.

'That's it!' Noel shouted and plonked himself on a concrete step beneath some rare shade. He shut his eyes, a good plan I thought, and joined him. A moment later our self-indulgent sulk was interrupted.

'Hallo, are you okay?' a local voice with good English asked.

'Bloody go away,' Noel murmured under his breath. The last thing we needed was someone asking for money. Being white, we stood out and looked to all like huge dollar signs walking down the street. However, this was no beggar, this was a knight in shining armour. I looked up and squinted into the sun, to see a brand new Lexus. Standing beside it was a young, striking man, handsome in his startling clean, white dishdasha (local tunic). He smiled.

'I have travelled a lot and know how difficult a strange country can be. Please let me help you.'

With a fair bit of scepticism, we told him of our plight. 'Come with me,' he offered the open door of his air-conditioned car. Thoughts of kidnapping, murder, mugging, and rape didn't enter our heads. We were so hot and defeated that we gladly stepped into the enormously plush car. We now had a chauffeur, tour guide, and translator, all wrapped up in a comfy air-conditioned car.

Our new friend, Murshid, drove us along dirt roads with deep potholes that you could lose a small person in, and parts of town we would have never known existed. A ramshackle old shed with smashed windows was the telephone company's headquarters. Here several minutes of intense conversation occurred between Murshid and many other jean-clad men, all with deeply creased faces. We just stood, watched, and sweated. Suddenly papers were shuffled and money offered to us for a full refund on our telephone card!

Murshid then invited us to his home for a traditional dinner. He dropped us off at the dinghy and waited while we collected fresh clothes and shower gear. We had learned to take any opportunity of another's' shower!

Murshid's home was simple, plainly painted with the odd fake gold, gaudy statue depicting reverence to a god. His bathroom was plain and unfinished, but his wonderful cold shower was used with much joy. Murshid was resplendent in his dishdasha of fine fabric the colour of ivy. Subtle patterns woven through the edges of his tunic with his smouldering dark looks made him look incredibly fetching (did I mention he was handsome?). A handful of his friends joined us for the evening. One lad wore jeans and he strutted with head held high; he clearly felt cool wearing western gear. I found myself frowning at his appearance. It was like turning up to a wedding in shorts – it just didn't sit right. Even Noel and I had gotten rid our western gear. Murshid presented Noel with a beautiful plain dishdasha and to me a huge, green tent dress, decorated with green flowers – not elegant, but we fitted right in!

Murshid's friends played homemade guitars and drums. They taught us words we didn't understand, and then rolled around in fits of laughter when we tried to sing them. We were served local foods, spices, vegetables, and dark meat. A young, pretty woman served us; she was subservient and glowed when we thanked her, Noel and I were the only ones that seemed to appreciate her. Murshid wore a slight scowl when she stayed too long in the room when we tried to engage her in conversation. He tried to hide the frown, but it was evident woman were not part of the social scene. I was grateful to be allowed an insight and grateful, too, of our western life and acceptance.

As the evening cooled, Murshid drove us back to the dinghy. We stopped for a stroll along the beach. Many other people had the same idea. I was the only woman. This was the men's time – women stayed at home, Murshid explained.

That night, we quietly approached the port entrance. Curfew back into the port was 7 pm. Sometimes, the officials stretched this to 10 pm. We got back at 11:30 pm. In a language we could not decipher, but with the meaning clear, the angry port authorities wagged their fingers and firmly held their guns. Noel and I stared at our feet like scolded kids. With our sincere apologies, they eventually let us back into the bay. However, our bowed heads were not just for the guards. We realised that we may have made it harder for following cruisers, possibly encouraging the authorities to instigate harsher rules, especially, perhaps for Australians. Worse, we had taken advantage of a warm welcome into a foreign country. A mistake we wouldn't make again.

The port's facilities in Salalah would sound good in any brochure, with fuel, water, and amenities, however the reality was a universe away. The shower block was communal, filthy, and the smell was one sniff short of making you heave. The shower doors, of which there were two, were held shut with grimy twine that you really didn't want to touch. Quickly, you learned how to balance the wash bag, towel, and fresh clothes on this piece of putrid string, which was the cleanest part of the entire building. Trying not to breathe too much or knock my gear on the floor, I'd shower frantically for as short a time as possible. Wearing decent footwear was imperative to help dodge cockroaches that were so big you could lean on them for support if you needed it. Why did we shower in such places? Well, at sea, you become covered in salt; it's sticky and uncomfortable. Apart from that, it is exceptionally hot. We had little other choice. The last clean, hot shower was in Thailand, about two months ago.

Let's get this straight: we *could* shower on board. But, at times it was easier to save our water supply. We had a pressure garden-spray that held four kettles of water (one warm if we were feeling indulgent). This was the shower we used when arriving into port. During the voyage, most days we would have a shower with the deck-wash hose using the chilly salt water of the ocean. Rinsing with salt water cleared the lather, and to finish up we used just one or two cups of fresh water to carefully rinse the salt from our skin and hair. We always arrived into port with plenty of spare fresh water, but at sea we didn't want to risk running low through using too much or suffering a problem with a tank. *Mariah* had three separate water tanks in case of contamination or damage.

There was a bright side to the showers in Oman. In the shower block, there was a big trough with taps (unending running water to a cruiser is close to heaven). We did our laundry here and filled up *Mariah's* water tanks via jerry can. Every drop was carried to the boat, unless we indulged in the rare luxury of a marina, or topped up the tanks when taking on diesel.

We learned another good lesson in Oman. When at anchor we used the VHF radio to talk to other boats (we hailed on channel sixteen, then changed to a working channel for longer conversations); we recently had a potentially rather embarrassing situation develop. A friend used our radio on board *Mariah* to organise a party. Unfortunately, she hung the mic back up, so the transmit button was pressed in! It wasn't until the next day when the whole anchorage was privy to our morning conversation, that we realised what had happened.

'Hey, *Mariah II*, it's all very nice hearing your breakfast conversation, but it's time to turn your mic off!' yelled the skipper of nearest boat anchored to us.

It all could have been very embarrassing. With a quick appraisal of what was said the previous night and during the morning, we believed we didn't do or say anything too shocking!

Sight-seeing and Oman are two words that don't really go together in one sentence. There's the dry and bleak vista, dusty camels, bleating goats, rocks and... well, that's it really. With a kind offer from another cruising couple that had hired a car, we took a quick drive up into the hills together. Great vistas of hot, stark land greeted our sun-burnt eyes. Wandering camels peered at us, keeping their distance, protecting their young, while also chewing on bleached thistles. Tents and basic timber huts speckled the hillside.

After about a week, we were ready to go. That week was spent fixing, maintaining, stocking up with food, fuel, water, hand-washing the laundry, and stowing everything properly, plus scraping the bottom of the boat again.

Soon it was time for the intrepid (read nervous) sailors to leave. We were in a group of six; together we would cross the pirate-infested waters.

The piracy plan was to stay in the group, and we were hoping this would make potential attackers think twice. If we were approached and their intent was harmful, the rest of the group were prepared to let off flares and put out a Mayday call on our designated channels. We hoped that we could scare them off.

In addition, we all agreed to use our running lights at night, (deck lights), instead of our masthead lights. This helped avoid detection from further afield. We agreed to only using the VHF radio to say, 'fleet to channel A, B or C.' These channels (A, B, C) were pre-arranged channels on the SSB (HF-long range radio); this was how we would communicate. Pirates could easily scan the few channels on VHF and then pinpoint us, keeping use of the VHF to a minimum and using HF for conversations could mean going undetected.

Tentatively, we set off. Our route took us initially south; the previous attack occurred close to the Yemeni coast, so we kept well out, away from land, in the shipping lane. We stuck close together, within about half a mile of each other, It was reassuring. No one came anywhere near us.

The excitement started early when Noel and I promptly caught a huge yellow fin tuna. With just fishing reels and a net, it took quite some effort to get the beautiful creature on board. He thrashed wildly and his blood splattered around the cockpit. As *Mariah* rolled, the blood ran around – it was slippery. The metallic smell suffocated the salty aroma. As he thrashed we grabbed the cheap bottle of vodka and gave him his last drink. The alcohol killed him immediately, and at last the fight ended. These beautiful fish are strong. I watched as his rainbow colours slowly faded and I felt sad. We thanked the sea for gifting us this food. This fine tuna fed us for most of the nine-day journey, with careful storing in the coolest parts of the boat. We didn't have a huge range of fresh food on board, so we were grateful. Although we didn't have a proper fridge, by this time, we did have a small built-in icebox. This helped keep the fish for longer.

On the second night out, amid the red and green lights of the small fleet, I noticed one boat turn around and head back the other way. I stayed silent for a while, waiting to see if anyone else noticed, or if the boat heading back would tell us why. Eventually, I couldn't stand the silence any longer and called up on the VHF.

'Fleet go to channel B,' I announced.

In just a few moments we all met on the selected frequency on the HF radio.

'Did anyone else notice that one of us has turned around?'

I received a few confirmations, and then the boat that had turned around came up and explained that they had some equipment problems on board and as we were still closer to Oman than anywhere else, they thought it prudent to turn around. A good decision, but strange just not to say anything. Now there were five boats in convoy.

When we thought the highest danger area was behind us, we pulled ahead. For many days we had been slowing *Mariah* down to stay with the fleet. Agreeing to a speed of five knots within our group was a total waste of time. No one bothered (except *Carmen Miranda*) to work with sails to maintain a good speed. A three knot speed was accepted by the rest of the group. Five knots was about our maximum, and we had no trouble achieving it with a bit of effort. Noel and I were completed miffed as to why anyone would want to go slow and spend more time in a pirate area. We were getting tired of backing our sails to stop *Mariah* and waiting for the rest of the fleet. Our sails were old and did not need the extra stress.

'It's hard for us to put our poles up,' one boat commented when we asked why we were not keeping to the agreed speed, a speed everyone was easily capable of – we were the smallest and slowest boat!

Why have the poles? We thought, *Why agree to something you can't be bothered to do?* These were our private thoughts and discussions. We made a decision then, and talked to the other boats about our choice to move ahead. The 'poles' were the spinnaker poles that helped keep the sails full of wind when the boat rolled, they weren't easy to put up, but a necessity at times. We were irked as to why some of the fleet didn't want to make an effort

'Stay safe,' the group called to us on the radio. We thought that they needed these thoughts more than us; we were heading further out of the danger area. With relief at being able to let *Mariah* go, we peeled away from the group.

As Eritrea approached, we were both keeping watch on our last night. During the night, we traversed a traffic separation zone, which is a stretch of water where you have to keep to a certain area. On our charts the area is marked like a road is marked, to show which side we must keep on, depending on which direction we were travelling. The traffic separation zone was between an island and the mainland, and the current was running fast. Fortunately, it was giving us a ride and we sped along at nine knots, watching islands fly past. There was plenty of traffic to avoid within the narrow "roads," shallow waters, and islands. At nine knots we felt a little out of control!

By 3 am we were both weary, but there were still plenty of ships around. The huge behemoths glided past at twenty-six knots: silent, dark, and foreboding. As I stretched out a huge yawn and rubbed my sore eyes, I noticed a light appear at the back of one of these ships. There was a small boat that was behind that ship, but now it'd come out from behind the ship and was heading our way! I rubbed my eyes again, my stomach lurched, and I noticed Noel had gone quiet too. I stared and felt the strain of concentration.

'Can you see that boat?' I asked Noel.

'Yes, it's coming towards us.'

It was moving fast, and although we were out of the main danger area, we were still concerned. If we could sail here, so could pirates. I picked up the winch handle, heavy in my hand, it made me feel better to be armed!

For a while we sat and watched, our hearts thudding with the imagined horrors, then it happened.

'Erm, I don't think it's a ship,' I said.

'It's not a ship. It's a light on an island!' We had figured it out at the same time. Where the 200,000 tonne ship had glided down our starboard side, overtaking us, it had hid a small island that had a flashing light on it. The movement of the ship going forward had made the light appear to be moving the other way. Our tired minds were playing tricks on us, but we were too relieved to care. With silly smiles, we had survived a potential pirate attack!

All in all, with adrenaline pumping at every light or fishing boat, a sleepless night, the traffic separation zone and a rampaging current, we were completely exhausted when we arrived, at dawn, into Eritrea. Our sagging limbs, scratchy eyes, and salt laden skin was mixed with the heady excitement of sailing into Eritrea. It was an interesting mix of emotions, which admittedly became a bit intoxicating and addictive.

Eritrea boarders Ethiopia, Sudan, and Djibouti; we anchored in the port of Massawa, which was quite close to the capital city of Asmara. We had traversed the worst of pirate infested-waters; the rest of the journey was looking to be beautiful and safe. We heaved a collective sigh of relief.

On entry, we tied *Mariah* alongside a wharf in order to check in. Once officials were happy, we could go anchor with the other boats. Meeting up with cruising buddies again was a delight, and we heard a rumour that the pirates that had attacked the catamaran were caught. Unfortunately, later we discovered it wasn't true. The pirates that were caught had attacked a boat last November. The rumour went on to reveal that they were hanged!

I'd never thought much about guardian angels until I noticed a friend of mine always leaving a mouthful or two of food at every meal. She revealed that she kept it aside for her guardian angel. Now on *Mariah*, with our safe trip so far, I figured I must have someone looking out for me (other than Noel). I elected my guardian angel to be Daisy, my Great Nan, who had passed away some time ago just prior to her 100th birthday. Daisy had kept her wits about her, well into her nineties. As a maths teacher, in her late eighties she had helped me with long division when I was struggling. I had loved her very much and admired the way she kept up with the racing modern world, while she had slowed so much herself. As my appointed guardian angel, Daisy would have her work cut out for her over the next few months.

14

Egyptian sand storm

We had left Oman on 12 March 2001 and arrived at Eritrea nine days later.

Eritreans are incredibly proud people. On 28 May 1993, Eritrea gained UN recognition as an independent country. A former Italian colony and under British rule through 1942-52, Eritrea became part of Ethiopia. The Eritrean people conducted a constant struggle for independence for thirty years. They are now poor, all their money had been spent on defence, and more importantly 65,000 lives were lost. The rubble town is saturated with evidence of bombings and shootings. But the people are happy, proud and friendly, giving a strong sense that they are pulling forward and Eritrea will flourish.

The town occupies a powerful strategic position, controlling all points of access to the Red Sea and beyond, leaving Ethiopia dependent on Eritrea for access to foreign trade. They tolerate zero crime here, the locals welcome you to their country, and are proud to explain that women can walk the streets alone day or night without fear, and it's true.

The anchorage was peaceful and calm, conducive to the rest our bodies craved. The dinghy ride ashore took about five minutes, and there was plenty to look at. As we puttered through the dirty water, bombed buildings lined the shore next to a flotilla of semi sunken ships, rusted, dying, and skewed in odd shapes, which seemed to highlight their agony. The concrete dock, where the dinghies were tied, was a hive of activity. Robotic crane arms stretched to load and unload freighters while sacks of dusty barley were delivered from the UN while brand new Red Cross trucks hummed around the bedlam. Noel tried to capture this on film and was almost rugby tackled by security – photos were strictly prohibited!

The rest of our convoy arrived the day after us, all in one piece. A meal was organised in a local restaurant to celebrate our survival. A couple of the cruisers were good friends; the others, well, were really just travelling companions. To be honest, the evening was dull, as one particular cruiser liked the sound of his voice a bit too much. However, it got worse: Noel and I had been living off fish and water for the last nine days, literally, and all they had on the menu was fish! Then we were told that they didn't sell alcohol; all I wanted was a steak and a beer. We ate bread and water for dinner and enjoyed a private chat with the girls on board *Carmen Miranda*. We were all grateful to be safe. Added to the feeling of comfort was the knowledge that we had missed some horrendous weather. Prior to traversing the Indian Ocean, there had been a cyclone nearby; after we had completed the journey across, there was another cyclone. My guardian angel, Daisy, must have been working overtime.

After dinner, Noel and I wandered around the unlit rubble town. Soft music caught our ears, and we followed the sweet sound. In a dim doorway, a group of young lads, with girls watching, sat playing homemade guitars. As we slowly approached, they beckoned us to join them in their coffee ceremony. Their English was broken, but far better than our Eritrean (their national languages are English, Standard Arabic, Tigrinya, and a few more). They had, what seemed like, a magic box that contained the necessary tools and a small brazier. The ceremony was serious, unique, and quite romantic. Small cups were set out on a round tray, and a show of washing them was made. The beans were naked, straight from the plant, added to a small saucepan and roasted on the coals. Once they were roasted, it was customary for everyone to smell them; the aroma was so strong it smacked our tastebuds and our mouths started watering in anticipation. The beans were ground and water gradually added. The whole process took about half-an-hour; it was slow and precise and actually very gentle. Two large teaspoons of sugar were added to the small cups, so we expected a sweet drink. But the coffee was dark and rich, the sugar just right. We sipped the perfect cup of coffee; a feeling of calm enveloped us.

Our small group was huddled around the soft brazier fire, the only light in the lane way. It flickered on our contented faces. It was like a small orange room created beneath the stars, and the endless darkness added to the intimate experience. Our different languages were no longer a barrier. We were all content to sit together and simply enjoy the moment. Cicadas chirped and the only noise was our soft murmurs of trial conversation and the subtle flick of fingers across guitar strings. The realisation that humans can be so distant in miles, yet share such a special moment in time, was a privilege.

Unfortunately for me, the water that I'd sipped at our thrilling celebratory meal earlier in the evening started to weave its way down my innards and demanded to be let out. There would be no sewerage system here. I felt shy, too embarrassed to ask for a loo within the hushed romance of the night and shatter the ambience. I crossed my legs and concentrated on the moment. Soft songs and stroking melodies were strummed out on the guitars and the night grew old. Our enjoyment swelled while my bladder almost burst.

The following day while walking the town to find supplies we ate a brief, odd, lunch in a cafe. I think some of it was goat. For the next two days, Noel and I played tag team match for the toilet. Our lunch clutched our stomachs and caused excruciating cramps. We were not alone: most cruisers suffered at some point during their stay. We were almost recovered when we set out on a Tuesday for some inland travel, in company with Cindy and Faith from *Carmen Miranda*, to Asmara, the capital.

Faith and Cindy are lovely girls from San Francisco. Their quirky humour and ability to bring fun to all situations was compelling. The most revealing story of their antics was about their cat named Toulouse. Toulouse had been on board for many years; he'd actually come with the boat. Cats suffer on trips, just like us humans. This resulted in a mid-ocean cat enema. They didn't provide full details of the story, but reported that, at the time Toulouse was rather put out and a bit huffy about the whole thing. Still, after the desired affect they were all friends again.

The journey into Asmara involved two bus rides: one to the main bus station and then four hours to the city. For an extra dollar, we opted for a smaller but more comfortable bus. The scenery was breathtaking: up and down and up again at least three almighty, barren hills. The hills accommodated stone huts that were perched on the sides of large precipices – one too many steps out the front door meant the express route to the bottom. The hills were horizontally lined with neatly piled stones, like a small wall, to help avoid erosion and to catch rain.

The journey, apparently, took us through three different seasons. To us it was stifling hot, uncomfortably hot, and then pleasantly hot as the cool, clear air of the hills refreshingly stroked our sweat caked skin. As we weaved around tight hairpin bends, we more or less followed the obsolete train track, which was intermittently spanned with the grandeur of Italian architecture. The barren hills were a casualty of the goats, who roamed freely with the odd shepherd herding them, it seemed, to the middle of nowhere. The superior camels, donkeys balancing on precipices – mimicking goats, and baboons all mingled graciously in the godforsaken land.

The town of Massawa was more familiar to us, a little more like what we are used to in the first world. The streets revealed the occasional Jacaranda with its familiar perfume and vivid purples. The Hotel Nyala had reasonable rooms. I stepped into the shower in anticipation, but alas it was tepid.

Feeling relaxed and happy to be in a large town that beckoned with its characteristic aura, we dined in the Blue Nile, an Italian restaurant. The Italians have had a fantastic influence in Asmara with the most exquisite pizza. The Blue Nile was spotlessly clean, had toilets where you could actually inhale without feeling like you should vomit, and the food was exceptionally cheap.

I was excited. Cindy and Faith looked at me as if I was slightly off balance. I was unashamedly energized to be in a clean place that served decent food, which you just knew was not going to take the express route out of your body. To top it all, I also had a nice cool beer. Noel just grinned at me; he had become used to me expressing my excitement, and I liked to be able to just be me – it's a rare thing to not be judged for your own eccentricities.

After a restful night, we all breakfasted at the Blue Nile then went our separate ways. We arranged to meet Faith and Cindy at the bus station at two. Noel and I found the Egyptian Embassy to obtain our Egyptian visas. We had thought that it might save some money and be easier in the long run. It turned out that it didn't save us time or money.

Our other main task was to catch up with family, primarily to let them know we were okay. The email was excruciatingly slow, but finally we were able to let our families know that we had not become pirate fodder. Eventually, we had achieved all we set out to do, so we could relax, pay our eleven nafka (a little over two Australia dollars) and watch the mystical and decaying scenery roll by on our journey home. The entire way, distorted Arabian music blared from inescapable overhead speakers and harassed our ears.

Suddenly, the world outside the window turned dark. Hail began to fall, and a thunderstorm hit. The fog swirled in like a blanket and reduced the vision down to about five feet. No longer did we lazily watch the scenery, but with adrenaline pumping we clutched, white knuckled, at our seats.

We watched as the brown water cascaded at an alarming rate down the hill and across our path, seemingly heavier at the tight hairpins, where the water dropped over the edge, spilling two hundred feet down. There were no barriers along the side of the road. Halfway into the journey, all of a sudden quiet descended, the storm cleared, and the clouds drew back to reveal the breathtaking scenery. Greenery seemed to spurt up, revived with a quenching drink. We became deaf to the music, and despite the numb buttocks the unique spectacle of this obscure land made the arduous journey more than rewarding.

At the end of March we said goodbye to Eritrea, happy to be on our way again. A perfect wind from the south pushed us through the water, and we sailed for about five hours, enjoying the flat seas and clear skies. We were heading up the Red Sea.

We anchored at a small reef for the night. We had all afternoon to explore, so we launched the dinghy for a spot of snorkelling; the coral was alive and fish plentiful. Spying a huge manta ray, a couple of metres wide, before I dived in made me a little nervous. But the sun was too hot and the water too clear to miss out. After enjoying the underwater world we cleaned *Mariah's* hull.

After a restful night, we set off at dawn the next day. We sailed for three days and nights with fantastic southerlies, so we had great sailing heading north along the Red Sea.

During the morning and evening radio Nets, we could hear the boats a few days in front of us. They were experiencing strong head winds, and our forecast was for strong northerlies. It was time to take shelter. The night before the northerlies were scheduled to hit us, we scanned the charts for an anchorage and turned *Mariah's* bow towards land. I was doing the 7 pm to 1 am watch. The moon was nearly full, so the nights were pleasantly lit, the sea calm. We had a perfect fifteen knots on the beam and a one knot current assisting us. This was the best sailing we had ever had. As I was sitting peacefully, keeping a vigilant watch, I heard a vessel call up another vessel on the radio. The ships were obviously heading towards each other.

'Vessel on bearing... I'm on a bearing of... my speed is fourteen knots and I am carrying a weight of 200,000 tonnes.' This was said twice.

'Yeah, well so what?' was the reply!

Funny, kind of, but I nearly picked up the mic and said, 'I'll tell you what – it means he is bloody huge and his stopping distance is several miles long, so get out of the way quick smart, you idiot!' But I thought I'd better leave that to the captain.

Within the Egyptian waters, we were blessed with three days of calm waters, cooling breezes, and clear skies. We found it somewhat hard to believe the weather report from the boats ahead of us.

'We have thirty to thirty-five knots; it should be with you within twenty-four hours,' came the gasping voice over the radio. The tinny tone, with the dramatic background of crashing winds, was like listening to a movie coming to a roaring end. In a few hours time, we'd be within the thick of that same mayhem.

'It's time to take shelter again,' we both agreed. We only had a few more days until we reached Safaga, our next clearing in port. Avoiding head winds was one of our main goals in life. Jarring waves smashing into *Mariah's* bow, stopping her forward momentum, was not only absurdly uncomfortable, but led to incredible stresses enforced on the boat. These stresses affected the equipment and us, so it was never worth the battle.

Before any departure, our charts would be thoroughly scanned and marked for possible hidey-holes. We always sought an opportunity to take shelter until the next weather window. This became a way of life: a few days of reasonable sailing, followed by punchy headwinds that we had to fight in order to reach the next shelter to rest.

And so it went on.

So much for only having a few more days until we reached the haven of Safaga; the weather was, what can only be described as, bloody awful. Continuous head winds of twenty to thirty knots made life virtually impossible.

The sky was completely swept clear of cloud. We could not move around the boat without holding on. The vertical posts within the boat allowed us to monkey-grip from one end to the other. Our limbs became sore and tired. Cleaning our teeth was a trial and as for having a pee, well, the sphincter is a marvellous muscle, but try relaxing it on a roller coaster ride, with a good bout of sea-sickness thrown in – it was something to be worked at. *Crash, crunch, BANG,* the noises were jarring: constantly side-to-side, up and down, forward and back.

And so it went on.

Between bouncing around the ocean like a ping-pong ball and throwing up, we took refuge within small bays. When the wind took a breather, we scurried out of our temporary sanctuary to head north. The trip was taking far longer than we anticipated, so food and water was starting to become alarmingly low; the menu was just noodles and peas. We'd eaten so much of this hideous concoction that starvation started to seem like an attractive alternative. Noodles (dried) and peas (tinned) was one of Noel's inventions. He creates amazing pairings of the most antipodean tucker: mustard and peanut butter sandwiches, vegemite, banana and cheese on biscuits, apple or nectarine (when available) in a meaty stew. Being a Brit, I grew up on meat and two veg. I enjoy cultural food and relish the opportunity to try new tastes in different countries. However, I like flavours that complement each other, that aren't vying for the attention of my taste buds! Bangers and mash, chops and peas (well maybe not peas anymore), and all that good old English food, I find enjoyable.

Two hundred nautical miles from Safaga, twenty-five knot head winds struck the water and caused mountainous waves, punching *Mariah* clean on the nose. Anyone who has suffered sea-sickness knows that when it is at its worst, you feel like you are going to die. Just when you have thrown your last morsel from your aching stomach, mal de mer demands more. It can be complete agony and I have, in fact, forced food down my stomach to ease the pain of constant retching on an empty stomach.

We pound our way towards another secure anchorage, some ten nautical miles away. Usually ten nautical miles at five knots would take us two hours. However, we were moving at three knots. A huge wave picked us up and slammed us down; the following relentless wave slammed straight into the bow. This stopped us dead in the water. It took a few seconds to re-gain the momentum of movement. Then we moved at three knots for a few seconds until the next wave. Our GPS told us we had six hours to reach our haven. There was nothing we could do but hang on, ensure the boat was not coming apart, and wait. If there were a way to step off the boat, I would have welcomed it with open arms.

While bumping into seawater that was as solid as a brick wall, a seal on the water pump on the engine expired. The engine was at a full throttle, as we could not sail into the strong winds and certainly not the seas. Indeed, we would have been going backwards, if it were not for our saviour, the Yanmar. However, the seal perishing was a bit of a problem. The engine was cooled by fresh water, which, in turn, was cooled by salt water. Raw water (salt water) was constantly sucked in and pumped through a heat exchanger to cool the fresh water, and then the raw water was spat out the exhaust. With the revs so high, a lot of water was in circulation. The sad thing was that with the seal gone most of the water that was usually pumped out of the exhaust was pumping straight into the boat, our home! We had bilge pumps, but they were not at the very lowest part of the boat and not able to cope with the quantity of water. We did have a hand pump as well, but it meant one of us pumping continually from below decks. We were both needed in the cockpit to traverse through this particularly sticky stage of our journey. Every half-hour, we took turns going below and scooping up the water into a bucket, and then lifting the bucket into the cockpit to empty it overboard. It sounds easy unless you are struggling to stay on your feet on a three-dimensionally lurching machine, to say nothing of carefully timing the next spew.

It was all quite horrendous. I would manage to scoop up half a bucket of sloshing water, and then I'd have to dash outside to empty the bucket and my stomach. Then I'd retreat back down again and follow the same process until the bilge was cleared and my stomach was unbearably empty. The exhaustion was two-fold. First, we had to hang on for dear life, while controlling slopping water in bucket. Secondly, our mal de mer intensified, particularly by being down below, near the diesel engine, where it was hot and stuffy. The six hours into our haven felt like six weeks. We just had to carry on; there were no alternatives. There was just the two of us, the boat, the sea, the sky, and the nasty wind and waves.

With exhaustion nipping at our extremities, we finally, achingly, turned into the protected anchorage.

The stark transformation from muddled seas to flat water was extraordinary. The crash of waves was silenced. *Mariah* glided through the placid water that was protected by pale yellow sand dunes. The sea-sickness vanished instantly and we forgot the horrendous conditions outside. The winds continued to howl around our rigging, unrelenting, while we made repairs. For two days, more noodles and peas were forced down when hunger consumed me. It wasn't a diet I'd recommend.

And so it went on.

Eventually, in April 2001, we bumped and ground our way into Egyptian waters and found another sheltered port. That was one positive thing about traversing the Red Sea, there were plenty of safe stops. As we entered this particular anchorage, we spotted a navy ship anchored in the middle of the bay. In the spirit of good manners, we headed towards them. As a foreign vessel, we had to ask permission to be there. Visas did not make any difference if they wanted you to leave. They asked us to tie up alongside them so they could check our passports and visas. With lots of undecipherable chatter, gesticulation, and dour faces, after an uncomfortable time, they indicated that we were allowed to go and anchor. But, they kept hold of our passports.

'We hold these until you leave. When you want to leave, ask us for permission, and if everything is okay, we will allow you to leave and give you back your passports.' This was said by man with a grave face; his uncompromising mouth wouldn't know a joke if it jumped up and slapped him on the chops. He wore a starched uniform and was heavily armed. What do we do? We were told to never surrender our passports. We tentatively explained that our respective countries do not allow us to leave our passports with anyone else.

'You are in Egypt,' (*really?*), 'this is my country. You do as I say, otherwise there are problems.'

Well, we really didn't want any problems in this country, so we smiled politely, thanked them profusely, and toddled off to anchor while muttering unprintable words about our welcome into Egypt.

Once again we anchored. Surviving the Red Sea's howling conditions was hard work and at times frightening, but getting through it and doing what had to be done was fortifying.

Anchoring had to be quick, clean, and precise, especially in strong winds. The protected water may be calm, but the wind was still howling against *Mariah* and causing her to swing erratically.

Much to our delight, a couple of hours later, a large catamaran puttered into the bay. These were our American friends, Chris and Roy, on board *Solmates* with their two English setters. After they completed the paperwork with the Navy, they anchored not too far away and called out, 'Come on over!'

Launching our dinghy could be a bit of an effort, but over time, as with everything else, we were becoming quick and efficient. Our dinghy was a little timber boat, which sat upturned on deck and lashed down securely. We would untie it, roll it onto one side, attach a halyard to the pre-rigged bridle within the dinghy, and use a winch to lift the rope and therefore the dinghy. The main halyard was a rope that runs to the top of our mast that was used to haul the main sail up. It took the weight of our dinghy, and I winched while Noel guided the little boat over the railings. It was smooth and relatively easy.

Now, we were an Australian registered boat, visiting an American registered boat – you'd think this perfectly normal. However, between our two boats was Egyptian water and the Egyptian Navy, and they would do everything they could to remind us of this and their power over us. They watched us launch our dinghy, and suddenly they were upon us in their dinghy. Our freedom suddenly felt uncomfortably squished.

'You cannot go to another boat unless we give you permission.' The irritating Egyptian's voice bounced over the water, coated in a thick glob of smart-arse power. He stared at us with what felt like a challenge. It took but a moment before Noel and I gathered our wits.

'Please may we have permission to visit our friends, sir?' I asked in my best British accent.

'You can go only if your meeting is about your journey and the boat.' The power-wielding maniac continued.

I didn't think it was appropriate to announce our intentions of enjoying civilised company, with the distinct possibility of behaving most foolishly with copious amounts of alcohol running around our veins. Instead I said, 'Of course, sir, it is related. They have a problem with their engine, and we need to discuss how to fix it and the best route to take from here.' I valiantly tried to conceal the sarcasm that so desperately wanted to escape my lips. A nod fit for royalty was bestowed upon us, and we headed for our good friends, interesting company, good food, and alcohol.

And it was here that things declined rapidly, the main culprit being the rum and vodka, which were supposedly mixed with a less innocuous drink. I think Chris waved my glass of vodka at the tonic and hoped the fumes would catch in the glass. Soon raucous laughter interspersed with, 'Sod the fake discussions,' was heard bouncing around the water.

Day after day, we had all been punching into nasty weather, eating boring food, and coping with the company of our partners in confined spaces. Radio relieved the monotony of speaking to the same person each day, but humans need other humans, and we all enjoyed new company.

As the evening progressed, the Egyptians came over to ask why the meeting was going on so long. Like naughty children, we picked up the strategically placed charts and navigation tools and tried to act in a serious manner, toning down the raucous conversation and furrowing our brows in concentration.

'You must return soon,' we were instructed.

Just for something different, the winds continued to howl from the north and, again, we were thankful to be tucked in safely. On the radio we heard that boats had found shelter; the couple that didn't had to hove to and sit it out. Hoving to, simply put, is just a technique to prevent a boat moving forward. It helped prevent the loss of any ground and could prevent damage to the vessel (and the occupants) if conditions were particularly bad, so it was a neat trick to learn.

So we learned, you have to sit and wait for "windows" that arrive every week or so in-between the howling gale force Nor'westerlys. This, I bet, sounds okay, lounging around on a yacht. Well, stick yourselves in a room, thirty feet long and eleven feet wide. Sprinkle over some sand, add more than a dash of salt (over everything in and out), takeaway all yummy foods, leaving just the basics of flour, baked beans and peas (all tinned!), and ration out the ever depleting water supply. Add to that constant creaking, scraping, and the banging of all equipment on deck. Add to that a view of sand, rock, more sand, more rock, and the odd camel. It could get a trifle tedious.

One day, at another anchorage, we asked *Solmates* for some flour to help boost our sad diet. Anchored about twenty metres away, we watched Roy kit up into his diving suit with air tanks. He plopped into the water, which though it wasn't sporting any huge waves, had a number of wavelets that made swimming a challenge. Chris passed Roy a package, tightly wrapped in plastic – our flour. We thought they would launch their dinghy (easier to launch than ours as it sat on the back of the boat on davits and could be hauled up and down with blocks). Roy took the opportunity to check all our anchors, but first he delivered the flour. Our knight-in-shining-wetsuit swam towards us with a bag of flour above his head, wrapped securely in zip lock bags (the flour that is, not his head); it was a sight to behold. He checked our anchor and informed us that our chain was nicely wrapped around all the rocks that were at the bottom. Oh well, at least we weren't going anywhere.

I spent a few hours rummaging around, cursing, and folding myself into compromising positions to view the back of the galley cupboards where all those boring foodstuffs lurk, all that gear you never fancy as it is too healthy and invariably tastes like cardboard. Using my special recipe (which means I am too embarrassed to reveal the ingredients), I cobbled together a batch of Samosas and Chapatis.

To pass a bit of time between staring at sand hills and the odd camel, while cursing the relentless wind, I had been writing out copies of crew lists for an easier entry in to ports. Meanwhile, Noel changed the oil and replaced the water pump seal.

At last, we felt as though we were making progress. We passed Sudan and only had about another three days until Safaga. Our excitement built at the prospect of visiting Cairo and Luxor and seeing the Pyramids at Giza and the Valley of the Kings.

Once again, we were on our way, and there were reports of good weather for a few days. We wanted to take advantage of this, but we were approaching Fury Bay, which reportedly had amazing snorkelling. Decisions, decisions: do we stop and enjoy one of the best places in the world to snorkel or pass it by and take advantage of the good weather? In the end, we stopped. We were definitely never sailing these waters again, so why miss this opportunity?

The water was extraordinarily clear; it felt like we were floating in air. The mountainous, lively coral scattered across the ocean's floor like a giant marble set, left to grow their own vivid garden with vibrant fish flicking, frolicking. Stingrays glided past, the waving seaweeds swayed in rhythm. There was a cliff of coral dropping off into the deep blue, providing the stomach turning illusion that we were suspended over a cliff face. Fan corals waved us on, while the fish fought the strong current alongside. It was hard not to smile too much and allow the water into our plastic masks. The silence of snorkelling and free diving transported us to another world. It was hard to imagine that hunting exists within this tranquil atmosphere. I felt as though I could see for miles, but wondered what could glide up the vivid cliff face to eye me up for lunch.

Back on board, lack of drinking water was now the issue. This was far more serious. We were at yet another anchorage, waiting for calmer winds. Our view was like a stone quarry where sand filled the gaps. A couple of small timber huts dotted the beach; within the huts a few uniformed bodies sat, and we hoped they would be our salvation.

We launched our dinghy and slowly rowed ashore, wondering what our welcome would be. As we beached the dinghy and took steps on terra firma, I gathered up our trading gifts, and the armed guards approached and smiled. Through miming and gesticulating, the guards were happy to provide us with water. They also gave us some thick, rather strange looking, purple fruit juice. Our bodies absorbed the goodness in moments; peas and noodles did not contain the same sort of vitamins! In return, we gave them colourful magazines, full of Hollywood stars and gossip. We also presented them with some boiled sweets and a little koala toy. They were delighted by these gifts and excited to see the American women in their splendour. We were relieved and equally thrilled with our bounty of water.

With exhausted jubilation, nearing the end of April, we arrived at Safaga, Egypt. The much needed social relaxing with fellow cruisers was put on hold while we dealt with the officialdom of checking in and taking on fuel and water. At the fuel dock, a huge oil slick managed to attach itself to *Mariah*, but at that moment we could not have cared less. We just wanted to get off the boat and have a decent meal.

Before we knew it, we were taking a two-day trip to Luxor with our friends Faith and Cindy from *Carmen Miranda*. A four-hour bus ride through amazingly arid, rocky terrain transported us to Luxor. Getting off the bus, we were literally bombarded with agents trying to convince us to stay at their hotel or go on their tour. Through advice gleaned from other cruisers, we knew where we were going and were soon settled into a reasonable hotel.

Luxor is one of the greatest capitals of the ancient world: charming and evocative. The Nile banks are lined with modern hotels. The feluccas sail along the quiet waters of the river and the Bazaar comes to life at night. This is the great ancient city of Thebes, capital of the Egyptian empire for almost one thousand years. The Pharaohs who succeeded to the throne left their mark by extending the temple or adding halls and chapels. The temple dedicated to Amon (Egyptian deity who was revered as king of the gods) is astounding because of its size. It is the largest temple with columns in the world; apparently it could contain Notre-Dame Cathedral in Paris within its entirety. In short, it is stunning. That evening we explored the temple, with its professional lighting creating eerie shadows and voices from the past imparting their grand history. The sphinxes that line the entrance stare hard at the thousands of trespassers. The imposing columns that stretch to the sky are filled with carvings – ancient words and pictures; the almighty statues stand guard. It's a remarkable sight with a heavy air of mystique.

Into the swing of being back on land and forever thankful to be safe, the next day we explored the tombs of the kings and queens, in the great Valley. In the middle of a desert, within steep, peaked mountains lie ornate buried graves. The hieroglyphics, carvings, and paintings completely cover the ceilings and walls of the tunnels that lead you down into the bowels of the rocks. There lies a huge granite coffin, extra rooms for the extensive gifts, and, in one, the skeleton of an unborn baby! Our guide orated a brief history lesson in each tomb as we stared in wonderment and touched where we could – where ancient hands touched before. I was awestruck and right in the moment; Noel was hot and bored. To him the tombs were all the same; to me they held the enchantment of the past.

We both got "the bug" and spent the last day avidly stuffing bottom-blocking tablets down our throats, in the hope that we would survive the return bus trip. There were no toilets on the bus or bushes on the road; if we did come across a café (and I use that word loosely), the toilet would be a hole in the ground. This hole was surrounded with stuff you do not want to tread in, but have no choice. It stinks to high heaven and probably contains some sort of life form you don't want to know about. Much to our relief, we made it back without an embarrassing incident, loaded up with fresh foods, and took off. We felt off colour, weak, and tired, but the weather was calm. We needed to take advantage of calm seas.

Mostly, the 240 miles towards Port Suez were calm and pleasant. We were on target to arrive in the afternoon. During our last night, a strong wind kicked up with vengeance. Windy and his mates tossed and buffeted us all night and did not give me a moment's rest. Fortunately, Noel had managed to have a sleep before the tumultuous weather bullied us north. In the morning, I was tired and cranky, but the forty knots of wind whisked us along at full pelt through the narrow, freighter-packed stretch, insuring our adrenaline was kept pumping at full flow.

Then the storm hit.

It wasn't your average thunder, lightning, and rain, but your face-stinging sand storm. Suddenly, the horizon turned peachy orange, as if someone had turned on a coloured light bulb. The horizon and its peachy companion came up to meet us. We turned on our navigation lights. Our below-deck lights were on, too. The sand was thick; it felt as though we were being sandblasted. It was scary. I was trying to think in two directions at once. We couldn't see past the bow of the boat. Sand worked its way into every orifice, completely covering the boat. Just as our stress levels had reached stroke-inducing levels, I thought that, surely, it couldn't get any worse. Then, I spotted the bow of an enormous, 300-foot freighter dead ahead, not thirty metres away and about to run us down! These behemoths can move through the water at twenty-six knots. As the monster loomed out of the gloom, I shouted to Noel, 'Quick hard to starboard'. I swore with the invention of a few, new colourful obscenities, my heart coming through my chest. We squinted through the peachy-fog and gasped as other ships emerged from the murkiness. Within a few moments, we noticed that the ships weren't actually moving. With tear-making relief, we realised we were in the middle of the anchorage! There were umpteen ships at anchor waiting to traverse the Canal. The smog was so thick we hadn't seen them until almost upon them.

As we approached our intended anchorage area, the sand started to clear a little. We entered the famous canal and travelled about half a mile to our designated area (the rest of the Suez canal trip had to be arranged by handing someone lots of money and taking a pilot on board). As we made our approach, there were more rather large freighters coming down the canal, and we passed these monsters within a few metres. With forty knot winds buffeting *Mariah* at their will, I was becoming more anxious. At least now we could see the ships, and it felt as though the wind was starting to ease a bit.

Just as we were about to anchor, the winds started to gust up to forty knots again and put on an almighty final display, reaching fifty knots, supplying us our greatest shot of adrenaline. I was operating the anchor winch, and Noel was steering. We were both keenly aware that anything could happen – equipment could fail, engine could die, we could get hurt. The winds had really gathered momentum now, and I was nearly blown clean off the deck; we were careering sideways in a tight anchorage. Somehow, Noel steered us to a good spot and I let the anchor go at the right time. We held our breaths, hoping that the anchor grabbed. It did, and the anchor chain pulled tight and finally gave a little; we were held firm for the first time in what felt like forever.

Some cruising buddies, who had already arrived, were full of congratulations, 'It's a real milestone you've just completed.' We were exhausted, our nerves completely rung out. We didn't know whether to laugh or cry.

Noel looked at me, his crinkled eyes exuded warmth, love, exhaustion, relief, and gratitude. He smiled and asked, 'Are we having fun yet?'

Boat jobs were tackled in a hurry; putting on sail covers, and the usual checks had to be done. It was a bargain of give and take: *Mariah* looked after us, we looked after her. Eventually, and at the earliest opportunity, I hopped into bed. My limbs were so heavy, my eyes so sore, I wasn't even able to undress. I had missed my sleep shift through the night and had been awake all day with adrenaline galloping through my veins.

'Hallo, hallo,' interrupted my slack-mouthed dribble as I floated off almost immediately. A local guy was hanging off *Mariah's* stern, looking into the cockpit. I got up to see what he wanted. Noel was still busy finishing off the anchor duties I had neglected, like tying on elasticised strops to ease the harsh movement. A warm welcome into a new country was always appreciated, and I usually asked visitors on board; this time I didn't. I was absolutely exhausted and my patience had become gossamer thinner.

The skinny, brown man, with a crooked smile and white teeth, asked, 'Do you want fuel? Water? Tours?' He was relentlessly trying to ensure our business went through him.

I couldn't get a word in edgeways and lost any sort of reason. 'Bugger off,' I said, and then I went back to bed.

He disappeared only momentarily. Just as I was drifting off into oblivion, I heard, 'Hallo, hallo, you have to move; you are in the wrong spot.'

A couple of tears escaped my eyes through exhaustion. *That'll teach me for being rude*, I thought. Once again, I got up. Noel was still busy ensuring everything was how it should be on deck. The whole episode started again, but this time I asked our visitor to come on board. However, I didn't offer him a cup of tea.

'Okay, if we have to move, you have to help us re-anchor.'

I could see his mind forming the reason why he couldn't help us. But then he looked at me. My hair hadn't been brushed for several days and had two attempted sleeps mussing it further, my eyes were dark, my mouth down, and I was tense. I could have taken lead role as a mad, murderous woman. Our new crew member swallowed and astutely thought about where he was and his options. Then he agreed to help.

I am just horrid when I am tired, so needless to say we gave him the worst job of flaking the anchor chain. He did a good job and turned out to be quite a nice man. We did give him our business – after I'd slept!

'We want to get off the boat as soon as possible,' Noel said to some friends.

'Great, join us on our organised trip.' All of a sudden we were on our way to Cairo to see the pyramids. We had been making friends along the way and having gained enough confidence to chat of my boating abilities, I was meeting people with a vast array of experience. Some cruisers had been living on board over ten years, some for one year, some were fledglings that had just joined as crew. We had been on board for three years. I was learning something new each day and had gained the courage to ask others for advice or information. I came to realise that everyone, whatever his or her level of experience, had something to teach us. Much to my amazement, I learned that I had something to teach others, too. I was feeling comfortable in my watery world.

I had changed so much, not just with learning to cope with new words, new items, and new ways of life, but my morals and beliefs had changed. I used to think that everyone should have a proper job. If they didn't have a good reason as to why they weren't working, I just viewed them as reprobates! I used to mount my moral steed and spout how I was paying taxes and paying them to be layabouts.

Being unemployed by choice, I lived on a tight budget. I had no regimented times to be anywhere. I was free. I shed those bigoted blinkers and realised how I had misjudged the world and my fellow humans. Now, I viewed people ensconced within the nine-to-fine with having no idea! Go and explore, have adventures, I wanted to preach. I had to learn to keep my opinions and views in check – just because I had found the freedom I had craved, didn't mean it was right for everyone.

Happy to once again step onto terra firma, we set off early with Joy (a Brit and a crew member from *Alien III*), Jimmy and Tineke (Dutch, on board *Gabba*), and a family of three from a French boat named *Balloo*. After a couple of hours drive into the bustling, dusty city of Cairo, we stepped into Cairo Museum. This huge gallery was stuffed full of tombs, statues, treasures, mummies, and even bread that was thousands of years old! But the best was the treasures from Tutankhamen. I hadn't realised they were here, the famous, stunning gold mask right there! The treasures from the young, handsome king's tomb were not found until 1923. So well hidden was the tomb that robbers hadn't found it, so present-day folk can enjoy the amazing sight of the most famous Egyptian king's burial treasures.

The discovery of Tutankhamen's tomb was one of the most exciting finds of modern archaeology. In 1922, Englishman Lord Carnarvon, an art collector and great traveller, had already invested about fifty-thousand British pounds in financing numerous excavations in Egypt, all of which had been fruitless. Lord Carnarvon and his mission director, Howard Carter, had almost given up hope of discovering another tomb. But in 1923, they had their day. Of all the precious objects in the sovereign's tomb, the most impressive of all was the great sarcophagus, which was a single, enormous block of quartzite that housed four gilt wooden containers placed one inside the other like Chinese boxes. Within these sarcophagus', there were three ornate coffins. When they lifted the tonne and a half granite lid off the third coffin and looked into the interior, they saw only discoloured linen cloths. When the cloths were slowly cast aside the king, though, the gold gradually appeared: a wooden sarcophagus entirely plated in gold and inlaid with glass and semi precious stones. But the most moving thing of all was a small garland of flowers, possibly laid by his young wife, Ankhesenamun; after thirty-two centuries those flowers still conserved a bit of their original colour!

In summary, Tutankhamen was in three ornate coffins, the third (or the first one he was laid in) was twenty-two carat solid gold, weighing 1,170 kilograms, the material itself was priceless in value. The carvings on these coffins were simply beautiful. After the three coffins, he was placed in a beautifully carved sarcophagus and covered in shrines. Tutankhamen was special, being the young pharaoh of transition who brought back the capital to Thebes, reviving the ancient cult of Amon-Ra and other gods. He was nineteen when he died, and he received the most royal of burials.

They must have been building his tomb when he was born! His mummy was covered in jewels, and his huge tomb was crammed full of gold, precious stones, gifts and offerings. I found it amazing that this tomb with kilograms of gold had managed to keep the immortal remains of the great king hidden from the eyes of the world for so long.

Just seeing all these treasure made the day, but there was more to come. We jumped back on the bus, en route for Giza, where the Pyramids stand. The magnificent pyramids are on the edge of the town. They are in the desert and spread over about two to three square miles. Our next decision was whether to walk, take a horse or take a camel. We opted for a camel, as it wasn't an everyday occurrence to be able to ride one and I felt it more apt.

After some serious negotiations, we were soon two to a camel, with four camels all tied to each other. Joy was in front with our guide. I had read that camels can be lovely friendly creatures. Alas, these camels had had the rough end of the deal and were completely fed up with being bullied into walking around the same triangular pile of stones day in and day out. They were not happy camels. When we approached them, they bared their teeth to such an extent we could see right down their throats. With protection from the handlers, we jumped on as fast as mounting a camel allowed us to. We were second in line; Noel was in front of me on our beast. We rolled along with basic instructions, but there was not too much to do, as we were tied to the lead camel. We were able to pad right up to the pyramids and the huge sphinx; the place had a magical feel, a feeling of ancient times gone by. Our guide was fun and full of history titbits.

Halfway there, we dismounted for photos. The camels expelled an ugly moan, bark, and groan. We were all giggling, bouncing, sliding, and rubber-necking around the vista, having a jolly good time. Later, when we remounted, the guide ensured we were all on, and he tried to hop on when his camel jumped up. Now, some sort of power play came in. He swiftly and violently whacked his steed right across its ears with a whip. I hate this sort of thing and promptly had a go at our guide. But the camel was perfectly capable of fighting its own battles and retaliated with the most violent bark. He was that angry a huge inflated bladder like bubble ballooned out of its throat into its mouth and beyond its lips. I was a little concerned that something quite horrible was about to occur. These camels were big, far stronger than us, and we were securely tied to the one with the 'ump (pun fully intended). We had no method of control whatsoever. With a few minutes of vying for supremacy, the handler finally won. It wasn't a pretty sight. We were somewhat relieved that we were safe and not about to be galloped off into the desert sunset dragged by an incensed camel.

After about half-an-hour of riding these beasts, my horse-riding background kicked in, and I was urging our camel on with my heels, using my weight to steer and trying to overtake the leader, much to Noel's disgust and my delight. At the end, we had a sprint finish and I was in my element, unleashing my competitive side.

We came to halt and the camels were prepared for the dismount. I was acutely aware that when the camels lie down, we'd be thrown forwards (as their front legs folded), then backwards (as their back legs folded), and braced myself in anticipation. I was in the front at this point and as the camel tipped us forward, Noel became unseated. As the camel's back legs crouched down, Noel lost all control of his body and his equilibrium with gravity and, beautifully, rolled straight off the back. I then had trouble dismounting, purely because I was in pain from laughing so hard.

Back in Suez, we spent a day or two in town provisioning. One evening, we fancied a beer and were guided to a place named St. George. An inconspicuous, shed-like shop was revealed after stepping through an unremarkable green door from the street. The bar was filled with men: strong Russians, frowning Polish, thoughtful Taiwanese, and serious Japanese who all worked at the Suez Port on the big ships. The small room was filled with once-white tables, timber chairs, and a general grubbiness beneath the haze of lingering smoke. There was no music, just the clatter of scraping chairs, deep masculine laughter, and hum of kindred spirits.

Timid at first, Noel and I sat quietly together and were just glad to have a cold beer. After a couple of beers and curious looks in both directions (from us to the port men), Noel was at one table and I at another! We both ended up in deep conversations with people from all over the world, all while only understanding one in ten words! I met George, from Greece. I could speak not one word of Greek and he could speak no English. He would start talking in earnest, and I would place my chin on my fist and nod at various pauses as if I understood; this would go on for a few minutes. Then I would grin and so would he. I started to laugh and so did he. We both performed these theatrics over and again and spent most of the evening in a fit of hysterical laughter. There were few words passed between us that were understood, we both grasped ideas of the meaning, or least thought we did. We said goodbye with a mutual respect – we both knew we would have become good friends, if only we could talk to each other!

On 4 May, we departed from Suez with an impatient pilot on board. We had waited over an hour for him to arrive. As soon as he jumped on *Mariah* he started shouting, 'Come on, hurry hurry, must go now!' Thankfully, our experience of working together smoothly meant we were ready to leave quickly.

To traverse the Suez Canal, you hire two pilots. It takes two days to traverse, one pilot per day. In the first instance, a few days prior to departure, an official comes on board from an agency called

Prince of the Red Sea, which Noel aptly renamed Prince of Thieves. The official took measurements and calculated our fee. No one had any idea how the calculations were made. We believe he comes aboard to assess your worth by the size and grandness of your boat.

As with all officials, we just tried to be as polite as possible and hoped he was in a good mood. We had been warned from other cruisers that he asked for shampoo for his wife and cigarettes and baksheesh (bribery being part and parcel of life here). We gathered these items and were ready to use them as bargaining tools to hopefully keep the price down. However, we were slightly thrown when instead of asking for soaps and cigarettes he asked, 'Do you have any computers or mobile phones I can have?' Noel and I looked at each other, then, blankly at him. 'What about binoculars or radios?' Our stunned silence continued, with the imaginings of a huge fee, as we could not bribe this particular official. 'I'll just sit here and wait until you find something for me,' he said!

The Egyptians truly believe that they are fully entitled to own everything you own. After some rummaging, we found an old mobile phone that didn't work. He wasn't too happy and left the boat rather abruptly, while we worried what our fees might amount to.

Surprisingly, our fees were not too high, in the region of a few hundred American dollars. Some boats were higher, some lower. We were quite happy with our quote.

The day came when we paid the agency fees, pilot fees, baksheesh and more baksheesh, and set off. This was the easy part, except you had an Egyptian on the boat.

Fortunately, our two pilots were nice; we provided a nice lunch for them both. The conversation was reasonable and, as per other cruisers' instructions, we did not let them below decks (except to use the head) – rumours of stealing were rife.

We knew that when we dropped each pilot off at the end of the day, we were required to give him or her a gift. The pilot's administration office advised that five American dollars was enough, plus a few packets of cigarettes. They actually asked us not to give any more and lift the pilots' expectations for the future, as it could create resentment. Of course, the pilots do not think this is enough. To save an argument on board your boat, we were told to wrap up the dollars (baksheesh) and the gifts tightly with plenty of tape and on no account give them their gifts until they were literally stepping off the boat. This was not as easy as it sounds, as they spent the last four hours on board continually asking for their gift like petulant children. As the pilot boat came alongside *Mariah* to collect our pilot, he was almost begging for something from us. We handed over the packages of soaps, shampoo, and money. Wildly, he tore at the gifts like a demented man and was instantly annoyed that we had given him just five American dollars. With resignation he stepped off *Mariah* and did not say farewell.

That night, on 5 May, we anchored at Ismailia, an overnight stop half way through the canals. After the first day, it was a relief to be in protected waters. At 6 am the next morning, the pilot boat dropped off the next pilot for the second and last day. As they approached, I had only just got up, so my hair was sticking-up in every direction, and my face still creased. I was drowsy as I tried to pull up the anchor, which was, as usual, splattering cold water and mud all over me as the chain wound in on the gypsy. As the pilot boat approached and asked for baksheesh for those on board, I gave them such an angry look that they withdrew the question. Noel, the pilots on the boat (about half a dozen), and the entire anchorage became quiet. They just gawped at this medusa looking woman who was splattered in mud, giving them a piece of her mind. Still, it worked and they left empty handed, leaving their slightly worried pilot on board to travel the last part of the canal with us. We all enjoyed a pleasant, easy going, final day in the canal under clear blue skies.

15

Finally ignored

At Port Said, the package-ripping pilot stepped off our boat, and we contemplated staying the night after receiving a weather warning.

'What d'ya reckon?' Noel asked.

'I reckon we can handle it,' I replied confidently, 'I've had enough of being constantly nagged for hand-outs.'

Usually we would anchor and await favourable conditions. But the port was exceptionally busy and full of Egyptians. We'd had enough of the constant nagging for money and gifts, so with proven faith in *Mariah* we ventured into the Mediterranean Sea and into gale force winds, and hurtled towards Cyprus. I knew I could cope in these winds, my experience now providing the courage.

For two days we bumped along, clinging white-knuckled and riding out nature's offering. Noel had picked up a nasty cold in Suez and was tired, so I tried to maintain longer shifts to give him some much-needed rest. This resulted in us both being exhausted, but we made it in to Cyprus safely on 7 May. Throughout the windstorm, I had done much of the boat work, sail changing, navigation, and watches by myself. These thoughts provided me with a self-satisfied grin that I carried around for several days.

Cruisers in front of us made a big deal of our arrival, as did we when boats arrived after us. It was quite a feat to traverse the Red Sea. Not just the threat of piracy, but ferocious weather and, of course, the Egyptian officials.

The first week in the port of Larnaca, we did nothing except eat enough meat to make up for our vegetarian diet over the last two months. We slept, rested, and gloated mightily at the fact that we were surrounded with cheap, nice wine, and way too healthy olive oil. I noticed, and felt somewhat guilty, that other cruisers had streams of washing out to dry the day after they arrived. We didn't tackle ours until about a week after landing. We had better things to do. I wanted to enjoy terra firma, quaff wine, and indulge in the Mediterranean way of life.

Different boats arrived each day, friends reunited and stories told. The social life was terrific. We felt mightily relieved just to be ignored as we walked the streets. Not one person harassed us or asked for money. It had been sometime since we were just one of the crowd.

We loved the Med but, as with everything, there was always compromise. We may have been gleefully ignored, but food prices were much higher than they'd been for a long time. It was what we expected, and we took more care with our expenditure, as you must when earning so little.

Our cruising budget came from savings. Over the months, we watched those savings dwindle. Before leaving Australia, I had completed a writing and photography course with dreams of earning a living via pen. Since heading off, I had tried my hand at fiction and had no success. We knew, in England, we'd have to bolster the coffers.

We didn't indulge in luxuries on board, but we could indulge ourselves in thoughts of reaching England; we were so close. It seemed incredible we had sailed the entire way here. But we had achieved this by baby-steps – one port at a time.

With thoughts in our heads of England, money, and work, we knew it unlikely we'd be back in Cyprus any time soon, so we wanted to explore. It was funny that Noel hired the largest motorbike on the island, but he deserved a reward for getting us thus far safely; we set off for Mount Olympus and Troodos. Avoiding large towns, we kept to the smallest roads and explored quaint little villages that speckled the countryside: beautiful crumbling churches, narrow cobbled alleys, crooked steps, and cheap stone walled cafes. We loved the unmistakable white buildings scattered between dried greens and blue waters and the friendly folk – all beneath sunny skies.

Back at Larnaca, we turned our minds to important tasks; we still had a long way to go. Our last week was spent hauling *Mariah* out of the water and slapping on some more anti-foul paint. We were happy to see that everything below the water was where it should be and that all our hard work last year had paid off.

Suddenly, we were casting off to Turkey. The first day out was calm, the smooth waters easing us into the three dimensional movements. Having been on the hard (out of the water) for a week, our sea legs took a while to re-appear. But the seas were kind and we were happy to be moving again.

Relaxing into the sail, we started to wonder what all the fuss was about sailing the Mediterranean. We had heard it could be quite a chore with either strong head winds or no wind at all. One day we'd learn to listen properly, as the next day the wind picked up. It wasn't super strong, but fifteen-to-twenty knots on the nose made for quite a bumpy ride. We were a little out of practice, having indulged so heavily in Cyprus; we became tired and scanned the charts for a more favourable course, a direction that was more with the wind, than fighting it. We altered course to the island of Rhodes. Suddenly *Mariah* calmed down and we skimmed along comfortably.

'Arrh, isn't sailing great?' and, 'So relaxing,' were odd phrases heard wafting over *Mariah's* deck. We were motor sailing now, as the winds had become light, which was perfectly okay with us. If a better sail can be had going to a different country, then that is what we'd do.

'Oh well, perhaps we'll see Turkey another day!' Noel said.

In the port of Lindos, Noel viewed his first castle. Unfortunately, Lindos was not a checking in port, so we could only step ashore briefly. In these situations, we had learned that most officials were sympathetic to circumstances, and if we were discreet, they were discreet. You had to choose your countries well when you want to bend the rules. We would not have done this in Egypt.

As picturesque as a postcard, Greece identifies itself with her white, concrete houses scattered across the jade of green hills. Clear water surrounded our timber home, a spotless beach was but a swim away, and nature put on a full show of fabulous weather. We enjoyed a day's rest, but before we knew it we were sampling our first taste of the Med's notorious weather. Forty-nine knots of harsh, skin-searing wind pummelled us around our anchor for one-and-a-half days. We were grateful that the harbour police didn't insist we move, as we still hadn't checked in; it was too dangerous to make us leave. To myself, I wondered what the Egyptians would have done. We stayed up all night doing anchor watch; we were boat bound during the day. Boat life can be crap sometimes. Anchor watch is hideously dull. If our anchor dragged or let go, we'd have little time to ready the boat before it ran aground or into another yacht. So we had to be ready to move in an instant. The clanging of the rigging and grinding of the anchor chain put a stop to any rest.

Crete was now scratched off the itinerary. Bob and Christine on board *Breakaway* (our Irish friends) were on anchorage in Crete and had tried several times to leave and kept getting beaten back by strong winds.

We decided to island hop a bit further north to try to avoid becoming trapped. Along the way, we caught up with some more friends, Tom and Leslie from *Obsession*. They had become our tour guides way back in Darwin that had talked us into going to Bali. It was their fault we had found ourselves in Greece! True to form, they had all information on the island's hopping route, which we gladly copied down.

Rhodes city on the northern tip of the island of Rhodes was the next stop, and the journey there was unremarkable, so it can only be assumed that it was reasonably good. Rhodes was, however, spectacular. The old town sits behind the castle's walls, and the castle stands proudly over the new city. Much of the castle has been rebuilt after earthquake damage, and what a fantastic job they have done. The Street of the Knights is a cobbled street with characteristic arched wooden doors and shutters. Here the knights slept with their horses stabled beneath them. So enchanting is the street, that you can almost hear the horse's hoofs on the cobbled stones and the raucous laughter of the heroic knights.

It was 9 June, and we were planning to leave within the next few days. We were moored on a wall with all the charter boats. The marina management were harassing us to move. We were reluctant to move as we had to med-moor, which was a tricky bit of manoeuvring.

Med-mooring required you to drop anchor a certain distance off the wall, about two boat lengths. Once the anchor was dropped, it was necessary to steer towards the wall and tie the other end of the boat there. Our anchor was set up on the bow, like most boats. We had zero steerage in reverse, which if we utilised our bow anchor, meant we'd have to try to steer in reverse. We decided to rig up the spare anchor astern and steer forwards into the wall to tie the bow on the wall. *Mariah* had a canoe stern, so her back part was as pointy as the front (making her a great sea boat in large, following seas).

At the right time (which meant Noel shouted, 'Now!') I threw the anchor over the handrails, trying to ensure it didn't hit the hull and that our feet weren't in the middle of the coil of rope that ran out at an alarming rate. By some miracle, the anchor grabbed. 'Perfect,' we smiled at each other, wondering what all the fuss was about. Tearing ourselves from our self-congratulatory club, we noticed our Scottish friends from *Athena* (John and Carol) were frantically waving at us, as our bow glided slowly towards the wharf.

'No, don't come in,' they shouted.

With our minds focused on anchoring and controlling the boat, we didn't see a mooring line straight across the gap! In the nick of time, Noel shoved our throttle into reverse, and we started to wonder how the hell we'd pull the anchor up. There was no anchor winch this end of the boat. With much grunting and grinding, a strong husband, and a well-behaved boat, the anchor came up without too many further dramas. We found another spot and achieved the impossible by comfortably mooring. These times were stressful and our kind friends John and Carol knew this only too well (as does any cruiser willing to admit it). They helped us tie up, calmed us down, and gave us a beer to steady the nerves, hence our reluctance to move. There would be a lot of practice with Med- moorings as we headed west.

We had to make a decision on timing, as we were running out of time to get to England that year. My two sisters (Denise and Josie) were planning a holiday to meet us somewhere, accompanied by Denise's boyfriend (Peter), her son (Kieran), and Josie's daughter (Trinity). We had not met Peter and Trinity, and I deeply missed my family. They booked a flight to arrive into the main airport in Greece on 18 June, but at that point they didn't know where to head. They patiently waited to hear from us to find out where they would be holidaying.

After umpteen phone calls, much uhhming and arhhing, and weather worrying, we all finally met up in Kalamata, home of those rather yummy olives and a port on the Southern side of Peloponnesus.

We left *Mariah* at a new, professional, and well-run marina in Kalamata and hired a car to meet the crew from England in a place thirty miles west of Kalamata. Here, it was quieter and much prettier. We spent a week catching up, eating, drinking, and getting to know each other once again.

Saying farewell left me feeling sad and relieved: relieved because the holiday went well and sad, as I hate farewells. I clung to the thought that I'd be seeing them all again soon in sunny old England!

Along the Messina Straits (around Italy's toes), there was a traffic separation zone, so everyone knew where they should be. Traversing this waterway at night, we were blessed with calm seas. We had a couple of scares when boats and ferries were crossing our channel and their navigation lights were camouflaged by the many shore lights on either side of us (in places the channel was only one-and-a-half miles wide). As we were both exhausted from being up all night, we found a small bay at the end of the straits to stop and rest. We found a spot on the end of the concrete pier, but then noticed that there was nothing to tie up to. With a bit of creativity, we managed to tie up to one of our oars, which was shoved into a crack in the concrete for our bow line; for our stern line, we found a two inch piece of rusted metal to tie on to. We collapsed into bed and tried to sleep with dozens of noisy fishermen as our neighbours.

When rested, we had a lovely evening with our neighbours on *Zigizoo*, who were great at providing us with much information on the French canals, as they had been through them two years ago. The canals were our target.

Our next stop was the Aeolian Islands, just round the toes of Italy and north-west, which was touristy, but pretty. We had our first Italian pizza here and it was the worst pizza we had ever eaten!

We visited the Volcano Island, where you can cover yourself in mud. I was all ready to wallow for a while, but when we got there it looked like a huge muddy puddle. No bubbles or mystery, so I didn't bother. It looked pretty hard to find mud anyhow – it all looked too watery.

From here we went to Sardinia and made it just as the winds picked up, so the last hour was a bit hairy. The marina was basic with just toilets and a small hut with a bar. The town (Olbia) was groovy and fun; beautiful men and women in the height of fashion draped themselves over walls and sat on grass. However, even though they were dressed fashionably, they were all dressed in the same beautiful clothes that bore no individuality.

We met some young lads who worked in a cafe. They knew about two words of English, and we knew the same in Italian, but we all tried to communicate and had good fun in doing so. We were glad we met these guys and had a laugh with them, as the people in the marina were straight-faced, didn't bother to communicate, and didn't know how to laugh. Still, we were glad of the shelter when the winds really picked up, and for six days we had to sit tight. Finally, we could leave, and we completed a couple of day-hops up the coast.

Next stop Corsica. We landed at Port Ajaccio, where Napoleon was born. We loved it there, and I think we liked it so much because of the people. They were friendly, happy, and enjoyed our clumsy attempts at communicating. I was enjoying the fact that not many people spoke English; I had been studying French for a few months, and was surprised that I could communicate, though only the basics. Everyone was so friendly, so I didn't feel shy about having a go. It became great fun and fuelled our desire to spend time in the French canals.

We became residents in Port Ajaccio for a week and whilst it was a nice place – and a good anchorage – we were eager to leave.

Time spent here was eating into our time in the canals. There had been strong winds in the Golfe Du Lion, where we were heading, but those winds were abating. We only needed two days for the 200 mile jump and our last overnight trip.

I don't mind overnight sails on the whole. In fact, I came to enjoy them more and more, especially when it was hot. Hot, hazy days hid boats on the horizon, whereas at night, you could spot the lights from another vessel from miles away. The cruise ships were so huge, you could see the loom of their lights before they popped over the horizon. I liked a good eight hours sleep at night, so that was the only part I disliked. However, I did enjoy a snooze during the day to catch up and of course the rewards of a safe arrival into a new port.

Darkness seemed to bring out the "night-horrors," and I had to work at not letting myself indulge in sorrowful memories or horror stories. During the day, I'd never think about death or feel fear. I trained myself to calm my thoughts and enjoy what the night offered, winking stars, cool air, vivid moon, and wonderment at, 'what was out there.'

We found the perfect weather window and skedaddled as fast as the Yanmar would allow to Port Saint Louis at the bottom of France. We anchored outside the port in calm weather near a huge industrial area and cracked open the champers. An enormous wave of relief lay on both our shoulders. Anchoring in the dark in unknown waters didn't faze us one bit. *Mariah* was our home; we knew every part of her and every part of each other's character. Our teamwork was like poetry or a fine song, flowing, easy on the nerves, and enjoyable. It had almost been a year since we had left Australia and three years living permanently on board.

There was little time to waste. The following day, testing my poor French, we were in the marina booking in for our mast to be taken down. We didn't know much about the canals, only that our depth of five feet was about the maximum you would want. There are many different off-shoots and routes to take, but we selected to traverse one of the main routes to maintain the necessary depth beneath. This route took us from south to north, right through the middle of France.

We had gathered advice along the way and knew that we could obtain additional fenders from boats that had just traversed the canals (from north to south) and wanted to be rid of their plastic covered tyres. As usual, the worries about how it would all happen dissolved with the patience of time.

We spent one day preparing for the mast to come down, removing most of the rigging, the boom, and organising a place for the boom and mast to lie. I became Noel's assistant; he had it all figured out and I was there to simply hold this, pull that, and hang on to the other.

The following day, we cautiously puttered over to the wharf where the mast would be taken down. The young lad scampered up the mast to fix the crane's loop in place; he was sinewy and quick, clearly having done this a thousand times. Our mast was timber and extraordinarily heavy, it was about thirty-four feet high, so we needed a good crane. The mast came down in minutes while we stood and watched. Hardly a word passed between us all. Our mast was as long as the boat, so it fit pretty well. That afternoon, we ventured into our first lock and into the labyrinth of the French Canals.

I was not sure whose idea it was to take this route. We wanted to get to England, spend time with my family, and fulfil Noel's dream of sailing to England. We could have sailed north along the coast of Portugal and France, but the predominant winds were north and therefore it meant bashing our way up the coast. We'd had enough of head winds and once the idea of France was planted it grew and made perfect sense. Plus, of course, there was the added enticement of French wine, baguettes, and poetic language.

This was the first time we had taken the mast down, and it was far more complicated than I ever imagined. You needed the mind of a technician, which Noel had. With the mast down, the dynamics of the boat completely changed. We were now on a motor boat. While sailing, we were a formidable team, but I couldn't help wondering how we'd cope in the canals. For a start, they were narrow and traffic was a constant consideration. The depth was shallow, too near the edge, and we'd run aground. Umpteen locks had to be traversed, which called for clever boat handling. With this mix of changes, potential problems, and caring for a timber boat in harsh metal constructed locks, I wondered if we would maintain our composure. Was our great teamwork that we were so proud of going to start showing some cracks? It became a whole new challenge to be met head on.

My first mistake was to say I was from the UK. Many French do not like the English for historical reasons and probably culinary reasons too. I did most of the radio work with limited French. On the radio I tended to have a heightened British accent, which wasn't helpful. We proudly flew the Australian flag, but on reflection I think it would have been better to start every conversation with, 'We're Australians!'

With a fair bit of confusion regarding the opening times, and with our mast securely lashed down with a web of ropes on deck, we were ready to tackle our first lock. It was not too scary as the lift was only half a metre. Once we had managed to clamber up the wall to tie to the bollards, yelled at the lock master not to yell at us, ('allez!, allez!'), everyone calmed down and the procedure was quite easy.

It was fairly simple, and my fear of what occurred in the locks vanished, replaced with a serene calm – I knew I was going to like this. All of a sudden, we found ourselves in the mighty Rhone!

We were moving through the water at six knots and doing three to four over the ground, the Rhone having a good flow to contend with. In Cyprus, we had received mixed messages about the French Canals. One such article in a sailing magazine had, within its opening paragraph, stated, '... and so commenced our long awaited canal voyage, which could only be described as two months of hell.' Cheery.

On our first day, we reached Arles. To travel in the locks, we were required to purchase a license, which was pretty straightforward. After a booklet of rules, navigation, and money was exchanged, we were let lose. It's amazing freedom. There's no lecture, just a few pointers, and off you go. The great thing was that we weren't allowed to travel at night. We *had* to stop. After endless nights of plunging into darkness, this was a welcomed relief. There were plenty of ports, anchorage spots, or jetties hidden away, where we could tie up or drop the pick and relax.

When we landed in Arles, we took a couple of days to sort the deck out. It was quite unusual to have the mast horizontal. We rigged up some shade, as frying in the extreme heat everyday was a trifle boring. We generally got ourselves ready to move further up the river and encounter our next lock. In Arles, we experienced our first bullfight, of the spectator kind, not the participating kind. We sat in a two-thousand year old amphitheatre, where many bottoms had sat before, and watched huge, black, powerful beasts become tense and wound up by skinny little white human. It was all quite fascinating.

Let me reassure anyone contemplating the journey through here that the canals are bloody marvellous. We state this even though we had had a robbery on board and that the locks, especially at first, can cause severe palpitations of the heart and generally made you wish that mummy was close to hand. It was beautiful. We were mostly surrounded by trees, parks, twittering birds, and people picnicking on the grassy banks. We puttered through the most handsome towns we had ever seen, stone houses, bending with age, cobbled streets full to the brim with character. It was like sitting in a postcard.

The locks deserve a mention, as they were quite incredible. The locks in the Rhone were huge, absolutely bloomin' enormous actually. There was still some commercial traffic on the Rhone (although not much), and large barges had to traverse the locks, too. The whole process was really amusing. I was in charge of communications, and I think it was fair to say that I gave the lock-keepers a good laugh. It is one thing ordering steak, chips, and a beer, but to organise for us to go through the lock via a radio was quite another.

The large locks were daunting, a bit like puttering into a horror movie. At some point the lock-keepers obliged by opening the doors. The doors were painted a lovely shade of black in order to match the decor within. This of course made it a trifle difficult to actually distinguish any difference in the door being open and the door being shut. But not to worry, we only had a three knot current against us and a one hundred metre long barge up our backside to contend with. When we'd worked out the lock was ready, we puttered into the big, creaking, groaning, metal chamber.

The walls, as stated, were black. There was the sound of dripping water, the groaning of some internal machinations and the occasional screech of a buzzer to summon the spectators, to witness yet another witch hunt trial; a trial by immersion. That, of course, was only my imagination, and the reality was much worse. First, we needed to slow the boat down, maintain steerage, and find something (besides each other) to tie on to.

The bollards were neatly hidden within the wall, identified as a darker vertical cavity running up the walls and spaced about fifty metres apart. These bollards floated within the cavity and rose with us. For the first three locks, we tied the stern on to one bollard and the bow to the next further along; we were also slow learners. Noel would try and steer the boat (as the boat slowed, steerage ability lessened), control the throttle, pay out, and add more line by tying knots and fumbling. Noel, of course, felt like a complete tosser, not in control at anytime and generally not enjoying the entire proceedings. Then I would simply loop a line onto the second bollard, and we would centre the boat between the two bollards.

Finally, we settled on tying the boat to the one bollard with lines running fore and aft and even an additional line amidships, so I could work all the lines while Noel concentrated on steering. We utilised a plank over two fenders amidships to save the fenders as well as keeping the boat steadier in the swirling current. Being a canoe stern, we also had a big, fat fender sitting on a tyre on *Mariah*'s quarter as well and yet another big, fat fender fine on the bow. All lines ran back to their own cleats for ease of release.

Most days, we travelled a little further north; the French wave at us from the grassy banks, offering us wine if we could stop. When we did stop and met people in cafes and bars, they were friendly, but knew little English, which was good for me as it was like having a French lesson every time we stepped ashore. My French was improving, so I loved having a go. I certainly kept most of the nation thoroughly amused and didn't mind one bit that I was making a complete twit of myself.

Unfortunately, I had to learn the words for "thieves," "stolen," and "angry,' along with just about every swear word you can imagine.

At a quiet jetty in a town called Roquemaure, we went shopping for a few hours, only to return and find the boat ransacked. We had been robbed. I marched straight off to the Gendarmerie. They couldn't do much until we had gone through and worked out what was gone: a GPS, camera, portable CD players and cassettes, Christmas presents, jewellery and jewellery box, and personal items that could never be replaced – about two thousand pounds worth of gear had been lifted. After the initial shock, anger, and helplessness all we could do was spend an hour giving a statement to the police (armed with French/English dictionary). So we packed up and moved on. Fortunately, they hadn't damaged the boat in any way and, of course, we were unharmed. So with that in mind, we decided to square our shoulders and just get over it as quickly as possible.

We tried hard not to let it affect the whole trip through France, and it didn't. We met some lovely people after that day, and our faith in humanity was restored. We were close to Lyon now, a place I visited a few years ago and had loved. We hoped to find email here to communicate with family, who must have assumed we had been snatched by aliens by now. So far, the tiny, quaint towns we had stopped in were marvellous for respite, but not keeping in touch with the world as we knew it.

All in all, it was wonderful, no weather to worry about, no waves, no big winds. It was peaceful and resting. Though, I do think we were becoming a bit travel weary. We looked forward to stopping in England for a while.

We reached the Canal Du Centre, where the water levels were a lot lower and the river was about ten metres wide. It was just like puttering along a creek, and most days were spent in the middle of fields. The cows and horses nonchalantly watched us putter by while chewing the rich, green grass. We ran aground a couple of times, but fortunately, only on mud.

When the big barges came past, it was necessary for us to move to the edge to allow them to pass, which meant we then became stuck. Often we managed to rock, reverse, or ram our way through the mud. On occasions, a friendly lock-keeper would let some water out from an upstream lock, which gave us a bit of a lift.

But, best of all was when we spied a bakery and a vineyard and an accommodating tree; we'd loop a rope around the tree and toddle off for supplies.

It was now August, and we found that the whole population of Southern France went on holiday in August. This made us explore hidden parts of the towns and seek small shops where the locals purchased supplies. The experience provided new tastes, smells, and a rather relaxed state of being.

Further north, our ability to adapt was tested further by different locks. They ranged between two-and-a-half metres high to about five metres high. The bigger locks had floating bollards and were the same as before. The two-and-a-half metre locks were a bit more interesting. Noel, controlling the boat magnificently, manoeuvred us right alongside the wall as I stood with a fore and aft line looped onto each shoulder, ready to grab hold of and jump onto the wet, slimy ladder. I found that usually there was no top to the ladder, and my tearing fingernails had to claw at the concrete wharf to haul myself up. To add to the fun, there were thick cobwebs with resident spiders near the top that I had to ignore – I was scared of spiders. Once I had traversed the thorny bush and stinging nettles at the end of the ascent, I could tie up the lines onto bollards, some metres above Noel and *Mariah*. I would pass the stern line back to Noel so he could control it, while I handled the bow line. Pulling a blue cord, which was always well hidden, operated the locks.

On occasion, a lock-keeper was there to help and sometimes they were a bit keen. I was glad when they weren't there as a race would ensue. With an evil twinkle in their eyes, they'd pull the blue cord just a few seconds before we were ready, creating superhuman efforts to make the boat secure while not panicking. When the water was let into the lock (by pulling the blue cord), the water swirled and caused the boat to whirl against the lines. At times, the water gushed in so quickly, it would create a bow wave, up and over the boat! The lines had to be tight, and you had to maintain that tautness as the boat rose. Our sailing gloves wore through, and my upper torso would have had the best body builders worried!

We were having fun, though, and at times the canal was much higher than the surrounding plateau. To be on a sailing boat and to look down at a magnificent view falling away from you was strange.

It was the middle of August, and we were on downhill locks now. These were pleasantly gentle, with the water gently flowing out instead of in. Starting high up, it was so much easier to jump on to the wharf and tie up, each of us with a line each, paying it out gradually as we descended. A couple of the locks were manual, and there was not always a lock-keeper to help. The closing of the doors, opening the holes for the water to escape, then opening the doors the other side was done via a large wheel that resembled a steering wheel. The locks were decorated with flowers, and we could purchase local fruit and vegetables from the lock-keepers.

We were once again a finely tuned team and relaxed in whatever the locks threw at us, until we nearly lost the boat – twice. The first incident I awarded solely to Noel. We were traversing an aqueduct, a large, narrow bridge some fifty metres above tumultuous water and rocks; they were narrow and perfectly safe. I had jumped off onto the path that ran alongside to run ahead to take a picture. Noel was taking a picture from the boat and forgot that one of us was meant to steer. He also forgot that he was the only person on the boat. *Mariah* hit the wall of the aqueduct. I had visions of the headlines, "First flying boat." Fortunately, one of *Mariah's* owners had put the fenders in a good spot (excuse me while I rub my halo) and the fender was the only casualty, (which we actually managed to rescue later).

The second incident occurred at another aqueduct, with helmsman firmly in place. We had the green light to go. Right at the other immediate end were two locks and what looked to be a drop in total of about nine metres. Two cruisers were ahead of us and the locks didn't look that big. The lock master had different ideas and crammed all three of us in together.

Mariah had to squeeze her bow alongside the cruiser in front (skippered by a Brit called Simon). I had nothing to tie the bow onto, so I stood on Simon's boat and hoped he had some control, as I didn't have much. The stern was tied onto a ladder, making us diagonal. When the water was let out in front of us, the over flow kicked up quite a stink behind us. Normally we didn't notice, but it created a waterfall, which this time, our stern was beneath. We were thinking we might just make it, when the lock-keeper bellowed, 'Avantez!, Avantez,' and explained by furious signing that there was a huge concrete ledge right below our stern. Noel powered on our engine, which in turned rammed us into Simon's boat, which in turn rammed the first boat. These boats retaliated and pushed back. Vying for space, *Mariah's* wind vane cleared this ledge by just half an inch. All in all, we had just one-inch gap on port, where I was fending off (with, I might add, a huge bloody great spider alongside me), and half an inch gap at her stern. *Mariah's* starboard toe rail scraped down the wall, despite the half a dozen now squished fenders. Luckily, the wall was completely covered in slime, so there was no harm done.

Simon, on the cruiser in the middle, was repeatedly shouted at by us to move forward. He was standing on his boat's port, holding onto his line for dear life (as I was pushing his boat this way and that). But at times, when he couldn't take our pleas for help any longer, he'd haul himself up by his two lines, so he was hanging by his arms. He'd walk his body across parts of his boat, so he was then hanging horizontally. His toe could then push his accelerator forward!

As we came out of this lock, we blew huge sighs of relief, only to realise we had to do it all again on the next two locks! Needless to say, later that day the three of us headed for the nearest bar.

We'd almost finished the Loire and were heading towards the Briare Canal, which is about fifty-four kilometres long with at least twenty-four locks. The Canal Lateral a la Loire is slightly wider, which was good as we met a few peniches (big barges). We did become well acquainted with the mud at the bottom at times though. But, it was all pretty easy, going down in the locks and they were becoming fewer, leaving us to enjoy the beautiful scenery.

Eventually, we found ourselves in Paris. Not near, or pointing at it in the distance, right in the heart of the most romantic city in the world. Arsenal Marina was a huge basin that housed a multitude of esoteric boats. Surprisingly, the marina was reasonable and we tucked ourselves into a good spot and jumped, literally into Paris. Becoming tourists, we ventured to the Arc de Triomphe, the top of the Eiffel Tower, every corner of the Louvre (our feet nearly expired), and plenty of yummy restaurants, cafes, and parks. I love the French and France, but even though Paris holds fantastic sights and sounds, some of the snotty waiters, shop staff, and local folk had their noses so high, they must suffer with neck strain later in life.

It was in the centre of Paris that I was run over. Our ever-faithful bicycles were used to the maximum around the city. It was rush hour, and the reputation the Parisians have of being the worst drivers in the world was justified. Admittedly, we were on the pavement, studiously avoiding the square-hatted policemen who had told me off earlier that day for riding on the path.

We were sitting at the lights, and when pedestrians were shown the green light, off I sped. A lady in a small car hurtled around the corner through the red light, we collided. Actually, I pushed myself off the car, only knowing too well that I could be sucked under. All eight lanes of traffic came to a halt; Paris came to a standstill. The lady in the car was distraught; I was shocked.

Without really knowing what happened, a tall, handsome man picked me up and almost carried me to the pavement, while crooning, 'Madam, you are ok, non? You are not hurt, non? Madam, you fell like a ballerina, like poetry. I am so sorry. You come all this way to our country to visit and this is what we do to you? I am so sorry, madam. What can we do to make it better?'

My knees were weak, not from the accident but from the smooth, poetic voice that caressed my ears. As I stared up into the handsome, dark face of my saviour, letting him lead me to wherever he wanted to go I felt a sharp pain in my ribs.

The magic of the moment was shattered with a, 'She'll be right, mate,' from the unmistakable Aussie twang from my husband as he elbowed his way between my saviour and me.

Reluctantly, the man let me go. As I thanked him, my heart sank as he disappeared. I think I loved him for a short time, if not him, then certainly the romance of the situation. In true Aussie form, Noel handed me my bike and said, 'Come on, let's go!' And off we went. I was somewhat shaky on my bike.

After a few minutes, the last twenty minutes of events caught up with me and once I realised that I had actually just been knocked down by a car, I demanded we stop and have a wee dram to straighten my nerves. Never one for turning down a drink, Noel stopped at a café and had a cool beer. I was still a little shaky, but Noel and I had a good laugh at the event.

'I had to hand it to him,' said Noel, 'he was smooth.' Noel had watched with amazement as I was led off. He wasn't sure what he was most amazed by: the skill of the Frenchman or his wife so easily led away with devotion in her eyes!

'I wasn't sure whether I should have punched him or shaken his hand!' Noel said.

Alas, it was soon time to leave. We arranged for the small lock of the Paris marina to open for us in the morning. Under a bridge, but in a lock, we waited patiently for the water to rise enough to release us into the busy channels that snake around the heart of the city. I was a bit of a worrier and constantly checked important functions on the boat. One of which was the salt (raw) water outlet. When we were in port, the salt-water seacock is turned off. I always made sure it was on when we left, but I couldn't help but check it every few minutes in the first hour of us moving. As we waited in the gloom of the bridge, I stuck my head over the side. No water spurted out. After a few more moments, I shut down the engine.

'What are you doing? The gates are opening. We have to leave,' said Noel, thinking I had sabotaged the boat in order to stay and find my rescuer.

We checked the problem. The return line on the heat exchanger had slipped off, and the water that should have been pumping out of the boat was pumping into our home!

The engine was okay to run. Noel completed a quick, temporary fix whilst we were tied up in the lock, and then we puttered into the canals. A foot of dirty water swilled around our home. As I was preparing myself for the cleanup, a police boat came alongside us, just a few metres away. They seemed to receive a radio call and suddenly on came the blue lights. The powerful boat was pushed into full throttle; they turned 180 degrees and sped off. Unfortunately, this had caused the stern of their boat to dig in so much a mini tidal wave headed our way. With no mast, we had nothing to stop us rocking and the boat flung herself side to side.

Each side of the boat went under water, right up to the gunwales. The water within *Mariah* sloshed everywhere, the mast nearly came off the boat, and a lovely pot plant in the cockpit fell into the boat, tipping all the dirt out creating a quagmire. Noel had to do everything he could to stop me radioing up the police to give them a piece of my mind.

As I settled into the task of cleaning up, Noel was steering, following our charts. I could hear little comments, 'Wow, that's incredible, beautiful.'

I rolled my eyes.

'You have to come see this Jack,' Noel called down. Reluctantly I peeled myself away from the boggy-muddy marsh inside our boat and stuck my head out; the Eiffel Tower, the Notre-Dame, and the Arc de Triomphe all stood near the banks, as if seeing us off; an incredible sight. I watched the beautiful buildings ease by.

'Lovely,' I said, as if I'd swallowed a lemon and grumpily got down to mucking-out the boat.

We were north of Paris, and it seemed to rain constantly. We rigged up more tarps, donned wet weather gear, and battled each day with our goal of England becoming keener.

We reached Dunkirk on a grey, rainy day. Tying easily into a marina, we looked back from where we'd come and sighed. I knew I'd miss France. We promised to return one day. That afternoon, we walked ashore and decided on some chips for lunch and a cup of tea. Standing in a small, steamy cafe, we ordered lunch and perused the French newspapers. We saw pictures of planes near tall buildings, explosions, death. Through broken French and English, we learned of 9/11. It had happened a few days before. With no newspapers or TV on board (and the radio hadn't been listened to for sometime), we knew nothing of this horrific event. The entire town was sad; the entire world felt sad, brittle. I cried a little. Disbelief hung over our lunch. I rang home.

'I haven't turned the TV off for three days,' said my mum.

The grey clouds seemed to darken further.

16

Noel fulfils a life-long dream

What struck me most as England appeared on the horizon and slowly glided towards us was its magical scents. The grass, dust, rubbish, trees and flowers flowed across the salty water and invaded my senses. I smelt the perfume of home. Tears pricked my eyes, and I foolishly grinned all across the entire English Channel.

At Ramsgate, we eased into the narrow entrance with the firm, but polite, British accent from the Harbour Master guiding us through.

In the secure haven of a near empty marina at dusk, we carefully secured *Mariah*. Noel handled the bow lines, and I was fiddling about at her stern. We stopped in unison, looked at each other, and at the same time realised we were both on shore. We were on terra firma. We were standing on England. We both did a ridiculous little jig and hugged, relishing our achievements. Actually, we were still on the water, standing on a floating pontoon, but we were in British water, British docks, and smelling British air.

Noel was champing at the bit to get to a pub, but we had to check in first. Customs came on board and stared at the white powder on our table. I blushed a little and said, 'It's talcum powder.' We had just taken a quick 'shower' in the sink and had dusted off in talc. They believed us and just thought we were a bit odd, but we were used to that.

They declined the proffered beer, and I batted my weary eyes to convince them to take a couple of pictures of us on English soil.

It was Noel's first time in England. What I found remarkable, and still do, is that Noel fulfilled a lifelong dream. He had always wanted to sail into England, not fly, and he had achieved that. How many of us have an unattainable dream, or even an attainable one, that we never achieve? I was very proud.

Once customs had cleared us in, we were free to roam. On the way to the pub, Noel wanted a meat pie.

'Remember,' I said 'if you ask for chips, don't ask for hot chips. You're likely to receive a smack.'

Across the oceans, I had been training Noel in English-speak. To ask for chips in Australia, you asked for hot chips. That is because they don't say crisps; they say chips if they want crisps. I giggled all the way to the pub while Noel practiced saying 'Crisps,' his lisp became heavier and thicker with each step.

'A pint please and some ccrrrrispssss,' announced Noel, as if he was an actor enhancing his esoteric character for the sake of an audience.

Nowhere in the world, do they have pubs like English pubs. Australia ruins its drinking holes with TVs lining bars with the volume up high, blaring out horse racing events, betting, and slot machines.

The low beams, dark cosy atmosphere, wrapped in hundreds of years of history and the occasional real fire is unique to our land; I love these places, the food and drinks are heightened in the palate by the splendid ambience. In one of these quaint English pubs, I rang home; I couldn't contain myself any longer.

'We're in Kent!' I exclaimed excitedly; Mum cried, which made me cry.

The following day, we untied and made our way up the mighty Thames River to where we would spend winter in St Katharine Docks in the heart of the city. Ironically, we had one of our best sails ever as we trickled past the Millennium Dome and sighted the London Eye for the first time.

'I've only ever seen this in books. I'm really here,' Noel said, a tear in his eye. 'I feel like I've come home,' he said, which caused a tear to appear in my eye. Some of the sights were new to me; I had come home, too.

As we expected, as well as being home, we were also in the land of uncertainty; otherwise known as planet numpty. It's that old familiar place, where one is not too sure whether to lead with the left or right foot. Where do we go now? How long do we stay? What do we do for work?

We arrived in London amidst great fanfare. Crowds thronged the foreshore. Tugs hooted, the masses where cheering. Tears were shed. We had arrived. Yes, after fifteen thousand odd miles of sailing, we had made our destination; our welcome was much appreciated. Success was rewarded by that rare bonhomie that we humans show when a spectacular and daring feat had been achieved.

Once we moved out of the way from the protesting tugboat, we dried our eyes and thus improved our eyesight. We could see that the crowd was cheering the streaker on the other bank. The long and short of it being that the welcoming committee was our heartfelt supporters, Roy and Valerie, my mum and dad.

In October 2001, we puttered *Mariah* into her last lock for a while, the gates slowly closed behind us. Noel stared at those gates. I was smirking and itching to get off the boat to hug Mum and Dad. Noel frowned a little. Later, he admitted to feeling a bit sad, 'Those gates closing behind me meant the end of a magnificent year; from here on out, I was heading back, not forward into the adventure.'

By the time we tied up in St Katharine Docks, it was near nine in the evening. Momentously, I was given the choice as to what we do. I wanted to go home, to Mum and Dad's house; it was late and a couple of hours drive, but I just wanted to get off the boat and show Noel where I had grown up. The house at Shenley in

Hertfordshire was called a cottage. It sat on two acres of land and was a square, pebble-dashed block, completely deceiving in what it contained inside its esoteric walls. With five bedrooms, three bathrooms, two enormous lounge rooms, dining and kitchen areas, a utility room, additional cloakrooms, and an entrance hall that was the size of lounge, it wasn't hard to believe that Mum and Dad were overrun with stuff. Until ten years ago, there had been four generations living in the house: us kids, Mum and Dad, Mum's mum (my nan), and her mum (my great nan). A house of all women except my long-suffering Dad!

On the land, my parents' owned were six breeze block stables, two double garages, a couple of caravans and various shapes of sheds. A JCB and a dumper truck added to the menagerie of fun. Various horses of different shapes and sizes were kept with various people of different shapes and sizes coming to look after, ride, and generally enjoy the countryside. Grazing fields, which were dappled with other horses, surrounded the house. It was blissful, and I loved it there.

Noel had heard about this house from Colin and his wife Brenda, who had both seen the house and added to its mystique by trying to explain the ethos of it. This is hard to do; it is hard to understand just how the house ran unless you'd seen it. It was an open house and the best way to describe it came from my childhood friend Sharon.

She said, 'If a stranger is sitting in your mum's lounge with a cup of tea, none of you would ask, '"Who are you,"' You simply say, '"Hello, would you like a biscuit with that!"' She added, 'On a second visit to Shenley, everyone is issued with a back door key.'

None of us ever used the front door. It was bolted from the inside, and you could not open it from outside. The back door was entrance and exit. Noel found it a bit disconcerting getting used to strange people walking in and out of the house at odd times, with dogs, cats, and children. But the house was alive, living. It wasn't tidy, but no one ever felt out of place or uncomfortable; everyone was relaxed and felt completely at home.

Amid the mayhem, Mum and Dad had kindly agreed to let us bring *Mariah* up to their garden for our stay in England. We had some savings left, and we could either continue our voyage and arrive back in Australia with nothing or use the money to buy a house, renovate it, and hopefully earn some rent, while completing our journey around the planet. Mum and Dad loved the idea of having a boat securely on land; it meant we were staying. There was an old, disused road that was now covered in earth and part of the garden, all securely fenced in with large trees and even larger black iron gates. It was here Noel and Dad dug and probed to unearth the road. We needed a stable base to sit *Mariah's* ten tonnes atop.

The big day came; we had sourced the only crane that lifted boats out in London. We had also enlisted the help of my Dad and Colin to help out. The firm we hired for lifting and transporting *Mariah* on a low loader came with two guys: a father and son. There was much organisation to be done with arranging suitable times a safe route under low bridges. We also had to take down the mast. Noel, Colin, Dad and I squished on board Mariah for several days while we prepared the boat for hauling out.

The big day came. The marina handled the crane that loaded *Mariah* onto the truck; I felt sick as I watched our home swing in the air, with just two slings holding her several feet above hard, unforgiving concrete. The truck guys took *Mariah* under their wings and spent hours sitting her properly, tying her down, checking, rechecking, and then checking again. It took many hours, but they were absolutely brilliant – never had our boat been in better hands.

It still didn't stop me becoming a jittery, clucking chook. I started fussing, asking, and pointing until Dad said, 'How about you and me go get everyone some brekkie?'

Everyone was delighted at the prospect of Maccie D's and wholeheartedly agreed that we should go. I loved adventuring out with my dad, no matter what we were doing; we always had a good time and a laugh. As we drove into the city to find some sustenance, I relaxed.

'I was becoming a pain wasn't I?' I asked with a lop-sided grin.

He laughed, 'You're alright; it's just a big day for you.'

I could streak through London naked, randomly shooting at people with an AK47, and Dad would understand and excuse me; he really is a special man.

Noel and I could ride in the truck with the lads. Colin and Dad were driving behind. As the huge lorry swept out of the marina gates, I cried, 'Watch it!'

The truck driver stopped. Turned off his engine, put his hands calmly in his lap, and regarded me with his deep, gentle eyes. The low-loader cab was separate, so swinging around the corner it appeared that we were going to hit the wall. I couldn't keep my mouth shut.

'Look, love,' he said, 'I have been doing this for twenty years; you have been in my cabin for twenty minutes, I do know what I am doing. You are going to have to trust me.'

I did, and I shut up. Everyone was highly amused; I was embarrassed. Watching our ten tonne boat do fifty miles per hour along motorways was heart-stopping. I continued to wiggle in my seat, biting my lip.

Dad and Colin were driving behind the truck, but soon slowly pulled right back. When we stopped to check all was well, I asked them why.

'As you approach a bridge, it looks like there is no way in hell you are going to make it underneath,' my Dad laughed. They both held their hearts, the whole adventure was great fun, but adrenaline and minor heart attacks were part and parcel of the escapade.

At last, we made it to the narrow lane where Shenley Lodge Cottage sits. We eased up the winding road; we were greeted by family and many friends. It wasn't everyday that an ocean-going sail-boat comes up the highest hill in Hertfordshire! The mobile crane was ready and waiting, a marvellous piece of equipment that everyone oohhhed and arrhhed over.

Everyone eyed the wooden props Noel had organised to hold *Mariah* up sceptically. But Noel had done this many times before; my confidence in him never waned. After just a few hours *Mariah* sat in my parents' garden. Her cockpit was under an enormous, old oak tree, resplendently vivid green leaves dangled over her stern. Sitting in the cockpit felt like sitting in a huge tree house. Her mast was tucked beneath the eves of the stable block, the length fitting perfectly, as if the stables had been made to measure.

Much to everyone's bemusement, Noel and I mostly stayed on board at night. The house at Shenley was huge, but we liked our home, our independence. We could watch what we wanted to watch on TV, have a drink, party, or sleep.

When *Mariah* was settled, we purchased a car and explored the lands looking for a house to renovate. We were about ten years too late to buy anything in the south and headed further and further north. In Staffordshire, we purchased a characteristic terrace house, which needed everything done to bring it back to life. We spent eight months lovingly renovating it and then successfully rented out the house to a lovely lad who loved the place as much as we did. We returned to the south and set about working, because now we had no money left at all.

Noel quickly landed a carpenters job, working in the glorious fields of Hertfordshire, converting old stables to offices. I refused to go into an office. I'd noticed that Mum and Dad's house was bursting at the seams. Shenley housed furniture and belongings that were my great nan's, nan's, my (and my sisters' gear), and now my nieces and nephews' stuff, and of course, Mum and Dad's collections. My parents and I came to an arrangement: I would clear out the house and renovate it. Dad was working full time and had just eased back to four days a week. He still could not keep up with all the repairs and renovations the old house needed. I set about clearing up. Auctions, garage sales, newspaper adverts... soon the gear was vanishing. Nothing was of any great value, but there was so much stuff that hundreds of pounds were earned by us all.

Dad wanted an en suite in the main bedroom. So Dad and I worked together three days a week, while the other days I battled on alone. It was glorious. I could give back to the house I had grown up in, the house that had looked after me all these years. The three days working with Dad were great fun; we both liked getting jobs done, no matter what time of day they ended. We always had a giggle and conversation, ideas and old stories bounded around the rooms while we worked in harmony.

Life was strolling along nicely, then it spiralled frantically downhill and made us all stare into the face of reality.

'Jack, Jack, wake up. JACK!' Thump-thump-thump on the hull. At 2 am, Dad had come running out of the house, across the garden, trying to wake me up in our well-insulated boat. I jumped up and followed Dad into the house. Mum was sitting on the bottom step of the stairs, holding her chest, gasping.

'Where's it hurt, Mum?' Her face was just a railroad of lines, the pain in her eyes almost tangible; she couldn't speak. 'Is it your chest? Does your chest hurt,' I said forcefully, I had to get some sort of answer. She nodded. I looked up into Dad's concerned face, 'I'm calling an ambulance.'

Dad still hadn't said a word. He simply nodded. Nervously, I made the call, worried about the ambulance finding us, as we were in an odd location compared to our address.

This terrifying occurrence happened many times, at least once a week before the doctors realised it was more than indigestion. As Mum deteriorated and became yellow with jaundice, the ambulance drivers started to grill her. They were frustrated with what they believed was a minor ailment. Dad and I were at our wits end.

Thankfully Noel piped up, 'You are here to take the woman to hospital. Please just do your job.'

The following day the doctor told an extremely tired Dad and me that kidney stones had caused a blockage, causing the jaundice.

'Your mum is lucky,' he said gravely, 'in these situations the best case is normally intensive care.' It took a while for this to sink in; we found out that when stones get stuck and block pipes, the body's poisons often cause death.

Mum is one of the kindest, gentlest persons I know, so I was quite amused when she became an awful patient. I would often tell her off for being so rude to helpful doctors. Despite the initial lack of correct diagnosis, the staff at the hospital was brilliant. I always admire these people; you have to be someone special to do this kind of work.

Dad and I became tired, and work slowed a little. Dad wanted to retire. He had worked all his life, giving his family a wonderful upbringing; it was his turn.

They started to receive details on houses for sale in a small town where they used to live. They wanted a bungalow, a small house so their children (me!) wouldn't keep coming home to stay. We were all frank with each other, and we all loved each other dearly, but really didn't need to live together anymore.

Mum was in hospital, and Dad wanted to view a bungalow in a street he had always liked. We snuck off, not telling anyone, and viewed the place. We both loved it and enjoyed telling Mum at the hospital visit that afternoon of our antics. Dad visited Mum every day in hospital, and I visited almost every day. Mum had done so much for me in my life that I had to see her to make sure she knew what was happening in the outside world, and that I cared. I know if I had been in hospital, she would have made the effort for me.

They purchased the first bungalow they saw (after viewing other properties too) and are incredibly happy, which in turn makes me exceptionally happy.

17

Whale collision

After almost two years in England turning the boat into a large garden gnome, working, buying, and renovating a house, we decided it was time to go.

'Why are you leaving?' One of my nephews asked.

My heart broke as his bewildered face was tinged with fear; it was the type of fear youngsters instinctively have in a situation they cannot understand. I could only hug him tight. 'I don't know. I want to go and have new adventures, but I'm sad that I have to say goodbye to people I love, like you.' Knowing that he'd never understand, because I didn't, I added, 'I just want to see places – something inside me just makes me keep moving.'

It was now June 2003 and launch day. In little time, *Mariah* was crane lifted in the air and swiftly secured onto the low-loader. By mid-afternoon, we were in Southampton waters, gently eased in by the mobile crane and relieved that there were no leaks. Feeling a little out of practice, we started to manoeuvre to our berth. Noel, Dad, and I were ready with ropes, fenders, and hearts in mouth; the engine started, and we eased backwards. Without warning, the engine stopped. Now we were totally at the whim of the wind. We slowly glided towards two pristine boats. With limbs flailing, voices wailing and fending off, we just managed to avoid colliding. With a look of despair, the marina staff towed us safely into our berth. With pink faces, we admitted to leaving the fuel cock off!

The next day we moved into a different berth; this time all went well, which boosted our confidence. After a lay-in and a hearty breakfast, Noel and my Dad worked at putting the mast back together while, I worked on trying to find a home for all our possessions, which lay in a hideous heap within the boat and on the deck. Trying to safely store every possession, tool, and spare part on a thirty-three foot yacht that was eleven feet at its widest was no mean feat. Attached to the inside of every cupboard was a list of each item that was stored within it. This may sound a bit pedantic, but in an emergency, it was a godsend. By 4:30 pm, we were exhausted. The last two months had been filled with fifteen-hour days, trying to get to this point.

On 12 July 2003, with a good weather forecast, we left Southampton. As it was a weekday, there was not much traffic. The channel was well buoyed and the tide carried us along nicely through the Needles (the narrow channel between Isle of Wight and Southampton). After feeling a little like we were in a washing machine, we were spat out safely into the open sea. For the next six hours a westerly wind blew. We were heading west, so it was a bumpy ride, which wasn't much fun while we were trying to recover our sea legs.

Eventually, the promised wind-change came, and we took off sailing pleasantly at over six knots. Thirty-three hours later, we made it to Falmouth, with not one problem and a fat-cheeked moon to light our way. Falmouth claims to have the third largest natural harbour in the world after Sydney. The beauty of the English countryside and the rolling patchwork fields encompassing the harbour was breathtaking.

We could anchor here. Once *Mariah* was settled we went to town to sample the local brew. We felt intoxicated with boat stupor. The bar was swaying with us and only another pint seemed to help.

After a rest, we provisioned for the next leg, destination Portugal; that meant crossing the notorious Bay of Biscay.

But there, in Falmouth, we sat. It was nice, but winter was coming, and there was all that wine in little Spanish taverns just waiting for little ol' us. We had conveniently forgotten the pain-in-the-arse factor of waiting for good weather. Fortunately, we hadn't forgotten the pain-in-the-arse factor of sailing in bad weather. So we sat, figuring the electoral roll would have our names soon. Mushrooms started to sprout from behind our ears, and our speech was starting to drawl: 'do yew liik or parschty then, Cornish parschty yew canna beat it mind' and 'Parschty und a pint, sets yew oop fa life it doz'.

Yes, we sat for a while.

I had two choices:
(1) Apply safety in numbers theory (wake up Noel) and
(2) Make like an ostrich.

Crack, lightning split the night with fierce ferocity. The Bay of Biscay was living up to its tempestuous name.

'Wake up,' I called to Noel. Hearing reassuring mutters calmed me down. Company is comforting when on watch.

Eventually, all was still and the lightning had moved off into the distance. In contrast to the angry weather, dolphins gracefully torpedoed alongside, a joyful sight that always generates a broad smile.

Amid gentle breezes and clear skies, we arrived intact at Rias de Muros, España (just north of Portugal). We anchored in the bay of this small, untouched town. With little tourist trade, the locals did not speak any English. We dinghied ashore, aware that we would finally be able to improve our non-existent Spanish.

Nearby shops made life easy to stock up. By using a series of signs we created, we communicated in a comical, clumsy way. The local butcher sold an array of meats. Unfortunately, Spanish for lamb did not exist in our vocabulary. Noel, the last person on Earth to be embarrassed, put his two index fingers on the top of his head, in the place of horns, pawed the ground and tried to make sheep noise. We didn't want goat and the difference between goat and sheep evaded Noel's hysterical miming. I think we ended up with beef that night, but to this day, I bet those giggling girls in the butcher's shop remember, 'That crazy Australian guy.'

In the bay, other cruisers were enjoying the peaceful anchorage and with local beer that was cheaper than water, we thought we would stop for some time.

Four days earlier, with heavy hearts, we had watched England recede. A sad farewell to friends, family and a beautiful, historic country; it was time to look forward, not back. We skipped down the Spanish coast, enjoying the small villages that were delightfully void of swarming tourists.

In September, we arrived at the river entrance to Lisbon. We survived a week in the capital where we obtained our USA visas.

There was thirty knots blowing outside as we sheltered behind the suburb of Caiscais, just a few kilometres from the heart of Lisbon. It was in Caiscais we experienced what it would be like to be a rubber band.

The wind created inevitably large waves on the windward coast. This, we happily reasoned, was fine. We were snug and rather smug on the lee of the headland. To quote from Abdul the poor quality carpet salesman, 'Nature, like my carpets, does not a vacuum like.' Nor does she like smarty-pant yachties lying comfortably in their bunks. Put the two axioms together and the result thus created? A two-metre swell rounded the Cape, entered the bay, and rolled with great stealth and accuracy, seeking out its prey. Contact! A perfect hit, right smack up the backside of the peaceful, if somewhat apprehensive, yachting fraternity. All things nautical were propelled fifty metres forward. The lonely swell, having completed its task, continued on its merry way. Leaving the vessels side-on to the ever present thirty knots of wind. Momentarily, the crew below thought that this okay, as there was relief from the constant grinding noise from their over taxed ground tackle... until windy and thirty of his mates decided to shove all the boats back where they belong. This was all very well, and things proceeded along without complaint or hindrance from any of the principals involved.

'It all seems so jolly peaceful,' one crew member was heard to say. Peace reigned supreme – for about twenty seconds. Then there was emitted a lot of horrible stretching noises, timbers complaining, and a general feeling of mal de mer prevailed due to stomachs protesting their being lurched violently from their bunks. What followed was the symphony of snapping ropes, bending steel, and fraying tempers. After five hours of this cycle repeating itself every sixty seconds, we eventually saw the sense in weighing anchor during the dark and wee hours and seeking out the relative solace of the open sea. Sines was our next town, where peace reigned once again.

In Portugal, I became an auntie again. Samantha Louise Lawrence arrived on 1 September. I was overjoyed, but a little sad. I ached to hold my new niece. Back on board, every blessed moving part seemed to have worn out while *Mariah* lay neglected at Shenley. Our motor for the dinghy would not start. Our anchor winch had retired. The camera had seized up. Noel had scraped his last vegemite and peanut butter jars and was becoming mutinous. (Portugal is void of these gastronomical delights.) Above all, I had my second grey hair.

Portugal's history, based on the cross, had become my crossroad. I was at a crux, pulled in every direction. I longed for the old world in England, to celebrate another generation, but I liked the new world and its excitement of voyaging to the Americas. Do we cross the Atlantic? Do we head home? We could see loved ones, make repairs, earn funds, and buy vegemite. Making decisions could be the hardest part.

Incidentally, we liked Portugal. We explored old Porto, an optical feast famous for producing port. Its narrow streets hug a wide shimmering river that is Porto's centre. Crammed with smug apartments and toppling slums, scrawny beggars wailed while blinkered, suited office workers clip clopped by. Cool stone arches crossed old cobbled streets. Drugs were openly available near respectable shops. Inside Franciscan chapels, wood-carved statues of beheaded martyrs and arrow pierced torsos of bloodied saints were on gruesome display. Visible bones laid in the catacombs, hence our excuse to inspect the winery and their cool, oak vat storage cellars. We were doing some serious thinking and hoping someone would find some vegemite, hankies, and hair-dye and send them our way.

Do you remember the game show *It's a Knockout*? We were the latest contestants.
Game 1: locate supermarket with askew map.
Game 2: guess which employee is truthful, 'Yes, we close soon', 'No, we stay open.'
Game 3: do not vomit when passing the butcher's counter, which displayed skinned goat's head complete with teeth, tongue, and bulging eyes.
Game 4: traverse beach, taking on hideous gait to prevent burning feet, splitting bags, and sinking.
Game 5: keep the shopping dry during dinghy crossing (impossible).
Game 6: perform miracles by finding space for supplies on an already bulging boat.

In the spirit of jocular games, we were great entertainment for the locals. Dressed for the evening, rowing ashore in a tatty little wooden boat, we managed to cock-up our beach landing with momentous brilliance. Simultaneously, we jumped out and the dinghy pinged up and away from us. I sat in the salty, sea. Noel lay down and chatted with the crabs two feet under. Through our tears of laugher, we noticed the beach dwellers were bent double watching us. Without further ado we wrung ourselves out and dripped our way to the bar.

Sines, Portugal is fifty nautical miles south of Lisbon and became our hometown for a few weeks while a gale blew. We had made repairs and were fully provisioned. We now felt ready to venture onward.

Scientifically choosing our next destination (eeny meeny miny moe), we headed for Morocco. From the corner of the Algarve (a place we didn't wish to visit), at midnight we fired up our laptop, tuned into a weather frequency, and waited. A few minutes after midnight, a clear weather report came through on our screen. We fancied visiting Madeira, but the weather showed gale force winds over there. So, what about the Canaries? Well, winds were strong there, too. The only place that looked safe was south east of us. We studied our charts: 'Casablanca it is,' announced Noel.

Safely in Casablanca, we soon learned that traversing the dilapidated jetty took SAS training. Thereafter, the four-kilometre walk through the lonesome industrial port felt ideal for an ambush.

In town, vivid Bougainvillea tangled its way through the evil barbed wire. Mercedes and the Hilton mixed with hawkers of fake goods, peanut vendors, load bearers, beggars, dust, and chrome; it all created a nose-curling hum.

Conversely, genial natives emerged in the vibrant nightlife, making the journey worthwhile. The harbour was incredibly sheltered, although anchoring between the shipwrecks was a little hard. Our end of the mighty port felt like the Mary Celeste. But we soon found a little man, in an even littler hut ready to 'watch over' our boat. He organised diesel and water for us, and for a few dollars a day enabled us to venture into town without coming home to a robbed boat.

Traipsing through the port, the interior became more heavily guarded, and soon we were asked who we were and what on earth we were doing.

Checking in was easy, officials in town stamped our passports and weren't interested in seeing the boat or performing any further checks. Wandering through the port like lost souls did us a favour, as the guards would stop a worker in his or her car and demand they take us into town. We found this highly embarrassing, although useful – it was a long trek. The people in the car, it seemed, were told not to take money. Indeed, none of them would take our offers. They were unhappy to be inconvenienced, but did as they were told by the guards and took us into town. The return journey was easier, as the taxis were allowed in to take us right back to the boat.

The next port south was Agadir, and it was incredibly touristy. We preferred exploring the locals' domain and made our way to the markets. The Souk was a heaving sea of bodies flowing amidst the alluring and dangerous shores of the stallholders. Never had we seen such a collective frenzy. We bargained for camel skin gifts; it was a hard business. Vendors thrust leather goods, carved wood, exotic spices, and mysterious vegetables in our faces, while the throng drove us on. Our senses were relentlessly yanked and stirred. It was an experience all at once bewildering, intimidating, and exhilarating.

Sucked dry of dirhams and battle weary, we plucked the traders off our sleeves and retreated. Hailing a cab, we cried, 'McDonalds.' Calming down, instead we made for the Kasbah (old fort). It was sparse, but the view was breathtaking. It gave us time and space to recover and enjoy the twinkling sequins of the city lights.

Completing the trip, our friendly cab driver tried to fiddle the fare. We'd learned long ago to negotiate and agree to the fare prior to stepping in a taxi. It was with enormous relief we arrived back at *Mariah*, our home and sanctuary. However, she now smelt of pungent baked camel skin. Apparently the smell grows on you, but then so do spots.

Eventually, we arrived in Puerto Naos in the Canary Islands. Safe harbours, good anchorages, and easy access to shore were our priorities. We had been lonely, because we'd been off the usual sailing routes. The cruisers we did meet were all going into the Mediterranean.

Friends were made quickly and lost even quicker. But once we arrived in the Canary Islands, we were back with the bulk of world's wanderers. One of the first friends we made was a Dutch couple, Dennis and Natasha, on the yacht *Frodo*. It was now February 2004.

The Dutch are incredibly resourceful, and Den and 'Tash were true professionals of their race. But, it took us a little while to figure out where they were from. As we anchored next to them, Den was on deck and gave us a friendly wave. We had just been sailing, which meant we craved beer, wine, food and rest.

'Fancy a beer later?' Noel shouted over to Den. He gave a big thumbs up sign and an even bigger grin.

That's the great thing about sailing: imagine pulling into a supermarket car park and calling over to a stranger, who is sitting in their car, and inviting them over for a drink; you'd be locked up, viewed as a lunatic. On a boat, however, this was considered perfectly normal.

Not long after, Den and 'Tash came puttering over. 'Welcome aboard,' we said in unison, 'come on down and have a beer. They're not cold though. We don't have a fridge.' Den just grinned a massive toothy grin and 'Tash politely said thanks, she'd have a drop of wine.

As I organised some biccies and dip in our galley, I looked at them both. With her blonde hair and fair skin, 'Tash was obviously Dutch. However, Den had blond streaks, a deep tan, and an Australian accent.

'So', I said pointing at Tash, 'You are obviously Dutch' (the Dutch flag flapping on *Frodo* helped), 'but where are you from? You sound Aussie,' I said to Den's enormous grin.

They explained that they had done much land travel, and most of the time they spent working, living, and exploring Australia. This was where they had learned English, hence the accent.

Quickly, we fell into a deep and rewarding friendship, and they would become an integral part of our lives for many years.

I had always wanted to be taught how to make bread. 'It's easy,' said 'Tash one day, shrugging her shoulders (it turned out that to 'Tash *everything* was easy!). 'I'll show you,' she said.

The following day, they puttered over, 'Tash armed with bread making gear, Den armed with a spear gun. It's here Noel is going to tell you of his adventures that day:

Dennis is a professional fisherman and is generally good at all things aquatic and can swim like a dolphin. All of which makes him somewhat of a burden, when we are not sitting in the cockpit having a beer and being sensible.

'I've got an idea,' he said, one morning. 'Let's go spear fishing; there's a spot just over there that 'Tash and I found, 's not bad, what ya reckon?'

What I reckoned was that a coffee and maybe a calm observance of the not yet completed sunrise would be a lot healthier. But you know how it is, one doesn't want to appear too lazy and actually the sun had been up for hours. I was on my second coffee and a simple splash round the rocks seemed fairly reasonable. After all, I used to be quite good at it only thirty years ago. Heavens, where was that Scotch?

"The Spot," turned out to be a mile down wind of our anchorage. As we were in our dingy without the motor for the return journey, I was already beginning to have my doubts.

'Ah well, yes, okay we'll go on, just round the corner you say?' Mutter, mutter, stroke, stroke, waves are getting bigger. Where is it again? How 'bout you bail, and I'll keep rowing. Better still, you row, I'll bail... What's that?, we're here,' pant, pant, 'jolly good, piece of cake. I'll walk home.'

We dragged the dinghy up the beach. I proceeded to sort my stuff out. Find flippers, snorkel, fit prescription sunglasses into goggles (so that I can at least see something), try to walk down beach with flippers and goggles on. Ignore laughing local brat's gestures in my direction. I reckoned I would show this Dutch bastard. How do you hold this spear under water again? I think it's better if I walk backwards.

What's this then? Dennis was coming back? He already had a fish! I was still practicing my snorkel breathing!

Half an hour later, I'd speared a three-inch whale, while Den had added another three fish to the larder. He swam over.

'Listen, there's an octopus over here under a rock, if I go down and lift the rock, you can spear the critter.' He then dove down fifteen feet and started heaving on this rock. I went down and started prodding. Ink came out from Octopus's hidey hole. I swim back to the surface to breathe. Aqualung man was still heaving on rock. I took a quick, frantic grasp and then dove back down to return to the fray.

Where's Den? He must have gone to the top for air, arhh well I'll do the deed. Jab, jab, I couldn't see the critter for all this ink, but I was prepared to put on a good show. Jab, jab, shit I need air, shall return after a few hours on oxygen. 'Never give up,' is the Parry motto.

At the surface, I was met by the horse dentures of the grinning Dutchman.

'Pass me some amphetamines and I'll get the bludger. I've got him on the ropes. I reckon one more heroic dive and we'll be eating like lords tonight.' I shouted between gasps.

'Before you do that,' said Den, can you get this off me? This thing's giving me some gyp.' The bastard lifted his hand to reveal the octopus wrapped round his arm with his tooth-like beak snapping at his arteries.

I was stunned. Apparently, while I was on my first search for air, the quarry had bolted twenty metres to another rock with Den in hot pursuit. With no spear, he only had his hands to grab the beast, and then he returned to the surface to have a laugh watching me doing the jab, jab bit. You just can't trust some people.

We travelled through the islands of the Canaries and headed for the Cape Verdes. We started to get in the swing of on board life, which was a good job as the Atlantic Ocean was looming. I looked forward to a few weeks at sea, away from dreary constraints of land life.

All was well until dusk, when we were three hundred nautical miles from the Verdes. *THUD.* 'What on earth was that?' In the middle of the Atlantic Ocean *Mariah* stopped dead in the water. A tingle of fear crept up our spines, the ocean around us bubbled crimson. Noel and I stared in disbelief. As the wind re-filled our sails, we slowly glided forward and watched as an enormous great whale turned to face us at our stern, his tail high in the air, flapping, agitated.

'We've hit a whale, and it's coming back for us!' I cried. We'd heard a couple of horror stories of whales hitting back. Frantically, we checked the bilges, started the engine, and hit full throttle. It was the first time I had looked at our grab bag thoughtfully. Relief flooded the adrenaline as the whale vanished.

We believe the impact mortally wounded the beautiful creature. We were shocked and saddened. We pulled in our trolling line and vowed to never fish ever again.

Luckily, *Mariah* was strong; there was no physical damage. Too easily this could have been fatal for *Mariah*. Every tap for the rest of the journey had us jumping out of our seats. We were glad to reach the Cape Verdes and finish that leg and put the incident behind us.

The Cape Verde Islands lie just over eight hundred nautical miles southwest of the Canary Islands, where by far the largest income was foreign aid. They didn't have much there, except, maybe cholera.

We, in convoy with *Frodo* decided to take enough food and water for a brief stop, and then gather ourselves together to traverse our biggest ocean yet: the Atlantic.

The Verdes was barren, poor, and quite bleak; however, lively, happy children brightened the landscape. Rowing ashore, we were bombarded with kids of various ages and sizes, asking us to be the one to keep a watch over our dinghy. For this they wanted twenty cents per day. We agreed to pay fifty cents. A tall, lanky lad got the responsibility of our dinghy, but he insisted on showing us where to purchase diesel in town. His Portuguese was too hard for us to understand, so he came with us, even though we were paying him to look after the dinghy! He helped us carry the diesel; of course this cost more, only cents, but it was all a bit strange.

Supplies were few and far between. Pens were like gold for the kids. I was almost trampled by the girls who saw I carried pens and pencils for gifts. One of the first little girls I gave one to took the pen as if it was made of silk, placed it in her palm, and literally gasped. My heart went out to them, and I planned to get back to *Mariah* and take every pen I could find to give them to all the girls on the island. However, I looked across to Noel and feared for his life. About fifty lads pawed at him, shouted, begged, and tugged at his clothes. He had loose change to hand out and the beach became a riot. He tried to be fair, but of course, as the larger change went he was left with small denominations. One boy came up to me with a look of despair; he showed me the twenty cents he had been given and I looked back at him, wondering what he meant. He violently threw the money on the floor in disgust. His actions infuriated me and I said, 'Well, if you don't want it, I'll have it back,' and I made to reach for it. He quickly snatched it back. What were we to do? We couldn't give them everything we had. The girls around me had been so different: gentle, giggly girls, patiently waiting to see if they would receive a gift. The boys had been violent, tough, and a bit scary. I didn't go back to shore with more pens.

We anchored at our last island, Sao Vicente and the capital town of Mindelo. It was here that we checked out. The other islands were so small and non bureaucratic, we could cruise between islands and not worry about officialdom. The HF radio was brilliant, because boats in front of us would give us the information we needed, where we could anchor, the laws of the land, and where to buy good supplies.

This island was a little more tourist-y, but for the more adventurous travellers. We met crew that had been dumped off by one boat and were stuck on this island. The story was odd, and we decided we were happy with just the two of us on board; we didn't need to take a stranger who had been dumped by a captain.

'Tash and I went ashore together to do the shopping. We left Noel and Den doing the last minute mechanical touch-ups before crossing two thousand miles of Atlantic Ocean.

As we had entered the last of the Verde Islands, our steering gear had stopped working. We had hand steered the last five miles into the anchorage. When we left the Cape Verdes, we were due to be in heavy winds for three weeks. The timing was incredible: if the steering gear had broken just ten miles later, we would have had to sail for three weeks, across the Atlantic, hand steering. It would have been too hard to turn around against the wind and waves. Imagine driving your car, at a slower speed perhaps, but for two weeks without stopping once, and just doing this with two people. To make a cup of tea or to have a pee, and just a walk around was necessary to enjoy and survive the trip. At sea the failure would be near impossible to fix and only then on a calm day. We thanked our lucky stars.

Tracking our supplies down was an interesting challenge. I chose the best fresh foods I could, the price for them was shown to me on a calculator (my Portuguese left a lot to be desired). I knew the prices were inflated; they always were for foreigners. They thought I was rich – if only they knew! Perhaps in comparison to them I was, however, my lifestyle was simple and cheap. We had no incoming bills. We bought gas and diesel when needed and purchased local foods. Noel and I worked when we could and lived with few luxuries – our lifestyle was the luxury.

Purchasing food in a local, foreign market was a bit like a badly scripted play. I played my normal role, but while viewing the price of my goods, I feigned shock, despair, with lots of shaking of the head. If this didn't reduce the price, I handed back the shopping – this time I had to hand it back, pick out each item and ask its worth individually.

I was shown an inordinate price for some bananas, I put them back, and then the price came down. This occurred for every single item I had picked up. It was tedious, but I had become used to the charade. The final price was almost half the original, and I knew they had still over charged me.

I put away the groceries with a bionic effort to stow everything on board. I had to ensure that it would all stay put in the roughest of conditions. The murky depths hid the water line on

Mariah, and I thought it would be a miracle if we made a decent speed.

The day of departure loomed, and I was anxious and fighting thoughts of, *Why am I doing this?* Later, after days of delay due to weather, I wanted to go. I was full of excitement for the challenge – which lied in endless views of sky and sea, and in bottomless depths that were unexplored by man – the great Atlantic Ocean.

For four years, I had lived on a wooden boat with my husband. *Mariah* was my home, and I loved her as if she were a living being. She moved as if she was alive, and after all this time on board, I could understand the old sea shanties of viewing material vessels as living things.

Thinking about the miles before us, I started to question our medical supplies – our first aid on board was more than lax. When I did my senior first aid certificate, my instructor made a joke that the bandages I kept after the course would probably double as our first aid kit. He was a little too near the truth. We didn't tell too many people we were going around the world with a few band-aids and aspirin! We'd coped thus far, so I just chucked in some extra strong painkillers and resolved not to worry any more about it.

Dried food would be our staple diet again: pasta, lentils, pasta, rice, pasta, chickpeas, pasta... so powders and sauces that could alter these bland foods were stock-piled. Fresh foods, tried and tested for their longevity, were hunted down. Finding dense, heavy cabbages was a great coup. I stocked up on flour, eggs, and yeast for cooking bread and muffins once the packaged supply was gone. Tinned food by the tonne was pushed, shoved, and cajoled into any space available.

Toilet rolls were purchased by the dozen, along with gallons of shampoo; the water and diesel tanks were swollen, jerry cans and containers with extra supplies were lashed to the deck. With gas bottles full and last minute checks completed, we were ready to leave.

The three of us had traversed waters from Sydney through to the Mediterranean, then England and on to Spain, Portugal, and Africa, but it felt as though the Atlantic was the big one. Reports from friends, who had already traversed this great ocean, were comforting.

'You won't notice the huge swells; you'll just lumber up and down with them,' said one.

'You'll jibe maybe once or twice. You'll be on the same tack for so long, barnacles will grow up the side of the hull,' said another.

All lies of course.

Preparation for the trip was a major undertaking. You would have thought we were organising a cruise ship. Practice and advice over the years had prepared me for most of the organisation, but with somewhere between two and three weeks at sea in front of me, it needed a little more thought. If we had a problem along the way, we could be out at sea for much longer.

Once we left port, it took three days for my tummy to stop somersaulting. Sea-sickness was held at bay by little round, magic pills, but the discomfort was still there. After four days, pill popping became less frequent, and Noel and I started to settle into our routine. It was like a tag-team match: four hours on, four hours off, twenty-four hours a day. Enormous ships glided silently across our path; through experience and hearing hideous stories, I knew that they did not always keep a good watch, they would never know if they hit us; Noel and I were vigilant in our watches.

The immense lumbering Atlantic swell our friends and all the books promised decided to split itself in two and slap *Mariah* on each side with relentless efficiency. I felt like I was in a washing machine, tumbling side to side, around and around. The minutes seemed like days, the days felt like weeks – more so at 2 am, during the graveyard watch.

One of us was either on watch or trying to sleep. After the years together, I could rest at ease in my bunk; Noel was as avid as I at maintaining watch.

The single bunks we used at sea could still feel too big when *Mariah* rolled from side to side. We would clip up a lee cloth, making the bunk like a cot, and then stuff many cushions and pillows down each side to keep our body still. Eventually, we became accustomed to our outer body remaining still, while our insides rolled around to rhythm of the swells.

At 11:30 pm one night, despite my whinging about the unruly swells, the night was peaceful, almost calm. Although the new moon had slipped below the horizon early, the clear sky allowed the stars to show off their mysterious lights, which kept the feeling of plunging into utter blackness at bay, at least for tonight.

I was sitting in the cockpit throughout my watch, listening to the reassuring trickle of water along our wake. I was enjoying the night, minding my own business. It was clear, cool, and I was content. The self-steering gear was working a treat, and I relaxed. Suddenly, without warning, a blinding spotlight from above lit me up as if I was on stage; in a split second, I dived towards our tiller ready to manoeuvre. I peered out, half expecting to see an alien spaceship.

'It can't be a ship,' my mind raced. I was over vigilant on my watches, and I always spotted ships from the horizon. As I scanned the surroundings with wide eyes and heart thumping, a huge ball of flames shot through the blackened sky, a glistening super nova trail in its wake. Distance helps you lose the perceived size of meteorites, to me they were usually star sized; however, this racing orb appeared to be the size of a small car. After many seconds that felt like years, it faded, and I assumed entry into earth's atmosphere blew it to pieces.

About an hour later, my heart regained its usual rhythm and I started to calm down. Throughout the rest of my watch every noise or change in movement had me achieving a personal best in the vertical jump and gasp event.

As quite often happened, Noel woke up before I called him.

'Everything okay?' he asked. It never ceased to amaze me that he was so cheerful upon awaking; it took me several hours to reach that point. With some adrenaline still skipping along in my veins, I recounted the story of the 'enormous light.' I was quite disappointed to not receive congratulations on being so brave (even though I wasn't!).

The following morning, on the radio Sched, an American boat piped up, 'Did anyone see that meteorite last night? It was incredible, just huge!' Noel and I were both up and listening in. My smug grin was not lost on Noel.

'I didn't realise it was true,' he said, 'I thought you were exaggerating!'

Two days later, I was back to my old self, enjoying the solitude of the watches, the times when I could think unhindered by land life racing around me.

Mid-Atlantic, the journey became hard; I just wanted to get off. I wanted to stand on something that didn't move all the time! My little heart was tired of the adrenaline shots that grabbed its beating momentum and shoved it up and down at alarming speed.

We did sail changes two, three, sometimes four times a day and night. We'd both be on deck within the cocoon of our deck lights, plunging into the black void; the sail adjustments meant handling heavy poles to fix the fore sail out, so it didn't flap while the wind pushed us along from behind. When going down-wind, the boat rolled; we kept the wind on *Mariah's* quarter, about twenty degrees from directly behind; this eased the rolling to a bearable motion. Umpteen ropes, clips, and cleats were utilised to keep the large, heavy spinnaker pole in place. It took two hands to lift the poles, while the knees were bent, trying to predict the boat's next lurching movement. It was always more daunting under the cloak of night.

One thousand, five hundred nautical miles slowly passed, and then it was Noel's birthday. Four days later and we were celebrating Christmas Day; the day after it was my birthday.

During the night, on Christmas Eve, Noel was sleeping so soundly I decorated the boat around him (between keeping an eye out for traffic). With the bright decorations and fun presents from my mum that we'd carried on board from England, our spirits were lifted. The hilarious talking toilet roll holder and the singing bottle opener diverted our attention away from the lonely days.

Mid-ocean, we heard a radio report of an abandoned yacht, sadly adrift, forever a mystery. Day-in and day-out, we experienced dull sunsets, blotchy clouds, livid squalls, and vivid bruises. For seventeen long nights, we plunged into darkness, watched shooting stars, and welcomed each dawn.

Squalls came and went and became routine, not drama. The deep grey, angry sky gave plenty of warning to close the hatches, reduce sail, and don wet weather gear. *Mariah* enjoyed these fun times, as the wind gathered momentum and the waves held hands, *Mariah* pitched up high, hovered gleefully as if holding the fun moment for as long as she could, then launched herself down the waves with all the excitement of a child on a roller coaster. We hung on and grimaced when we looked behind to see the wall of water catching us. The squalls passed quickly and all became calm. The crew was relieved, and settled back to routine.

The best time was dawn. The long, black night had slowly receded and the first glimpse of light silently stroked the sky. We had a long, bright day ahead. Although the ships were easier to spot at night, the days were less sinister and it was a time to relax, read novels, and to try to forget about the possibility of containers lurking beneath the surface.

At last, after seventeen long days and nights, the night-lights of Barbados came into sight. As I stared up into the inky infinity I watched a star slowly move towards the west.

'West! What the...' I watched and tried to calm down. It was 3 am, and I was quite good at imaging horrors at this time. I took a breath and tried to think logically through the haze of weariness. It occurred to me that the star was moving awfully fast. It finally dawned on me that it was a plane, the angle of its light causing a slow trajectory and my imagined horror that the world was upside down and inside out. A little chuckle escaped my lips – sailing makes you laugh at yourself... or go mad. I chose the first.

The sweet smell of land tickled my nose: the grass, the trees, the rubbish, and the people. We made landfall the following morning, with calloused hands, fatigue, and elation. Barbados would witness our celebration of a successful landfall and crossing the Atlantic, but first sleep beckoned.

We rested well, which was good as we'd have to face the results of two smashed boats in the coming days: one ours and one a friends'.

18

Working in a brothel

Checking in to Barbados followed the usual script: find the required papers, locate the bank, track down the right officials, fill in inordinate quantities of paperwork, and hand over cash to everyone you met.

The first anchorage welcomed in the Atlantic swell that had over 2,000 miles to build itself into a solid, continually rolling wall. Having just spent two weeks sitting in these swells, we didn't need to experience it any longer so we decided to move the following day.

We had arrived a day before *Frodo*; the ever frugal Dutch had not used their engine once – indeed since Holland they had used an incredible ten litres of fuel in total! They claimed they could live on $1 a day! We admired them, but could not do it ourselves. Our life was about safety, then comfort, and then speed. If, occasionally, it meant using the engine to incur one less day at sea or spending a bit over our budget to have a fun night out, then so be it. We were living for today and although to most standard landlubbers we were frugal, compared with *Frodo* we were big spenders!

Frodo arrived with a big fanfare, provided by us. The skies were translucent, the rolling had calmed a little, and the water was crystal clear; it was perfect. They anchored smartly, and we promptly joined them on board for a party, celebrating the successful crossing. The Santa and fairy outfits (another inspired gift from my mum), were donned, which provided plenty of laughs. The pictures of me wearing fairy wings and Noel's white beard appeared all over Holland, within a magazine following *Frodo's* journey. Needless to say, we all became quite merry, and late into the night we poured our satisfied selves back into our dinghy and collapsed into bed.

At 3 am, the wind changed direction, and all the boats on anchor swung around; the wind was now coming across the vast ocean and pushing all the boats towards the shore, their anchors straining to hold them still in the pounding swell. The swell built higher and higher, and as *Mariah's* motion changed Noel and I leapt up. Accompanied by the seedy feeling of excess wine and heavy eyes, our bodies were so in-tune with *Mariah* that we instantly knew there was a problem.

Other cruisers began awaking and started up a loud racket. We watched as an American boat glided past us and up onto the rocks. We had joined in with the cacophony trying to arouse the drifting boat's owners, but they couldn't hear us from below their insulated decks. We all watched in horror, and as they went past us, Noel said, 'I'll switch on our engine, just in case.' As he did so our anchor let go, and we started to drag towards the land, too.

Other boats were in our destructive path, and Noel grappled against the large seas and howling wind to keep *Mariah* from clashing with other bucking vessels. Noel was doing a great job on the helm, so I jumped on deck to haul in the anchor. Kneeling down on one knee, with one hand grasping the stanchions, I pressed the anchor winch button with my heel and tried to feed in the chain. It felt like sitting atop a bucking bronco. I was terrified. It was pitch black; we smashed up and down in the waves, each one coating me in fine salt and skin tingling icy water. I could barely hold on.

Gritting my teeth, I knew Noel was working hard with *Mariah's* engine and the tiller to help me haul in the chain. As *Mariah's* bow lifted, the chain became bar taut. As she theatrically plunged into the dip, the chain slackened and I hauled in as much chain as possible – breaking equipment now was not an option.

The electronic winch was powerful, and I had remembered Noel's lesson of, 'We can fix the boat, but we can't fix missing fingers,' so, I kept my hands well clear of the moving parts. Gradually, painfully, the anchor came up. Noel had kept us in one spot so we didn't latch on and haul up someone else's anchor chain with ours. I had achieved my goal and was still in one piece, as was our equipment. We both concentrated on our own jobs while working together. Talking was pointless, as we were at either end of the boat, with the wind whipping any sound cleanly away. Once the anchor was clear, Noel turned *Mariah's* bow into the mountainous swell and pushed the throttle down, asking the Yanmar to get us out of here. By now it was about 4 am, and as we bounced into deeper water, the waves reduced in rowdiness.

All of a sudden, we were in a different world: the black sea mellowed, the moon shone to light a pathway, and the stars glowed serenely. Behind us, the shallow bay was a nightmare. A tangled boat sat on a reef, and the pumping seas continued to pummel the boats on anchor.

Away from the shallow water that heightened the swell and the wind that bounced around the shore, the waves were moderate, and as dawn approached all was back to normal on *Mariah*. We headed an hour south towards Barbados' capital and an alternative anchorage.

Bridgetown anchorage was much better protected, but we had to anchor a fair way out to gain the depth we needed. However, the violent, swearing, ugly music that boomed out across the anchorage at full, distorted volume, made our boat vibrate each night. It was hideous. For a few days we alternated between different anchorages: when we were fed up with rolling we headed south, when we were fed up with the music we headed north.

Soon the resourceful 'Tash had sourced the cheapie shops and we obtained supplies, did some sight-seeing, and paid attention to our need to move. We decided to stay for New Year's Eve and were safely anchored in soft, pulsating swells from the ocean, ready to welcome in a new year and new adventures. Little did we know that in just a few days' time, Noel would be working in a brothel. This is where Noel joins us again to tell us the story.

We've made it across the Atlantic to Barbados, arriving just in time to celebrate New Year's Eve. Two weeks later, Den and I were still hard at it, every day, in a Bridgetown brothel. There wasn't much privacy either, as we worked at the rear of the establishment, in an open shed, exposed to the derisive laughter and unasked for advice from the local Cajuns.

'Hey mon! Wat cha doo-in?'

'Well g'day. We're makin' a little dinghy.'

'Oh, you makin' a little boat for the big boat, dat's good. Hey, mon, you gonna fiba glas dat ding?'

This was the basic conversation, repeated on the hour with each new smiling face.

As our cupboard-bred collection of materials begrudgingly transformed into an object of nautical symmetry, the laughter increased. What I looked upon as fine lines, the locals viewed as a receptacle for ice and cold beer. If only we would '... fiba glas dat ding, mon.'

The head honcho of the establishment was accommodating and made us feel welcome. He seemed to run the joint at the command of the boss lady. Mr. Honcho stood at 190 cm (6 foot 3" in the old money), had a solid build and had a flashy smile that should have been fronting a toothpaste advert. Dripping gold from his wrists, neck, ears, and even his mouth, I swear he was a walking dubloon. The glow from his jewellery made me squint, and when he started laughing, I slipped on the sunnies. The red bandana on his cannonball shaped head, the vivid shirt, and the baggy trousers, neatly rounded off the whole Pirates of Penzance performance.

As he swaggered over, as if in a joint conspiracy, he whispered, 'You don wanna laugh with dem Cajun's, mon. All dey wanna do is steal yo' tools, rape yaw wife, and den kill you!'

As he was Cajun himself, I returned to work, wondering whether to laugh or take note.

'We're 'aving a party this Sat'day,' our host continued, 'celebrating a return to work for dis joint, we've been closed a year since dat murder dat night. You guys be finished by den, wontcha?'

At this point, I decided to take note.

'No worries,' I replied, gazing at our two made up frames and sheets of furniture grade ply. 'We'll be out of 'ere Friday arvo.'

Deciding to build a replacement for our smashed dinghy named Penguin Jack (PJ), sourcing materials and finding a building site took about a week. A week of bus rides complete with Bob Marley blasting through the speakers, pounding our ears. The driver danced in his seat, chatting with his mates while scattering pedestrians, all with his right foot firmly on the peddle. It took a week of relying on our good friends, Den and 'Tash, to be our taxi to and from shore several times a day. It was 'Tash who bravely asked the woman behind the three metre corrugated iron fence and barbed wire whether we could use the shed out back. Mrs. Barkly was most accommodating, letting us leave our tools locked in her hallway. Mrs. Barkly, as we soon found out, was the madam.

For three days, we cut out frames, trying to bend Honduras Pine stringers into something resembling a boat frame. Honduras Pine looked like Radiata Pine without the knots; it had greater density, and therefore more weight. Its oily feel, I thought, indicated longevity and resistance to rot. What I failed to notice, until much later, was its natural abhorrence to being bent.

On entering the yard one morning, I found one of the girls, all fifteen stone of her, sitting stark naked on a stool, all limbs akimbo as she was hosed down by another woman, similarly clad. Not knowing where to look, I thought I would stare at one of the stencilled signs indicating that no credit was given and that guns were forbidden. That's nice, I thought.

It was now Tuesday. Crossing the Atlantic only two weeks ago, I had images of coral sands, palm trees, scantily clad women, and Pina Coladas. The images proved correct, except that instead of a deckchair and a cool drink, I had a workbench and a screwdriver. Cruising reality was a hot tin roof and sawdust. Enjoying a new country this time, meant traipsing miles carrying or looking for supplies. It also meant that a shimmering crime-lord was custodian to all my worldly tools of trade. What went wrong?

We almost stayed on board that night, as the swell was swallowing the concrete jetty each time that we tried to land. We were about to return for a rave up on Mariah II, i.e. a tinned meal and our favourite book, when our American friends, Roy and Chris from Solmates, suggested that we tie up to their dinghy.

'It's anchored off as well as tied, so it'll be fine,' they called. Their four metre, hard bottomed rigid inflatable boat appeared to be sitting as comfortably as Mariah out on anchor, so what could go wrong?

'Successful cruising is a matter of continual awareness.' This adage was not followed. Sitting at a beach bar, boasting about crossing oceans to the only people who care to listen, other cruisers, was not awareness. With my back firmly placed to the worrying scene of two dinghies porpoising in their attempts to ride the increasing swell, I figured the Ostrich Theory would work. Could we not relax now, tonight of all nights? After all, we had just crossed the Atlantic. We deserved a break, didn't we? The result answered that question.

The concrete wharf ripped the large, sturdy RIB to shreds as if it was paper thin; its 15 horse-power outboard dragged what remained of the planing hull into the depths of swelling sands and coral sea. Our beloved servant from Aussie, PJ, was shattered; the remnants floated off in the moonlight.

We stood on the jetty and with moist eyes wished each other an ironic 'Happy New Year.' We piled into our Dutch friends' dinghy, headed for Solmates, and dutifully awaited midnight. We soberly repeated our 'Happy New Years' and 'Goodnights.' Then I remembered that PJ was gone. This began the first of many pleas of, 'Give us a lift, mate?'

Two weeks later, on the promised Friday arvo, we launched PJ II as the sun set. It had been a frantic, albeit interesting time. PJ II had been prime coated, but was barely dry. The next morning, our home, Mariah II, turned into a work-shop. So we could finish the dinghy.

PJ II, built in Barbados, in a brothel, by an Aussie and a Dutchman, was unique. As we puttered along, people pointed, stared, and the odd snort of laughter could be heard. We heard children say 'I want one!' I think it was the green fenders that were cunningly made from swimming floats that turned their eye.

But, we had the last laugh. No one would steal PJ, he looked too 'unique'. Each year many shiny, new dinghies were stolen in the Caribbean, which caused heartache and drama that we knew too well. With the glue holding and the timber staying in one piece, PJ almost made it home to Australia.

A new hard dinghy would have cost us at least one thousand Australian dollars, a new inflatable dinghy around two thousand Australian dollars, Penguin Jack II cost us two hundred dollars and a bouquet of flowers for Madam Barkly.

Frodo and *Mariah*, were together day in day out. Never had we made such good friends; they were easy to be with and had no expectations. 'Tash's parents were visiting to spend some time with them on one of the Dutch islands, whereas we were heading north to Puerto Rico. A sad goodbye loomed before us.

Roy and Chris, had become our good friends, too. They had helped us in Egypt by supplying and delivering flour; we had enjoyed many a social night on board their huge floating home.

They owned two apartments in Puerto Rico, which needed some renovations. When they heard that Noel and I had renovated houses previously, we came to an agreement to renovate their apartments.

Noel and I had to make a decision with the hurricane season looming. Were we going to go south to Trinidad or north to America? We had heard whispers about the inland waterways in America; we had both visited America some years back and wanted to see more. The work offer in Puerto Rico fitted in nicely with our plans, so north it was.

To fulfil these needs and wants meant a tough farewell with *Frodo*. Den and 'Tash came on board *Mariah* for the last time, and we anchored between the two main anchorages in Barbados to dive with the tourists. At midday each day, a tourist boat headed to a certain area and fed the giant turtles. We anchored nearby and joined in the excursion. Snorkelling amongst these graceful creatures in their silent world was spectacular. Den and the largest turtle had a face-off: the turtle sat inches from Den's masked face and they stared into each other's eyes. I nearly drowned from laughing. The turtle retreated, and then Den realised he had some turtle food on his shoulder (some weed). After swimming with these gentle giants, we headed to the rolly anchorage, where the wind had subdued and the roll had settled down, creating just a gentle rock.

Den and 'Tash were staying on *Mariah* for the night and were going to help us check out in the morning at the wharf, where they could jump off and walk back to *Frodo*. As the evening progressed, Noel and Den drank beer in the cockpit while 'Tash and I sat below chatting amicably, both trying to ignore the approaching farewell. 'Tash was a tough girl. She was strong, adaptable, and just got on with whatever needed doing. She'd straightened me out a few times. 'Come on, girly,' 'Tash would say, 'get on with it.' I knew I was going to miss her terribly.

My girlfriends in the UK were becoming just a memory. The four girls I was close to were all quite different, but all had been incredible friends to me, helping me in my most difficult times in my life before I had left for Australia. I sent emails, postcards, and letters, but I would only receive the odd email back. I was not there, so it was hard to be a part of their lives. At the time, I took this quite hard, but later I would understand. Life moves fast, it's hard keeping in touch with those around you, let alone those farther afield. In England, I had seen my friends briefly, but I was so different and the comfortable, relaxed friendship had altered – I was now from a different world. They spoke of the latest car, phone, and computer. The most important thing to me was favourable weather and a safe anchorage. I had to remember it was I that had changed, not them, and I had to accept the fact that if I was not physically there, then the friendships would alter.

Our final night with *Frodo* wore on, and the guys decided to go into town to get some more booze. 'Tash and I were just happy chatting. We actually went to bed before they left, and once they went out, we got up for another cuppa and a chat. We were so relaxed together, even the silent pauses in conversation were comfortable. The guys came back, singing and giggling; it was great that Den and Noel got on so well, too.

The following morning at dawn, I could hear someone clomping around on deck. I got up to find Den had had a swim and was sitting on the deck making noises in an attempt to wake everyone. He had only been to bed for a few hours and had had mountains of beer. This guy had the constitution of a bloody ox. In the cockpit sat the leftovers from the night before. The guys had run out of papers to roll up tobacco and had therefore tried to make a tobacco bong. Parts of the boat had been dismantled to make this thing! They were just like naughty children; they thought it was hysterical. 'Tash and I laughed and rolled our eyes.

Mid-morning, we puttered over to the dock to fill with water, diesel, and check out of Barbados. The process became frantic; other boats were there, we were tied alongside them, and soon after they wanted to leave. I took the paperwork into the office, while Noel filled the boat with diesel and water. Noel and I were both captains, so when it was easier (and acceptable) for me to check us in or out of a port, I did so.

I sat down with the customs official, and he read through the papers. He looked up at me and grinned and said in the most patronising voice, 'Arrrh, he's let you be captain today, has he?' I just glared at him. When I was faced with narrow-minded views, I didn't trust my mouth with my thoughts. I bit my lip.

Later I realised I should have said, 'No, when we checked in, I had let him be the captain.' A lot of people assumed the boat was Noel's, and that I had seen a good thing and married him. But the boat was *ours*, we had purchased *Mariah* together and both worked just as hard on her. Over time, I learned to deal with this temerity and realised that people with these types of opinions had the problem, not me.

Suddenly, we were ready to go and the boat that we were tied to was pressuring us to hurry. Den stepped off and waved farewell; he wasn't a tactile person. That was just the way that he was. I thought 'Tash would give me a quick hug and go, and I bit back my tears, as I thought she'd say 'Don't be soft, girlie.' We hugged hard, and as we let go I looked into her face and saw the tears streaming down her cheeks. I held her again and let my emotions flow; she jumped off and waved farewell with Den. The silence on board was tangible; what was there to say?

Barbados provided fond memories of swimming with giant turtles, graceful, fearless characters, which nipped unsuspecting toes, sunsets and balmy nights. It also provided not so fond memories of ear splitting music until four in the morning and evening strolls where shady characters offered *'dessert'* to smoke after our chips.

We had a calm two-day sail into St. Lucia and anchored at Rodney Bay. In the vivid green of St. Lucia, we felt sad. We had said a sad goodbye to our good friends. Itchy-feet syndrome meant constant goodbyes, as new friends followed different paths. Meanwhile, back home, nieces and nephews were growing up and my friends were moving on. Maybe there was a patch of land waiting for us, somewhere where we could be still. If only our damned feet would stop itching.

We puttered our way north stopping at Dominica.

Through time and nature doing its thing, a small island had joined to the landmass of Dominica. Shirley Fort was built in c1780 and occupied this "island". The fort itself had been occupied until 1815, and then abandoned in 1856. Between the years of 1982 and 1992, it was renovated. The fort was built by the English to hold territory between the French terrain of Martinique and Guadeloupe.

The rusty canons were littered around the maintained lawn; the big joke was that never a shot was fired in anger or war. Shirley Fort sat within gardens that resembled secret grounds: velvet lawns littered with artistic trees that were interwoven with vivid pink, red, green, and yellow leaves. The area was peaceful, calm. The silence pressed against our ears. We learned about cotton silk trees, which had half-inch, hardy thorns that covered the entire trunk like a carpet; surely a means for medieval torture. Teak trees were prevalent, with their straight trunks and big leaves. They were too young, though, and made us wonder if they would be allowed to mature before being slaughtered for humans to build their trinkets.

The thirty-minute walk to the east of the hill had us zigzagging up and up, watching lizards scarper, iguanas stare, and the shells of black crabs line the walk. We reached the peak, and the air was sucked in as we gasped in wonder. The Southern Bay, where we were anchored, opened up to allow us to view the speck of *Mariah*, the carpet of vibrant green, the blue sky, and a pretty rainbow framed the picture. Why wasn't this place overrun with tourists? It was perfect. There were no beaches to speak off and such a terrain that electricity and water wasn't commonplace. In twenty years' time, I thought, this island would look very different. This beauty could not be ignored. We were thankful we had found somewhere in the world that we had the opportunity to see before it was deluged with people and the twentieth century, and quite possibly, destruction.

After a few hours' walk, we deserved a cool beer. The Purple Turtle was the nearest place for a cheap beer, so it was here we sat and reflected on the wonders we had witnessed while getting eaten by mozzies and sand flies. The following day was carnival day, commencing at 4 am.

As the day gave way to evening, ashore the gentle groovy beat became a soothing backdrop. We watched the white anchor lights of the many yachts swing in the soft breeze; the black night, new moon, and stars were all conducive for sleep. We felt satisfied, content at peace. I wondered if we'd still feel the same at 4 am!

I had gone to bed early, and Noel was unusually awake around 11 pm, sitting in the cockpit. Suddenly, two dark guys sitting upon surfboards were hanging on to our boat.

'What are you doing?' Noel asked as he jumped out of his skin.

The two men pulled balaclavas over the heads and said, 'We're fishing.'

'Bugger off!' Noel shouted, 'I'm radioing the police.'

Fortunately, the guys paddled off. I don't like to think what would have happened if Noel wasn't in the cockpit to stop them from boarding us.

'We should give that information out on the Caribbean Net,' I said to Noel, a little shaken when he told me the story the next day. He made non-committal noises, and we both thought that maybe it was a bit melodramatic to tell everyone, as nothing had happened. How wrong we were.

Each morning the Caribbean Net boomed into every boat that had tuned in with their HF radio. It was filled with lots of interesting information, we'd try to listen in regularly. The next Sched would send shivers up every cruiser's spine.

'Good morning everyone, this is the safety and security Net on Tuesday, the 24th February, at 08:15. First off, does anyone have any emergency or priority calls?'
'This is yacht Blue Sky; we are in Marigot Bay, St. Lucia, do you copy?'
'Go ahead, Blue Sky.'
'Last night at 10:30 pm, we were boarded by two locals. They threatened us with knives and beat me up and stole various items. When they left, we desperately tried to call police on the radio, blow our horns, anything to attract attention. It was over thirty minutes before we were heard. We are okay, but this bay is packed with boats, so everyone should be on their guard.'
SILENCE
There were many of us living in the Caribbean for the season; we were all stunned and a little scared.

We were looking forward to reaching cooler climates. We began to slowly make our way up the chain of islands, and Puerto Rico was looming nearer. We were also looking forward to earning some American dollars.

As it was a French island, I loved Guadeloupe; however, the weather had been too hot and everything became too wet. To reach the butterfly shaped island, we did several dawn starts, which was just heavenly as it was the only time of the day we were cool. By the time it got to 8 am, the sun had so much strength that Noel and I almost came to blows over the tiny bit of shade in the cockpit.

We arrived at the butterfly's tail at a town called Point de Pitre. We chose this town as, apparently, we could sail between the middle of the islands – i.e. along the butterfly's body, the narrowest part. There was a bridge that needed to be opened, but we had to be ready at 5 am, otherwise the bridge's operator saw that there are no boats ready and tootled off home!

This suited us, as we enjoyed these mornings. Even though the bridge was closed for three days due to maintenance, the anchorage was protected and safe. Plus, the forecast foretold of a big wind coming through for a few days, so staying put was beneficial.

We tried to get some more jobs done. The water catcher, in the form of tarps tied across the boat, with pipes tied at the bottom of said tarps, had been quite a success – we managed to fill up with rain water in Dominica. Noel had a great idea for an improvement, using hooks instead of ropes. After about four hours of fiddling, grunting and cussing, the whole set up looked exactly the same! I was wishing it would rain; I had this perverse satisfaction in watching the water trickle into our tanks.

19

Sinking in Florida

'Stop chewing my ear!' I cried. 'Great, there goes the paint.' It was playtime for Mancha, the English Pointer and beloved pet of Roy and Chris.

In March 2004, we were sharing a condominium with Mancha. She wanted walks and attention, but we were there to do painting, fixing, and repairing.

We had arrived in Puerto Rico with the pressure of time against us. My parents were meeting us in Florida, but first we had a couple of months' work. Roy and Chris were anxious for us to arrive to get on with it. We chose our weather window carefully and blasted our way through to Puerto Rico. As always with sailing, or any kind of travelling, you just can't stop and see everywhere. This time we missed out on the Virgin Islands. Neither of us had been there before, and we felt sad that we had to sail past. As we were adjacent with the islands, a weather warning was issued: strong winds were heading our way. We could either stop and probably become stuck for a good few days, or continue on. After much uhhming and arrhing, we made the hard decision to continue. The pressure to reach Florida on time, coupled with much needed work, meant that the decision was already out of our hands.

Puerto Rico is the land of good coffee, colourful Spanish, a magnificent fort, endless road works, and police who wear bulletproof vests on traffic duty. Amongst the mayhem, we had our own turmoil. Our house back in the UK was empty; the tenant had left, which meant no rent, which meant no income. Whilst working, we had to think carefully about what to do, whether to fly to England to sort out the problem and do some work or even fast-track sail to Australia to earn dollars. We needed an income to live on. We discussed our problems, but with a salary coming in we had the luxury of waiting to see what happened.

We had decided to stay in a marina whilst working. We didn't need the worry of being away from *Mariah* all day, leaving her alone at anchor. We walked to and from work each day and arrived back at the boat each night exhausted. After two days, we met the owner of the boat tied next to us. Sporting bloodshot eyes, a stagger, and a glass of rum tightly grasped, our new neighbour in San Juan Bay Marina, Puerto Rico, greeted us.

'Great,' we mused, 'this is all we need after a hard day at work.'

There is nothing worse than dodging spittle while listening to the same slurred stories. Typically, our first impressions were as useful as a chocolate anchor. Bill was not a drunk. At seventy-five, his eyes had earned the right to do as they please. Throughout his life, he had traversed many oceans, losing two boats to a watery grave. His second lost boat, sunk by hundreds of attacking pilot whales, left Bill and his wife to survive in a small, rubber life raft for sixty-six days. Each day, sharks attacked, taking them within a hairs breadth of death. Amid the laughter, the tears flowed as I read their remarkable book, *66 Days Adrift*, detailing their plight.

Bill became our friend; he was full of useful information for two foreigners lost in a new city. We discussed our dilemmas with Bill, and he offered his thoughts.

'Go for it,' he said, 'live for the now.'

He was right; we realised that something would work out. Besides, the next adventure was nipping at our heels. We wanted to head for the Intracoastal Waterways on the east coast of America. Here, we hoped to see Washington and New York. Best of all, these waterways should be void of whales, and there was no night time travel – bliss!

San Juan Bay Marina, Puerto Rico was an interesting stop for a few months; not just because the rich, the poor, the colourful, and the dull mingled around this historical part of the world, but because of the constant reminders of momentous events in our past were present at every turn.

Noel will join us again here, to describe the sights and sounds:

Our history lesson started at 5 am. The drone of a twin-engine plane climbed to a crescendo of air grabbing propellers and oxygen sucking internal combustion engines. The re-enactment of the Berlin airlift had begun! Fifty metres above our sleep bemused brains, the first of the day's constant air traffic began to educate us. Thoughts of the German Blitzkrieg on Poland occurred in the evening, as the returning planes gave their version of dive-bombing stukas. We were told that they once were a little more realistic and used live bombs.

Next on our historical journey were the morning ablutions. Cold showers in the marina, provided the Elizabethan background. Black soot in a fine layer had been spread over all surfaces. Placing one's clothes on the peeling laminex of the basin shelf, as they had thoughtfully omitted the tedium of hooks, was always rewarded with an authentic smudge.

With the day's preparations completed, we returned to the boat, learning the method perfected by daring buccaneers in assailing a vessel via the moving target of the bowsprit. Mind you, we thwarted reality somewhat and only juggled our shower bag and towel. I was sure it would have been more fun with a cutlass. This all led to the desperate need for coffee, which was prepared under the continued presence of piston engines skimming the masthead. This, of course, plunged us into the heavy nostalgic trip of imagining the days of post-rationing with the marvellous return of caffeine and victory rolls by "one of our boys" returning over the white cliffs of Dover.

With these reminders of history to start the day, we were now ready to hit the town of San Juan. San Juan was approached from the Marina after crossing eight lanes of freeway interspersed with three Bailey bridges and the construction team building their replacements. This gave a glimpse of things to come, a time when there were no demeaning problems to consider, such as, the pedestrian. In San Juan, they had planned and will one day complete the ultimate monument to Henry Ford: The Perfect Highway. Finally, a place where the driver does not have to worry about the wandering lower class members of our race. The pedestrian will not exist if we simply follow the guideline, to wit, "Make No Provision For Them!" We were clearly aware of this directive, while walking and dodging cars, to and from work each day.

At last, the laborious task of working for someone else was finally over, and we got to do what we do best: making plans for our next trip. Doubling the profits of Puerto Rico's telephone companies, we placed numerous phone calls to England. They knew that we couldn't really answer their questions, but my parents still asked, 'When are you going to be in Florida?' and 'Where will you make landfall?'

But a date had to be picked. We made weather predictions and hoped equipment failures on the boat still alluded us. The date was like the Mecca, everything seemed to hang on it.

The day we left Puerto Rico, our American friends Bob and Carol on board *Star Cruiser* arrived into San Juan. Again, the decision to delay our departure another day was upon us. We decided to leave. We had to allow plenty of time to reach Florida, as Mum and Dad's return flights were committed. With heavy hearts, we said our farewells to Roy and Chris in person, and Carol and Bob over the radio.

Having spent what felt like a long time in San Juan, recouping the coffers, and with the looming hurricane season, more decisions had to be made. After meeting my parents, did we head south to Venezuela and pirates, or north to New York and muggers? It was possible to avoid both obstacles; however, our hearts held hope of exploring inland. Actually, it's remarkable that we were here at all. Pessimistic sailing friends thought the inland waterways of America boring (and oceans aren't?) and for retirees. We were a headstrong couple, and if it felt right, we did it. We tried to live by this philosophy in a world of people telling us what we must see and do.

The Atlantic Intracoastal Waterway (ICW) facilitates navigation along the eastern seaboard of the United States. It's made up of natural river channels, estuaries, bays protected by barrier islands and man-made canals. Not too many people know about the ICW. I think the US is trying to keep it a secret to avoid attracting too many frightful foreigners.

We had already organised our visas, as we had heard about the ICW from sailing friends in Portugal, and we knew that it may become part of our itinerary. America can and will turn away boaters who arrive without a *bona fide* visa.

We decided to make a beeline for Florida, trying to get further north than Miami to avoid the busier waterways, but it all depended how kind Mother Nature would be.

Dominican Republic had troubles, so we avoided its shores, but halfway along our time-fraught journey a strong wind warning was issued. We could take shelter in the Bahamas, but it cost hundreds of dollars to stop there, and we had no great urge to see the place. The brochures looked beautiful, but it was busy, full of boat-wrecking shoals and packed with tourists. Reluctantly, we had to find a place to shelter until the blow had passed. Around this part of the world, currents were strong, with opposing winds seas would kick up and create a tough and dangerous journey. Our schedule had just enough allowance for a few days to wait out unfavourable conditions.

We puttered in to Mayaguana, in the southern Bahamas. The town was not worthy of the title of "town". It had just one shop that opened when you could find the owner.

The shallow, heavily reefed water became our neighbourhood for three days as we sat on board and waited for the thirty-knot winds to abate. Boat bound and restless, we accepted an offer of a ride to shore. A couple on a motorboat anchored nearby ferried us in and I found a phone to call home.

'If we aren't at the airport to meet you,' I said quickly, for I did not know how long the connection would last, 'call Denise or Josie and give them the name and address of the hotel you end up in. At least then I can call them to track you down.' Mum and Dad just giggled; it would be an adventure for them too, the excitement heightened as they could arrive with no one to meet them and nowhere booked to stay.

With butterflies bouncing around in our stomachs in tune with the ocean waves, we grabbed hold of the Gulf Stream and flew up the east coast to West Palm Beach, Florida. As land rapidly approached, we proudly hauled the American flag. Our tired smiles hiding the questions that we both had lurking under the surface – was the one thousand mile trip out of our way going to be worth it? Had we done the right thing bringing a yacht to inland waters that was saturated by motorboats?

Two hours later, we learned our first lesson that things changed fast: from the mayhem of a busy inlet, brimming with weekend anglers breaking free from domesticity, to a secure, peaceful and well-sheltered anchorage, where we drank to our safe arrival.

We arrived the day before Mum and Dad flew in. We booked into a marina and promptly sunk the boat – well, almost.

The night before collecting the hire car to drive to the airport, we were sleeping well in the sanctuary of a marina, tied securely, within protected waters, what could go wrong?

At 2:30 am, a loud clunk woke me up. I peeled back my eyelids, lying still, listening. My heart was clattering, as I'd jumped when I heard the noise. Over the years, I had become accustomed to odd noises and squeaks the boat can make in different weathers, circumstances, and currents. This noise was alien. The full moon was piercing through the hatches, and I turned in my bed and watched the moonbeams hit the floor. The small mats on the floor levitated towards me. *That can't be right*, I thought. I decided to get up and promptly stepped into water that reached my ankle!

'We're sinking,' I stated, surprisingly calm. Noel didn't need much more encouragement to leap up. Immediately, we turned the bilge pumps on. The mats were saturated and thrown out onto the jetty. Our tinned food that was stored in the bilge floated around us. Cans of coke sprung open and shot their sticky contents all over the cushions. 'How lovely,' we both muttered, interspersed with more colourful language of the bluer kind.

Quickly, our pumps won the battle. After mopping for hours, the boat was almost dry. But we had to source the problem. We could find no leaks, no holes – what was going on? Whilst pondering the problem, we washed-up the tins and washed-down the carpets to remove all the salt. I was mindful of my parents' arrival, so we grabbed a couple of hours sleep. Later, after much detective work, we found a pump tap dripping: an easy fix, but a bad set up. The seacock on this tap had been inadvertently knocked open by me and slowly dribbled thereafter. The laundry bag sat near this seacock and when I had moved the bag, I think I had moved the seacock lever. We needed more security than that.

Arriving just in time at the airport, with bleary eyes, we met Mum and Dad at Orlando. It was great to see them again.

'We're going straight to the boat,' I told them. We had planned to stop in a hotel for the night after their long flight, providing a rest before a lengthy drive. But the near sinking of the boat had left us a bit jittery, and we didn't want to leave *Mariah* too long.

Mum and Dad slipped easily into boating life once again and were not too shocked when we over-filled our water tanks, because we were diverted by chatting to other cruisers, and nearly filled the boat with water – again!

We were now motor-sailing north, along the Intracoastal waterways, watching the cotton wool clouds scud below the azure sky. The east coast of Florida glided by, while we caught up on all the home news and hoped we'd stay afloat.

With the boat trying to sink since arriving in Florida, we had another leak near the propeller shaft. To fix the problem, we would have to haul the boat out of the water. For the time being, we tightened the bolts and crossed our fingers, which really wasn't akin to good seamanship. We monitored things closely and could not leave the boat for any significant time. In the meantime, we enjoyed being in protected waters and with family.

As expected, Florida was teeming with gleaming boats, and anchoring at weekends kept our sanity in check. Many boaters had no clue what the collision regulations were, let alone what action they must or must not take when two vessels met. It was interesting, at times, being the stand on vessel; (depending on the type of vessel and area, when two boats meet, one is the stand on vessel and one gives way). It was like playing chicken with half-a-million dollars of boat (their boat not ours!). Listening to channel sixteen on the VHF radio became daily entertainment with boaters bickering for all to hear.

The predominate southerlies and straight north channels granted us a good ride. The soft breeze stroked our sails and pushed us through Florida at five knots. Here, sailboats were in the minority, foreign sailboats were rare, and as for foreign sailboats that were actually sailing – it was almost unheard of.

Each day, landlubbers enjoying their water-front gardens waved and gave us a thumbs up. Most days, they watched their gardens slowly disappear, snatched by the relentless wake of ill designed motorboats. We trickled past, silently accompanied by the waterfall symphony of towing a dinghy. Conversely, busy towns lined the banks, so we were glad to leave the plastic cities of Florida with its sun-bleached inhabitants, where even the trashcans were new and move into smaller towns, with simpler folk, just like us.

The four weeks with Mum and Dad came and went far too quickly, and again we were on our own. But not for long, as *Frodo* had reached their own crossroads in their adventures. They wanted to explore America; they travelled a massive two-thousand miles for a spectacular *Mariah* and *Frodo* reunion along the ICW.

Carting a keel through shallow waters was not ideal, as shoaling was common even within the well-buoyed channels. However, wind assisted propulsion and a steady speed left most boats in our wake, as far as diesel consumption was concerned. But running aground was a problem. We had become proficient at hauling aloft all sail and hanging off the side to lift *Mariah's* keel. It could become scary when the tides were high and the swift current quickly lowered the water, but with soft bottom landings, the help of fellow sailors, and a dash of common sense, we rectified the situation in no time at all. Our most frightening grounding occurred near a starboard marker on a bank of mud, with the racing current lowering the depth rapidly. *Frodo* came to our rescue, pulling our main halyard from atop our mast via their sailboat, hauling *Mariah* over until we were almost horizontal. We were dismayed to see many rescue companies lurking in the tricky places, awaiting boats in distress and then charging a large percentage of the boat's worth to assist.

The waterway winds itself around the towns of Georgia. Tacking became constant, and our engine was called upon. Side channels snaked us away from the main channel each night, and we felt like the first to explore these untouched estuaries that teemed with life. Unfortunately, that life included tenacious flies with an insatiable hunger. Mercifully, at dusk they faded away, and we were left to enjoy the wondrous wildlife; dolphins spurted by grinning at us, manatees rose, blinked, and then were silently gone. Alongside uninhabited islands, alligators ruffled the silky surface and snatched at unwary birds. Never had we witnessed such bountiful life. My favourites were the gracious pelicans, swooping, diving, and swallowing their catch.

Amid the glorious, gentle days, the heat became relentless and the skies threatened storms. A half-hourly cool soaking from our shower combated the discomfort.

Hurricanes became a threat as the sea temperature crept up. We started to cram in more miles during the day to reach the safer latitudes. Each night we were thankful to find safe, secure anchorages where we could relax and regroup for the following day.

In the beginning, finding an anchor spot was easy. There were plenty of marinas, but we had no need to blow the budget. Occasionally, there was a free marina. They had no electricity or water, but we were grateful for letting our dinghy have a day off.

Throughout the murky waters of Georgia, we began to have great difficulties in deciding and agreeing on where to anchor. We had comprehensive charts, but off channel the depths were dubious. We had travelled far without a pilot book identifying anchorage sites. With frustration and fear co-mingling on my tongue, Noel and I had two huge arguments over where to anchor, so we decided it was prudent to buy a good pilot book. Skipper Bob's book, *Anchorages Along The ICW*, saved us a fortune in post argument drinks.

As we puttered along the litter free waterways towards Carolina, we enjoyed the company of 'Tash and Den on *Frodo*. It was fun to have good friends to share these adventures with. Den was an angler, and he seemed to find a small fishing harbour for anchoring nightly. This was not a bad idea. The locals loved for us to sample their fresh shrimp, as well as to help ourselves to ice and as much water as we needed. Lifts to the supermarket and marine shops for spare parts were part and parcel of their generous hospitality. Coupled with their fine southern drawl, this place captured our imagination and we expected to see *Deputy Dawg* swagger around the corner at any moment.

Den and 'Tash were great at keeping to budget and keeping us in line too. Visiting protected islands via "the back door" – where wild horses roamed amongst the armadillos – was their speciality. All perfectly legal, but you had to possess an extra dose of daring.

Without a jetty to tie the dinghy to, we sludged our way through eight inches of thick, black, squishy mud, trying hard not to squash the scattering black crabs. Buried up to our ankles with mud so thick you could sun-dry it for ballast bricks, we struggled and giggled as we tried to haul the dinghy to firmer ground. A fresh water hand-pump, thoughtfully installed amongst the gracious trees, gave us all utter relief after our five-hour hike through dense vegetation. Washing naked on an island, picking ticks off our soggy flesh, and sharing soap, was considered quite normal between the four of us. We stayed in company with *Frodo* for a few weeks. We girls relished the opportunity to natter, and the guys enjoying their blokes' chat. Putting the world to rights was almost a nightly meeting, with the iridescent dragonflies flitting around us in the fading light.

As close as we were, our boats moved at different speeds. Ironically, our boat speeds were similar; it was our *desired* speed that differed. Noel and I liked to keep moving, letting our thoughts flow through our minds as we watched the changing scenery. *Frodo* was content to sail at two knots and preferred to spend more time in each town. Our life was full of goodbyes and, once again, it was upon us.

I received a useful piece of advice some years ago, when I became over-whelmed with the constant departing of friends.

'Don't say good-bye,' a fellow sailor said. 'Don't actually say the words; we all know that it's good-bye, but by not saying it, it might make it a little easier.' It does.

Without *Frodo* watching our guilty key turning antics, we could go as fast as our engine pleased and quickly we munched through the miles. The channels were becoming deeper, so we could relax. We watched the houses challenge each other along the banks, the rolling hills, resplendent trees where deer frolicked, and the vivid arrangements of colours that I had thought were unique to England. The constant flow of welcoming people was tidal in every port.

Chatting to locals, we discovered a new opportunity, a new adventure. If we made good time, we could turn west at New York and go through the Great Lakes to Chicago, pick up the famous Mississippi and adjacent rivers, and reach the Gulf of Mexico. This route is called The Great Loop, or The Great Circle. The ICW is just one small part of this incredible journey. It is a continuous waterway circumnavigating the eastern portion of North America, covering over six thousand miles, over one hundred locks, and many low bridges.

Another stage of decision-making was upon us. Despite every person we met saying we had left it too late to complete the Great Circle, we decided to do it. The Great Lakes freeze in winter, so we needed to pass through these lakes and be in Chicago by September. We buried ourselves in books, doing in-depth research of miles, mast stepping requirements, and visa expirations. Considering Noel had a longing to get back to Australia in 2005, while not having to double back, this won the decision for us, for friends it just confirmed their doubts of our sanity.

At any given time, we could have leap-frogged up the coast and caught the current, but by North Carolina the ICW had straightened itself out, and we were happy to avoid gut wrenching Atlantic swells. We decided to do some overnighters, to help with the miles, speed, and seasons battle, which we were currently losing. The cool nights were a welcomed break from hot sticky days; we felt the pleasure of wrapping up in warm clothes.

The famous Chesapeake Bay gave us a full moon, positive current, and clear skies, so we kept going all the way to Washington DC. To reach the capital we turned west half way up the Chesapeake into the Potomac River. The city was two hundred miles out of our way (there and back), but after careful thought, it was an opportunity we just couldn't miss. The wide expanse was all ours; unexpectedly, it was lined with emerald greens of woodlands, with just a splash of imposing dwellings here and there.

Entering Washington DC was chock-full of adrenaline rushes; we held our collective breaths as we skimmed under a forty-five foot bridge, while watching the constant aircraft landing just one hundred metres off our bow. It was a great thrill, anchoring right in the heart of the city. For a small fee, we could use a secure dinghy dock that came with a plethora of freebies (our families have never received so many emails!). We anchored within walking distance to the Smithsonian Museums and the magnificent monuments. Adding to the stimulation, we coincided our stay for the July 4th celebrations, which came hand-in-hand with ear-splitting, dramatic fireworks that we watched from our prime seats on the river. As time was tight, we carefully chose the main attractions that appealed to us, ignoring the nagging yacht next door stating that we should stay longer and not bother with New York.

With the autumn of July approaching, we had to move on. The three day and three night sail to New York was comforting for our sightseeing-weary bodies. In the well-buoyed channels, the black nights heightened other senses. The breeze picked up the sweet perfume of flora carrying it blindly along. The deep throaty calls of the dawn chorus hidden by the fresh, heavy mist made us feel alive, in a new world. The bonus of calm seas as we traversed the only outside stretch made the trip a memorable gift.

Not quite believing where we were, we entered the mayhem of the wildest city in the world. The Statue of Liberty welcomed us while we weaved, dodged, and dived around every conceivable boat out to play on a Sunday afternoon. The East River runs alongside Manhattan Island, enabling us to view the Empire State Building, the canyon streets, and the Brooklyn Bridge while on board *Mariah*.

Eventually, we found a mooring up stream in the Hudson River for thirty American dollars a night – not bad for living in the heart of New York. Time's Square was a long walk or a short subway ride away, where we rubbernecked around the streets and stared at the shows on the side of buildings that flew at us from every angle. We treated ourselves to a theatre play and a movie. We visited the Empire State Building and the strangely peaceful site of Ground Zero. These were the most remarkable days of our trip.

At dusk, before leaving, we sat on board our faithful home, watching eagles sweep by, clutching writhing fish in their talons. The evening light on the water was like the caress of an angel's breath. We felt as though we had discovered America's hidden secret. Viewing the city lights flickering along the unmistakable coast, we discussed *The Phantom of the Opera*, which had blown our minds. It turned our conversation to the next part of this magical trip and this theatre show that was our lives. And, with some disbelief, we revelled in what we had achieved so far.

The following day, as we freed *Mariah* from the mooring in New York and watched the skyscrapers shrink, we started to focus on what was to come: a trip up the Hudson, the DIY mast stepping, the Great Lakes, the snow capped mountains, and the autumn golds. It was all there for the taking, just waiting anyone with a sense of adventure who desired a rewarding voyage.

Noel threw me a look as my loud sneeze bounced off the vast pink, glimmering rocks; the alien noise echoed around in our secluded, staggeringly quiet anchorage. We wouldn't have been at all surprised if a salivating T-Rex crashed through the profusion of trees that were begging for the company of ramblers. This was just one of our countless, superb anchorages we had found within our expedition around The Great Loop. We were on the second half of this fascinating journey and were preparing to say our farewells to a remarkable, ever changing country.

We had puttered along the Hudson River, housing an exotic cocktail of anxiousness and intrigue, wondering what further adventures inland America and Canada would hold for us. Planning here was critical. Tidal waters creating sturdy currents could make the difference between a stressful battle and a peaceful glide. Wide, green, and deep, the Hudson was easy to navigate, leaving ample time to view the manicured lawns, tree covered banks, and tumbling castle ruins. It all seemed effortless, and if you took a peek at dawn, the hills cloaked in opaque mist momentarily transported you to the eerie Highlands of Scotland.

The dependable cruisers' grapevine assured us that mast stepping was easy and cheap, it was the DIY bit that worried me.

Castleton on Hudson was friendly, funky, and frequently made us feel like movie stars as the locals became intrigued with, 'The funny sounding foreigners.' It was here that we were turning *Mariah* into a motorboat. The next part of the trip squeezed us under low bridges and up and down hills via large formidable locks.

After a day of preparation, early the next morning *Mariah* and crew were the guinea pigs at the de-masting process. A French Canadian couple were next to take down their mast, a single-hander (American) wanted to put his back up. We all agreed to help each other. As the crane took the weight, our mast was perfectly balanced. Ready with wooden cradles for support, we eased the heavy lump of timber and its metal stays along the length of *Mariah*. When the mast was secure, we were ready to tackle the next boat. Backs were aching and tempers fraying as the unbalanced mast caught us in uncompromising positions. Lastly, we all helped the American put his mast up. Unfortunately, as the mast reached its vertical limit, we noticed that the rigging was clutched around the mast by the crane's straps.

As lunchtime slinked up on us, we tightened the last shackle and sat in comfortable companionship, sipping cool beers. Our new friends, work colleagues, and fellow travellers gave credit to Noel: his planning and forethought made us look like professionals. Cruisers are a wonderful breed; it was the most inclusive club we'd belonged to.

We approached our first lock in the New York Canal system (the Erie Canal). Casting our minds back to our France experience, when we could not figure out whether the lock doors are open or closed, we were pleased that the locks here were clearer and cleaner. In France, the lock doors were a lovely shade of black to match the decor within. Feeling more at ease in the States, we tentatively coaxed *Mariah* into the dungeon. Our full keel meant little steerage when we slowed down, with powerful currents carrying us along it made somewhat of a stressful situation. The tumultuous locks in France taught us that you could not have enough fenders. So, *Mariah* looked like an inflatable boat, covered completely in plastic and timber boards. The huge door ground shut, and the water started to rise. The water swirled and bubbled; the chamber creaked, groaned, and we stared up at the green slimy walls. The lock master suggested that we should remove a few of the planks of wood that rested on the fenders, 'As they'll just get in the way.' Our France experience suggested that they may not be enough. But after rising up hundreds of metres and descending back down again through a plethora of locks of varying heights, we realised the US lock designers knew what they were doing. The locks were mild, painless, and really quiet enjoyable. It was astonishing to think we were hill climbing on our boat.

At either side of the locks, or in an accommodating town, free, clean tie-up places were provided. It was here that we met locals interested in our voyage. I interviewed people for my writing, and they, in turn, interviewed us for their local papers. We were the furthest travelled, foreign sailing boat most people had seen, and we felt a little humbled at all the attention we received.

I had begun to see some of my sailing articles published: mostly destination pieces and a few technical articles. It had taken a long time and a lot of work and editing, but at last I was starting to fulfil my dream of earning some money while doing what I love. The fact I was writing about a subject, that not long ago I knew nothing of, gave me a remarkable sense of achievement.

Each day, as the northern evening arrived and the unique light to these latitudes softened the view, the mouth-watering smell of BBQs smothered the fragrance of freshly cut grass. For us, it meant that it was time to stop for the night, to relax and study the charts for the next day and our trip across the border to Canada.

The Great Lakes are just that – great, vast expanses of water that are really inland seas. We were unsure what to expect when entering Canada. We knew that they charged for locking through and for mooring up at the locks. (However, if you were over seventy-seven years of age and were operating a vessel under eighteen feet, you got a free lockage pass!). The pilot book explained that leaving the main channel for anchoring could be dangerous with shoaling and debris. Preferring to anchor, we decided to take a gamble and cautiously picked our way off the channel and found that we had not one problem. In fact, we had no need to hand over any of our hard earned cash to Canadian officials for moorings throughout the entire trip through Canada.

There were alternative routes to choose from in order to traverse The Great Loop. The Great Lakes beckoned with an ideal opportunity for some good sailing. However, with time and budget against us, our mast stayed prone. Warily, we approached open water. Staggered at the might of the lakes, the inland seas, we selected our weather judiciously. The shallow, lighter fresh water allowed hefty, cube like waves to build swiftly in a modest breeze.

The air smelt fresh here, like home; it was inviting with the promise of adventure. Not once did we tire of the endless pink and black glimmering rock formations that lined our pathway through the shimmering water. Here, inventive builders pieced together esoteric houses on rocks that were scattered throughout the canals and hidden in picture book bays, nestled in with their own jetty. It left us wondering which movie star may hide there. We made plans to return someday.

It was here that we experienced what it would be like to drive through treacle. With numerous places to anchor, we guided *Mariah* from the main channel and suddenly she turned into a languid lump. Suspiciously, we peered over the side to see that a bushy weed, just visible under the surface, had *Mariah* in its clutches. Little by little, we extracted ourselves from the embracing triffid, back to the main channel. It was like working our way through a syrupy paste. This, thankfully, was a one off phenomenon.

Night after night, alone, we revelled in the serenity, our contentedness. Looking east from the partly protected bay, the horizon was a tiny speck. From our deserted surrounding we could see for miles. Perhaps the world had ended and no one told us.

Ashore, we were acutely aware that this was bear, snake, and spider country. Stepping into the vibrant forest, we raised our voices to scare off any prowling bears.

'What's your plan if we're confronted by a bear? I asked.

'If a large grizzly approached me, I plan to play dead.'

'Good,' I said, 'I intend to look it in the eye and slowly back off.' I felt more at ease. 'If my plan fails, at least the bear would deal with you first, and have a hearty meal before attacking me!'

We collected wood for our modest potbelly stove that kept us snug on board. The nights were becoming chilly, but the clear sparkle of the water still beckoned us in each day. On the shore, the pink, blue, and quartz stones were like jewels, each one I lifted for a closer inspection made a creepy, long-legged spider skitter in one direction, while I scurried in another. Some of the rock formations stirred our imaginations; they were reportedly over one hundred million years old. I wondered what had trodden here before us. If only they could whisper their secrets.

As we gathered information on the Peterborough Hydraulic Lock, a stranger took great pleasure enlightening us that farther along the Trent Severn the depth was down to three feet. With our five feet draft, this caused some anxious creasing of the crew's foreheads.

'The lock-keepers will tell you about it, but everyone is having problems,' he expounded. But the fearless *Mariah* carried on in the face of adversity, knowing that somewhere along the line, someone would tell us what to do. Well, at least we hoped they would. Twice we bumped our bottom; there was no damage and no water less than five feet.

The locals we met along the Trent Severn Waterways were intrigued with our travels.

'You sailed all that way in *that* boat?' they'd say with what seemed to me unnecessary emphasis on 'that'.

But *Mariah* had her own exclusive claims to fame. In England, she'd been perched on the highest hill in Hertfordshire and sped along the M25 motorway; now we were going to put her in a large bath tub that lifts into the air and then on a railway track, quite a feat for an ocean going vessel. Canada has two unique systems aside from the usual locks. The first is a Lift Lock. We drove into a large bathtub, and a door rises out of the depths behind us to secure us in. Another boat at the top does the same, and his weight pushed water from somewhere below him into somewhere below us. He came down, while we went up. Underneath us both was a large, hopefully strong, hydraulic ram. The ride was speedy and smooth. Peering over a twenty metre ledge in a boat was bizarre.

The second unique system is the Marine Railway or The Big Chute. For economic reasons and as a barrier to prevent migration of the parasitic sea lamprey, a huge one hundred tonne open carriage was built over granite that separates converging waterways. Riding on twin tracks, it lifts boats out of the water, over the rock, to off load them into the river on the other side. *Mariah*, held by slings, was over seventeen metres high, looking out over a sheer drop of hard rock. As she rattled in the air, our hearts rattled to the same rhythm.

Aside from the fairground rides through Canada, the scenery was by far the most breathtaking we had seen anywhere in the world. In the translucent water, lilies did a Mexican wave in our soft wake, and sentinel silver birches stood tall on pink granite next to proud pines that mixed within a surplus of greens, tinged with an autumn flush. Each night, swinging on our three-hundred-and-sixty degree panorama, we savoured the views like a fine wine, trying to taste, absorb, and never forget.

Bidding a sad farewell to the dramatic Canadian scenery, we eased our way back into the States and picked our time to go south along Michigan Lake.

While the wind gathered spirit, Penguin Jack II (our dinghy) had been surfing behind us and trying to overtake *Mariah*, skewering violently. Ropes snatched for the last time and yanked loose the towing line. We shifted *Mariah* around to search for an eight-foot boat in a three hundred mile long lake. Fortunately, PJ's bright green paint caught our eye, and we fought the growing waves to salvage the wayward dinghy. Having been born in a brothel, PJ was clearly independent and lacking in any manners. The white-knuckle ride that was our boat made the retrieval challenging. Eventually, with skilful boat manoeuvres and ungraceful lurching, we reclaimed our rebellious dinghy. Abruptly, the winds gathered momentum with the fresh water and heaved the waves higher, the clatter of shifting equipment, plates, and books made me cringe. Noel gasped through the stinging rain to re-tie the prone mast that was trying to break free. Noel relied on his flexing knees, his earned balance, and a bit of luck while he weaved a spider's nest of nautical knots to secure the heavy lump of timber.

At last, rocking and rolling into a safe anchorage, we turned to the task of mucking-out the boat. Again, we were surprised and caught off guard (as we were in France) at how changing the dynamics of the boat, by dropping the mast, so radically changes its performance.

After a couple of moon-lit dashes along Lake Michigan, we arrived in Chicago at 2 am on the first day in September. The towering, opalescent city lights welcomed us into its still bay. The next morning, bureaucrats turned us away from the shore. We could not step onto land from the anchorage area; we had to go into a marina. As budget conscious cruisers, we took advantage of being dumb foreigners and sweet-talked the marine police into allowing us to dock at their private jetty, while we explored Chicago's sights and did the paperwork.

Actually, the best way to see Chicago is via boat, puttering through both its adolescent and mature, tall buildings, watching the rat race scurry by. This was the beginning of an entirely new adventure, heading south in mid-west America.

From Chicago, there are two routes to take; we opted for the Sanitary and Ship Canal that offered superior scenery. This leads to the Illinois River. Not too far into the Canal there was Barge City, my words for a place where there were two hundred foot long barges parked bow to stern, as far as the eye could see; the channel between left just inches leeway for any traffic.

As I squinted through our tatty binoculars, I was convinced a barge was heading our way, and I could not see a clear way ahead. With little time, we squeezed into a small gap, dwarfed by huge, rusted monsters. From behind the wall of barges around us, a monstrosity glided past. This thing, with the tug pushing it along was over a quarter of a mile long and one hundred feet wide! We were a little awe struck at the captain's deft handling. We waited until four of these monsters had gone by and slowly poked out our nose. After a mile, we caught up with yet another behemoth. Politely, we asked if we could overtake (knowing the mile marker you were at was a necessity at all times). We had to wait for the captain's permission to pass and obey his requests. We finally grasped his southern drawl after many whispers of 'what d'he say?' He gave the signal, so we upped the revs and started overtaking a boat over 1200 feet long, that's seventeen barges plus the pushing tow boat! Halfway alongside, we saw an approaching barge was static, tied to a bank, but we would not fit the three of us alongside, so the throttle received an extra shove. With our mind taking great leaps from, *yes, we'll make it* to no, *we won't*, and the throttle receiving the abuse that matched our thoughts, we slipped through just before we created a unique type of boat concertina.

We had been chatting about it for months, and with a giddy blend of trepidation and anticipation, we crossed the threshold onto the famous Mississippi River. We had only heard negative experiences about this part of the trip, which heightened the emotions. This corridor of commerce runs, in total, for over seventeen hundred miles from Minneapolis, MN to New Orleans, LA. We traversed just two-hundred-and-fifty miles of this fast flowing, muddy water, where often you'd see historic paddle-wheel boats gliding past. The current was with us, but running fast, giving us an extra three knots; good for speed, bad for mistakes.

There was little information available for this section, so for the first night we had to find our own anchorage. Tip-toeing off the channel (the charts had no depths), we found enough room to anchor. With the new trip line tied securely onto our anchor with a floating fender, I dropped the anchor and miraculously the knot unravelled. I watched in wonder as our fender took off on its own.

Without thought, Noel and I grappled to fix the outboard onto the dinghy and I jumped in, feeling a bit like Jane Bond on a mission to rescue. We had anchored behind a submerged wall (a wing dam) which gave us a little reprieve from the dominant current; however the fender had, by this time, built up some speed. Racing towards it in the dinghy, I caught up with the fender and scooped it up in a heroic fashion, I turned just before reaching the unforgiving current of the main channel. I revved the two horsepower outboard hard, the engine coughed, and I prayed. Somewhat late, my mind decided to offer some thought. If I were caught in the current, in the main channel, our small outboard would not have coped; I'd have been whisked off down the Mississippi with only PJ for company. I upped the revs more and was shaking by the time I reached *Mariah*. What a foolish thing to do, risk my life for an old fender!

The Mississippi was an exhilarating cruise. The clean sandy beaches, parks, and lush vegetation possessed an unexpected beauty. Along the way, we found some fabulous rest stops out of the channel, out of the current, and away from the commercial traffic. We were approaching the Ohio River turn-off and poignantly ended our trip along the Mississippi.

'Hurricane Ivan is heading for Mobile, Alabama.' The radio updated us on the relentless hurricanes that were only a few hundred miles away. Being inland, we felt safe from the awesome winds, however, when hurricanes move to a large expanse of land, the rain comes.

'I'm standing here near the Tennessee River, watching pleasure craft and yachts break free from their moorings and crash into bridges,' gasped the commentator on the radio, fully in tune with my horror. The Tennessee runs into the Ohio, our next river. The Ohio was running at three to four knots current – against us. That meant our average speed would be a monotonous one to two knots. Luckily, there was a protected, pretty anchorage just before the raging river, near a town named Cairo. We sat there for a long week, waiting for the Ohio River to calm. We tackled jobs on the boat and took trips to the town every other day.

The outing to town was a marathon. We dinghied ashore, climbed a ten foot muddy bank, and trekked a mile across fields overgrown with a mesh of weeds. Mozzies were fearsome and waged a full-on war. We then climbed a levee bank, which was ideal rattle snake foliage, and ultimately reached a gravel road. We were now half way there. The rest of the journey was a bit easier and after dragging our push-bikes (and many sock burrs) thus far, we were able to enjoy a ride. Loaded on the outward journey with bags of rubbish and all our groceries homebound made for a somewhat challenging exercise.

With flood waters still rampaging down the Ohio River, we prepared for battle and turned into the thick brown, debris-ridden river. Our speed slowed to a laboured two knots speed over the ground, while we played dodgems with the floating trees. The Ohio River houses two locks, which raised us up higher, away from sea level. However, water levels were so high, we motored right over the top of the locks, walls and all! At the second lock, while going over the top of the huge superstructure, we stopped dead in the water. Our hardworking Yanmar was pushed to the red as an enormous tugboat, thrusting fifteen barges, crept up our rear. As the barge crawled nearer, we stared at the land that was not moving by, and the Yanmar started to scream, not much before I did. Suddenly, Noel had the bright idea of tacking. Weaving left to right, we broke through the current, and the shore started moving along again.

We continued on and motored for long days, trying to get through this laborious section with haste. When we reached Tennessee, we started going down-hill with the current flowing south, the same direction as us, into the Gulf of Mexico.

The Cumberland River was enchanting. Well, I am not sure if it was the magic of the place or the fact that we were reading Harry Potter at the time. That evening two hooting owls, perched on a tree across the narrow river, entertained us for hours with their mystical calls.

After the Cumberland and Tennessee River, we entered the last stretch of the system that would lead us south into Mobile, which was just east of New Orleans, into the Gulf of Mexico. The Ten-Tom Canal connects the Tennessee River with the Tombigbee River; this was our last fresh water canal. The locks appeared newer and quieter in the Tenn-Tom. The waterway was sparsely populated and we took delight in watching the majestic Blue Herons sit in the almost naked trees with the onset of winter.

The cold nipped at our extremities, a price we paid for completing this trip in winter, but the cloak of warmth from people of the Deep South warded off the chill. We lived through part of winter, in Demopolis, Alabama, experiencing the way of life at first hand, while we worked on *Mariah* in preparation for the Pacific Ocean.

Living within a community such as Demopolis, Alabama was what travelling was all about, not the latest tourist attraction, but the people, the culture, the feel of the place. The locals instantly accepted us, and their welcoming smiles were contagious. We easily slipped into their ways and their rhythmic accents. Listening to their voices was like pouring dark molasses from a warm drum, thick, rich, and leisurely. You could hear the melodic beat of country music beneath their day-to-day conversations. We knew their laid back attitude was absorbed deep into our hearts when we tentatively thought about making a decision tomorrow.

While working towards departure, and victualling the boat we had ducked into a rather plain looking cafe. Situated within a semi-industrial area, we were surprised at the cleanliness and comfortable surroundings. We were on the run, between picking up fuel filters and our last supermarket shop.

'Two burgers and two glasses of milk, please.' That's all we wanted.

The burgers were nothing short of brilliant within a toasted bun that was full of fresh, crisp salad, too.

'Thank you,' we said to the waitress, when she collected our plates, 'we just have to tell you, we are from Australia and that is one of the best hamburgers we have had since Australia!'

'Well, sir, ma'am,' the waitress smiled, 'that is so very nice of you to say so.'

But, what we didn't realise, was that our "waitress" was the owner. As we gathered our belongings to leave and pay at the counter near the door, the entire staff stood in a line. The owners, waitresses, chef and washer-up, all smiled at us.

'We just want to say, it has been a pleasure to meet you and an honour to serve you today.' The owner said sincerely.

Noel and I then walked down the line of employees while they shook our hands, and refused to take any money from us when we left! They were so thrilled to have foreign visitors that took the time to thank them for their food, they treated us like royalty. And, that just about sums up the Alabamian way!

We said our farewells to PJ, our dinghy, in Alabama. The kitchen cupboard sheets were slowly separating, and it was only fair he retired. We searched for a replacement without much luck. Until, rather despondently, we were strolling around the yard and called up to a guy standing on his boat, on the hard.

'D'ya know anywhere we can buy a dinghy?'

'You can have this one.' And with that he tossed over the handrails a perfect, beautiful fibreglass dinghy, complete with brass row-locks, oars, and a neat little plaque.

'I was about to throw it away,' he said.

We named her Matilda, and she was destined to travel home with us.

During our river cruising we had felt that things weren't quite right with our house in England. A tenant had left and the estate agents said they couldn't find another. So, with winter becoming chilly and causing boat work to slow, and with a longing to see my family we decided to do some land travel in Europe.

We left *Mariah* on the hard in the marina in Demopolis, Alabama. Mum and Dad had offered to buy us our airfare back to the UK to see them for a few weeks. Organising the trip before Christmas was a rush, but with the boat in a safe and reasonable marina, at one hundred American dollars per month, we were happy to go. We could also visit our great friends, Den and 'Tash, in the Netherlands.

'We can't wait to see you,' 'Tash and I had declared simultaneously.

They were about to become parents to twins! Their boat, *Frodo*, patiently waited for them in the USA.

Getting around America on land was only easy if you had a car. We researched public transport and found the only way to get to an international airport was via coach. Locals in the marina were horrified that we thought about travelling this way and quickly a cruiser offered us a lift to the airport via his home. It was a four-hour drive to his home near Nashville and a further hour's drive to the airport. En route to his place, he told us of his time in a straight-jacket; we started to feel a little vulnerable cooped up in a van with a stranger who had officially been on the wrong side of sane at some point. The couple were hospitable, and a few days in the middle of the country was relaxing; however, the odd tic the guy produced and the unstable emotions, plus the gun, made us a little tense. The hour's drive to the airport at 4:30 am wasn't fun, and the hour long argument with his wife was disconcerting, and I shivered at my imaginings at his actions if we were not there. We knew we would return back to *Mariah* a different way. Being cut off, with strangers, in a remote location in a foreign country seemed a rather daft thing to do.

I loved being back home in the warm arms of my family. It was our first introduction to Sammy and Zino, our newest niece and nephew. The whole bunch were a joy. Dad surprised me by insuring me on his brand new Jaguar, so we could have some freedom.

Our house had been empty for over six months now, and we decided to go and check it out and surprise our estate agents. They *were* surprised. They had neglected to tell us about the fire that had engulfed the kitchen, the holes in the walls, the dirt, the stains, the damaged door and doorframes throughout the entire three-bedroom house, and the stripping of everything that wasn't nailed down (and some things that were!). The vivid, deep pink paint that the last renter had used to try to cover the smoke damage hurt our eyes and didn't work. We sacked our agents who, "couldn't park on the yellow lines out front to do a proper bi-monthly look at the house," ignoring the free car park fifty metres up the road. We received a little compensation from them after they stupidly made this admittance. Never had I seen such an unprofessional, shoddy business; I wished them everything they deserved.

Two months later, we had renovated the entire house – *again*. We had missed our flights back to the boat; it was now February and we had no money. Noel quickly got a carpentry job in Yorkshire, which was almost the coldest place to be in England in the coldest month of the year. I worked in an office, it was a good, temp, job, but it was in an office. We worked for a few weeks, but as our track record proved, we couldn't stick to it. We had a deeply emotional meeting in a pub one Sunday.

'This is not where I want to be,' said Noel and I had agreed. Decisive action was what was needed and decisive, if not a bit odd, it was.

Two days later, we flew to Romania. Noel had been working with a few Romanians and had got on well with them. Romania was scheduled to transfer their currency into euros some years down the line. It had been a dream of ours to buy land in a country that hadn't gone to the euro yet, but intended to. Soon we were following that plan, heading for a country we knew little of and was currently experiencing the worst winter in one hundred years.

We noticed the thick snow as we swooped around to land. We quickly got off the plane and stood in a grey building for a couple of moments about to step into another weird and wonderful adventure. We had arranged for a work mate's father and family to meet us. We even had an apartment to stay in. What could go wrong?

I walked through the passport control and waited for Noel.

'Is this your only passport?' he was asked.

'Yes,' Noel replied.

'Where is your visa?'

Oops.

Having UK residency was not enough; we had neglected to arrange a visa for Noel. Despite, begging, and pleading, they would not let Noel in.

'You can stay,' they said to me. But, I was not staying alone.

Within just fifteen minutes, we were put on a plane back to the UK via Holland.

We sat in first class, our distress clear.

'We have a full bar, what would you like to drink?' the steward with deeply sympathetic eyes asked.

'A cup of tea would be nice,' said Noel. But I had picked up the steward's nuances within his question.

'We have a *full* bar, sir, madam,' he said again.

'I'll have your finest wine,' I said and Noel looked at me. Our wine was normally from the budget section. I explained to Noel and it took a moment for it to sink in, but soon doubles of this that and the other were wafted down with a marvellous meal.

We had planned to spend just a couple of days in the Netherlands on our way back from Romania with Den and 'Tash. Now we would be there early and have plenty of time.

With a frenzy of hurried phone calls, we suddenly found ourselves on the train from Amsterdam on our way to see our good buddies. Noel and I sat opposite each other on a chilly, grey, winters' night, the sun just starting to disappear. Suit clad workers sat around us, and I looked at Noel and giggled; he giggled back. A station sign shot past, and we had no idea whether it was ours or not. Soon, filled with the despair and lost in the bizarre situation of the last few hours, we were in fits of giggles. It wasn't just muffled snorts; it was breathtaking convulsions. We lost complete control. How could world travellers neglect to get a visa? We became hysterical. In these odd situations, we rarely argued or shouted at each other, we simply laughed. The people sitting around us covertly shuffled away, which made us laugh even harder.

It was pure delight to be together once again with Den and 'Tash. We each had the same philosophy of life and each succumbed to land-life only for necessity, while we planned our return to our floating freedom. The chatter was flowing and the underlying feelings did not need words, we were all comfortable together.

We discovered the pleasures of other freedoms in Amsterdam and floated, carefree, around the structured city. To add to the excitement, Noel and I had organised to fly home to *Mariah* on 14 February. As we said our good-byes to Den and 'Tash, my tears confirmed my dislike for farewells, as did 'Tash's. They were desperate to get back to their boat. They took comfort in the thought that they planned to bring up their children on board *Frodo*. This shocked a lot of people, but after sailing for almost seven years, the boat children we had met were level headed, un-materialistic, and happy. Besides, it was far safer moving along at walking pace, than one hundred kilometres per hour along our motorways.

We wished our friends luck and headed back to disrupt my parents' home, commandeering the washing machine while we organised ourselves to fly back to America in February 2005. The whirlwind week flashed along, with exhausting social events and playful games with my young nieces and nephews. Though our heads were already back in Alabama, it took a little while for our hearts to follow.

Back in America, with our sails aloft, we glided into Florida and our last stretch of the magnificent adventure on The Great Loop. It felt a bit like coming home to a favourite comfy chair. Leaving the rivers and entering back into the ICW brought a familiar feel with it, along with the comfort of smelling the ocean. We could see the hard, tenacious work Floridians had done to repair their pretty state after the bashing of ruthless hurricanes. Unfortunately, we also witnessed the telltale signs that remained: submerged boats, dismasted, left for dead, and bright blue tarpaulins streaking along the horizon, covering gaps where the roofs had taken flight – a carpenter's dream. We were back in salt water and tides and were elated to be able to dip into clean water that tightened our skin with its sharp chill. The view was now dappled with the promise of spring.

It was an honour to be able to do this trip, to watch the seasons come and go and see parts of the world we knew nothing of. Our heads were starting to think Panama Canal and Pacific Ocean; our hearts were, for quite some time, still in America.

20

Dolphins

'When are you going to be at the Panama Canal?'

This question plagued us.

'If you can predict the weather for the next two months, I will tell you,' was my frustrated reply.

Our delay in the UK meant we had to move fast to reach the Panama Canal in April. Thereafter, we would traverse the magnificent Pacific Ocean, and timing was of the essence. If we did not reach Australia by the end of November, we would be caught in cyclone season. We had made a pact that we'd never be in a latitude at the time when hurricanes or cyclones could develop. We hated thirty knots of winds let alone one hundred knots. Why would we gamble our lives and our home with nature?

My dad, Roy, and Noel's brother, Colin, had firmly staked their claim to be our additional crew when we went through man's majestic Panama Canal. They both knew we could not predict when we would reach there, as our timing laid in Mother Nature's hands.

It was going to take some organising to figure out where and when to collect them. Dad fancied Jamaica, and although we knew we could get to Cuba, winds and currents were the other factors that could make it impossible to reach Jamaica. Noel and I had much chart studying to do. We needed to figure out the best route for us and learn about the predominant winds and currents. We could study the usual weather for this time of year, but that was never completely reliable. We calculated how many miles we needed to cover and how long it would take. We averaged one-hundred-and-twenty nautical miles per day (over twenty-four hours), but good and bad currents, wind, and weather changed our speed anywhere from fifty miles a day to one-hundred-and-fifty miles a day.

It was all on a toss of a coin when we plumped for the Cayman Islands on 5 April 2005. That was our target to collect my dad. Colin was heading to Los Angeles and would wait for our call when we were nearing the Canal, so he could hop on a short flight down to Panama.

We waited for good weather at the Dry Tortugas at the tip of Florida Key West. Our next stop was Cuba, but we were already behind schedule.

The sail to Cuba was unremarkable, but checking into Cuba was extraordinary; six tall men with polished boots and pressed uniforms stomped around *Mariah* for an hour. The sniffer dogs enjoyed a pat from us and wagged their tails, while the officials scowled. I bit my tongue as they flicked through private paperwork, but once they had left, we could relax in a safe harbour. Tied to a concrete wharf along a narrow stretch, it was faintly odd to be amid Cubans and other cruising nationalities, but not one single citizen of the United States.

Old Havana, Cuba, bustled around us as we walked as bewildered tourists do. A free bus ride dumped us in the heart of the city, with just our wits to find our way. Decaying and refurbished buildings fought for space, and we felt as though we had stepped back in time as the clot of American Classic 1950's cars wrestled for road space.

Amazingly, we found the Ship's Chandlery easily, and they had the charts we needed to help find our way to the south of Cuba. This was where we would make our exit to pick up my dad at the Grand Cayman Islands.

Time was ticking. It was two days before Dad landed at the Caymans and started to twiddle his thumbs. Meanwhile, the narrow channel to exit the marina was stirring up into a wild, white frenzy with the whipping winds. To attempt to leave would have been suicide.

We left Havana the day before Dad's arrival in the Caymans and had thirty-six hours of our best sailing ever. 'What a glorious life,' I said. 'Dad's going to love this.'

As usual, our illusions were soon in shreds as we turned around Cuba's western extremity and were met with ferocious head winds. The wind got together with the waves and they continually launched water over us. We had to carry on, sail changes, engine checks, ropes re-furled and, of course, our continual look out for other traffic. We experienced our worst ever and best ever sail, all in one day.

Mariah's engine was thrusting her hard into the walls of water that slammed undeterred; great geysers of water showered down, drowning us in sticky salt. The lurching became unbearable. Imagine the worst (best?) tummy lurching fair-ground ride, and then imagine doing that for twenty-four hours, non-stop while you try to carry on normally: cleaning your teeth, using the bathroom... *Dad's gonna hate this,* we thought.

Off shift, we could not sleep. The soaring waves lifted *Mariah,* and then released her. She dropped like a rock, slamming down; this left us levitating in our bunks before plopping back down in a muddled heap.

Twenty-four hours later, exhausted and salt ridden, we reached the anchorage on the south of Cuba, where we could rest and await favourable winds. With much relief we were away from towns (and bureaucracy), surrounded by rocky hills, mangroves, and the odd coconut tree.

We spent our rest day working; salt-water had found its way through a dogged hatch and had soaked our bed. We washed the mattress and linen in fresh water and pinned, tied, and clipped it around the deck to allow it to dry. Noel ensured the engine was okay and carried out routine checks and maintenance. In the afternoon, we plotted our course for the Caymans, listened to weather reports, and tidied up the mayhem that the fierce weather had left us in. Right at that moment we hated sailing, but had a destination to reach. We were already five days late.

'We're coming, pa!' Noel and I started to quote dumb phrases from movies. Sailing could still have its dull moments and coupled with the endless horizons, we could become quite daft – anything to keep us amused.

We were just two days away from Grand Cayman and looked forward to seeing my dad. Things were not normal; we couldn't pick up the phone or drop a quick email to find out if he had safely arrived and to let him know where we were.

Our route from Cuba to Caymans was a scenic one. We added over ninety miles to our journey to try and out guess the usual winds and keep them on our stern.

Like any kind of life, sailing has its ups and downs. One day, dozens of dolphins frolicked on our bow wave, Mums with babies sharing the ride, a sight that always brought a sting of joy to my eyes. We believed (and had tried and tested) the theory that sighting dolphins on our journey was a good sign, meaning a good journey – we had seen none on our last trip. The moonless night enabled us to witness the miracle of phosphorescence, the biological phenomenon that dazzled us with explosions of vivid blue and green.

The following day, three swallows had tried to find a stable place to rest their weary wings on board *Mariah's* constantly shifting deck. One brave bird kept us company in the cockpit, chirping a pretty tune and turning his beak up at Noel's favourite oatmeal biscuit that I tried to entice him with. Finally, bored with my company, he flitted below and snuggled on a sleeping bag, tucked in his head, and slept. I would take in any waif, so I felt delighted to offer a reprieve to these pretty birds that reminded me so much of home.

Our small feathery pal took flight, leaving a reminder of his visit with two little messy packets, a small price to pay to be so close to wild birds that had put their trust in large, clumsy humans.

Our feathery friend returned to our safe cockpit and sang his last chirp before suffering a swift heart attack right at my feet. With a different kind of sting in my eyes and lump in my throat, I carried the delicate swallow to show Noel, so he could say his farewell too. We gave the colourful swallow an official burial at sea. It was a poignant moment. Alone at sea, we became especially attached to any living creature that was braving the elements hand in hand with us. The afternoon was quiet and sad, but the small sprinkle of rain was refreshing; the clouds coupled up with the sun and rain to form a beautiful, horse-shoe rainbow. The water was flat, seas were calm, and things were well. I started to wonder what would happen next.

'I felt just like Robinson Crusoe,' my dad exclaimed.

We mirrored his relief that we had finally arrived to collect him from the Caymans. For five days, he had sat on the long shelf of white sand beach and watched for us to make our entry. We had snuck in at night and went searching for Dad in his plush hotel the following day. Actually, the hotel was the only one open after Hurricane Ivan walloped Grand Cayman. Other hotels were closed and undergoing repair.

As weary travellers, we took advantage of the luxuries of a holiday hotel. Hot showers, laundry, free Internet, and TV! For one day only we lived as kings. Dad then somewhat downgraded his accommodation, squishing into a thirty-three foot boat that disturbingly lacked fresh towels and maid service.

'Where's the air-conditioning then?' Dad asked with a sly grin.

'Same place as the running hot water and TV,' I replied smartly.

We made plans to dive with giant stingrays and explore the island, but again Mother Nature waved her dominating hand, and the weather dictated an immediate departure.

Since selecting the Caymans to collect Dad from, we had found out that the Caribbean Sea was notoriously rough with big, ugly waves. Noel and I were anxious – Dad had spent holidays on our boat, but always in dead calm, flat water. Actually being at sea was a whole new ball game. We decided to beat east to Jamaica, which would take two days. At least then Dad had the opportunity to jump off and fly down to the Panama if it all became too much.

We re-introduced him to boat life with a different, more in-depth, preamble on safety.

'This is your harness, always wear it and always clip yourself on. Tablets to curb sea-sickness are to be taken each morning.'

We were all ready to leave, but first we needed fuel.

For us, the simple task of filling up with fuel was not quite the same as driving a car into a garage. However, this time our task played out a sequence that was a hot contender for the next *Carry On* film.

I called the dock for the third time to confirm that we could pull up to the concrete pier to refuel.

'George Town Port Authority, this is the sail boat Mariah II. 'Mariah II, this is Port Security. When you see that large, black ship called Mona leave, you may tie up and refuel; we'll be there waiting to show you where to go.'*

We waited, one hour, and then two hours. At nine o'clock that night, Dad released us from our mooring, and I guided *Mariah* to the dock. Noel was flat on his back with a good book, not because he'd suddenly become perversely lazy, but because lifting the dinghy up the beach earlier that day had caused an imperative muscle to pop. Dad and I were on our own.

'Port Security, this is Mariah II, we are approaching the dock, please indicate where we should tie.'

Silence.

I called again.

Silence.

I called again, my voice revealing my impatience as I circled Mariah.

'Mariah II, this is Port Authority, have you paid for your fuel?'

This was the first we had heard that we should pay first.

'We'll be ready for you tomorrow, once you've paid,' Port Authority said over the radio.

'We'll see,' I said, the cutting anger in my voice was as clear as a glass.

At 8 am the following day, after estimating our required fuel and paying, Dad and I took *Mariah* to the dock – again. Noel was still on his back.

Nearing the assumed tie up location, we saw that the huge fenders for the ships on the dock would prevent Dad from leaping onto the dock to secure our lines. I couldn't expect him to leap about like a teenager. I knew he'd give it a go and would probably do okay, but I could see him become a bit contemplative at the thought. As only Jane Bond could, I eased *Mariah* alongside the wharf, pulled the throttle into neutral, leapt on deck, grabbed a line, and took a gamble that the fender would hold my weight. I took a further leap onto the filthy concrete with Dad right on my heels and between us we secured the boat. Noel adjusted his pillow and turned a page. Then we saw that the only place to tie up, where we had tied, was too far from the fuel!

With diesel now dripping from my neck, and the sweat covering my burning skin, we were finally ready to leave. It had taken six hours of running ragged, the sunscreen slipped down my face together with the sweat. Dad and I were suffering in the relentless, breeze free heat. Meanwhile, Noel adjusted his fan.

Now we had paid for more fuel than we had taken on board. With much relief, the refund was easy, as was the clearing with customs and immigration, although the diesel/sweat perfume coupled with my extraordinarily red face caused a few odd looks.

Dad was now officially on the crew list, I looked like a crisp, Noel was enjoying his book, and we were ready to leave, with only the notorious Caribbean Sea to tackle.

'Anyone for a cuppa?' Dad asked. He had become the official tea-maker on board. Mother Nature had taken pity on us and presented a stalling low pressure system, enabling us to gain plenty of easting and a restful night on Jamaica's shores. Still wary of the fickle weather that apparently stalked yachts in this area, our stay in Jamaica was brief and only on anchor. Soon, we were watching the land disappear with four days and nights of sailing in front of us with our new crewmember.

As we steered south towards the necklace of Panama's San Blas Islands, we were impressed with Dad's ability to handle the oddities of sailing. As if Mother Nature was witnessing Dad's adeptness, each day she pushed the wind a bit harder. The prevailing south easterlies were constant and strong across the Caribbean Sea. We took advantage of the gift of a suspended low. After two days, we were riding eight-foot waves, which provided us with a rolling ride that would earn a few casualties at a fairground park. Dad coped with the odd, three-dimensional, continuous, movement with a cheerful smile and more offers of tea. On day three, the dolphins came.

'Look,' Noel whispered to Dad, 'over there on the horizon.' Dad peered into the sun, and a huge smile spread across his face.

Dad pulled his weight and matched our hours on shift. It was really odd that both Noel and I could sleep at the same time while sailing. I got up every hour or so to check on Dad during his watch, not because I thought he couldn't cope, but because I felt it was a lot to ask. Standing night watches on a sailboat while traversing a difficult sea, is not easy. But, I needn't have worried.

Four days after leaving Jamaica's shores, the bouncy but speedy ride delivered us safely into the sanctuary of the San Blas islands. We all relished the dawn welcome into what would reveal itself as paradise. On asking our newest crew member what he would remember most about his first off-shore sail, he grinned and exclaimed, 'The dolphins! The dolphins were the highlight, seeing them leap towards the boat I could almost hear them sing yippee!' Watching over twenty of these beautiful, friendly animals guide *Mariah* along, while taking advantage of a free ride on our bow, was a gift he would never forget. I was elated that I could be part of that with him and perhaps I had finally given something back to him, after everything he had done for me.

As for me, the weirdest thing was sleeping, while sailing, at the same time as Noel. Normally one of us was always on watch; my memories of Dad surviving within our strange world with a cheery smile and willingness to learn and take part in all aspects of the boat, left me feeling proud.

21

Man-eating crocs and muggers

'You gife mi fiv dollar,' the abrupt stocky Indian pointed sharply at me, himself, and our timber boat with his leathery finger.

Here we go again, I thought, with vivid memories of cunning Egyptians, shrewd Malaysians, and darn right calculating Caribbeans. His worn hands reached to his pocket and revealed a slim printed receipt book. For once, I was grateful for my indecision of reaction and the official booklet declared the five American dollars fee for sailing boats to stay in the San Blas, for up to a month. Our new smiley friend showed his relief as he witnessed the proverbial penny dropping in our salt sluggish minds. We gladly exchanged cash for receipt.

'Bambino,' he nodded his wrinkly head at the young girl curled up at the end of their sturdy, dugout canoe. Her dazzling smile lit up her eyes, the sun had yet to perform its harshness on her smooth, brown skin. 'Mag-a-zine,' old smiley pronounced with some difficulty. We were pitifully short on glossy magazines; it was a rich request. The one tattered, but colourful, publication exhumed from the bowels of *Mariah's* burdened hull caused the youthful youngster to hold her breath. A small whimper confirmed she was breathing again as she gratefully clasped the smooth pages and immediately became lost within the colourful pictures and foreign printed words.

'A gift,' the next words, painstakingly practiced from her cheerful dad. He handed over three large, un-ripe avocados. 'Quatro dias,' he said with a more comfortable tongue, they would be ready to eat in four days.

Behind schedule by three months (due to problems on terra firma not nautical), we had hurriedly sailed two thousand five hundred miles in just six weeks to enable us to witness for ourselves why the San Blas was "a place to see." We were also preparing for the Panama Canal experience, traversing the magnificent Pacific Ocean, and heading home to Australia.

It was not what the San Blas Islands had so much, but rather it was what they hadn't got that made them special. The necklace archipelago that threaded its way along the northern Panama coast was happily void of ugly, noisy jet skis and thumping music. Absent were the flamboyant tourist boats skimming our bow, housing burnt faces straining to peer into our home. The glorious silence with only the backing rhythm of the gentle rolling ocean was soothing, even the flies buzzed in a soft key.

I think most cruisers have a certain respect for places they visit, such as the San Blas Islands. As we took our first steps in paradise, it was extraordinary to feel and witness the respect. There was a display of pretty shells left untouched for all to enjoy, a pile of coconuts set in neat piles next to a mismatched bench in a welcomed shady spot, no litter to tarnish the beautiful picture. Our mementos were, more often than not, gathered at beaches: a shell, piece of washed up coral, and even an old Cuban paddle hung precariously around *Mariah's* innards. Here, we did not want to touch or take anything, this place should be left as it was found; it was like an unwritten, unspoken rule.

San Blas has 365 islands, but some figures say there are up to 379. I imagined appointed island counters kicking back and enjoying the peaceful scenery, and then losing their place. Besides who really cares exactly how many there are! On each flat atoll the strapping, vivid, green palm trees bestow cool, dark shade to the Kuna Indians that inhabit some of the islands. This indigenous group offered us a warm welcome, but they were a tough bunch.

After decades of conflict and a short war with the Panamanian government in 1925, the victorious Kuna won a self-governing region of 2,360 km² they call Kuna Earth (Kuna Yala).

Around 35,000 Kuna's lived here, scattered from thirty to a few thousand per village. The brawny Indians, as you would expect, fish and cultivate their coconut plantations. They didn't do too badly from cruisers, too.

The vibrant women paddle daily in their tough, dugout canoe to each boat swinging in the welcomed breeze.

'*Molas, molas,*' they called, which was wasted on our inadequate Spanish tongue. Gran, mum, and daughters made it clear that each pile of *molas* they tried to sell were individual to each of them. To keep them all happy I felt I should buy one from each, but that was not going to happen at around fifty American dollars a-piece! *Molas* are intricately hand stitched, many layered, cotton panels, which depict colourful turtles, parrots, or indigenous patterns. Muddling the separately crafted pieces left you on the end of some severe tutting.

'Don't tell anyone about this place,' our new neighbour on the New York boat said after we bid them good morning and exclaimed our astonishment at the beauty of our surroundings. As we gazed around the picture book islands and reefs that formed a perfectly protected anchorage, we felt like we should have been in that glossy magazine we gave away. Crystal clear beckoning water, model palm trees that were the healthiest thing we'd seen since vegemite sandwiches, and glistening sandy islands that appeared to have just had a make-over and were ready for their photo shoot with *Vogue* magazine.

The sandy islands summoned us to explore their shady secrets. We exhausted ourselves by snorkelling within the dazzling live reefs, matched only by the Great Barrier Reef. My weary limbs were cajoled by the excitement of further exploration, and I took a solitary ride to a partially inhabited island. Tacking through the abundant waving shallows, I was alerted by whistles showing me where to land the dinghy. The natives hauled up the dinghy and tried to peer into my bag for goodies. Endlessly embarrassed by my lack of Spanish, I tripped over words spoken in English laced with a Spanish accent, hoping something would catch. 'Salade, Banan, tomat,' I chanted in a poor mimic of their tone. We all ambled into their tiny village centre, where two strong huts weaved down into the dirty sand with dried palm leaves surrounding a ramshackle table amidst the dust. Fresh lemons, avocados, and bananas were assembled by the excitable children who stared at me – a stranger daring to enter their home, alone. The small bounty was just four American dollars. I did not attempt to negotiate, but pulled out of my bag two extra dollars, popcorn, and a small magazine to show my appreciation for making me welcome and perhaps enabling me to take a couple of photos. Sighting the camera, the chief put on his shirt, lined up two incongruous pink and blue plastic chairs, and sat down stiffly with his wife.

'Not what I had in mind,' I muttered, but obligingly took the picture. With a bit more chocolate and even a coke (I felt a tad stingy with yesterday's coke purchases), a lot of hand movements and miming, I convinced our smiley, avocado gift-friend to take a picture with me, the fruit on the dusty table, and all his family. Trustingly, I handed over the camera with foreign instructions and frantically waved at all the kids to gather around. Many smiles, giggles, and shaky pictures later, we bade farewell with the promise of my return with a black and white print-out of their pictures.

With Dad in tow, I returned with the printed pictures. Squeals of joy permeated through the solid palms out onto the flat, green-blue water as the chief unrolled the photos.

'Come, come,' beckoned a new arrival. She trotted off east, with my dad and I trying to keep pace in the dusty path, dodging falling coconuts. Summoning her husband, she expounded the details of the new pictures that I presented, and we were met with a toothless, mischievous grin from her cheeky husband. Raucous laughter bellowed from the gathering crowd as our new friends posed for pictures, calling us to sit with them and cuddling each other, a tactile show that I think was usually for private.

An hour later, on board *Mariah,* we handed the remaining pictures to the younger girls of the family who had paddled over to see us. They could hardly wave farewell, as they tipped the canoe by gathering at one end to grasp an early peek of the pictures. The thrill etched on their faces and eager fingers gave us our own joy and memory that was equally imprinted in our minds.

As some sailboats drifted silently away and others puttered in, we wondered if it was too late to keep San Blas as it was. On the well-worn routes, sailors ply around our planet the San Blas islands were an ideal location to stop at before dealing with, and ironing out, the mountainous rumours that cloaked the Panama Canal. The cruising grapevine would keep growing, weaving its information to all who explore, revealing this enchanted archipelago. I wrestled with myself while writing an article about our experience in the San Blas, advertising such a place in a popular magazine.

After three days, it was time to leave. We opted for a night sail to Colon City on the mainland of Panama. The cool night with its bright full moon brought a welcomed reprieve to the still, sticky days.

A shroud of mystery enveloped the modus operandi for traversing the Panama Canal. Gossip, rumour, and dare I say, a little tittle-tattle gave the crew of *Mariah II* some serious frowns as we approached the infamous isthmus.

There were assorted methods to choose from to achieve the same thing; whether at anchor, or in the mosquito-infested marina, there was a standard three days to complete all the paperwork. Once you had handed over all your dollars to everyone you met, lied through your teeth, and signed your life away, you accomplished your "go through" date. Depending how you reached this highly sought status, those three days could be effortless or could feel as though you had a three-day pass into hell.

Colon was a dangerous city. It had been for years, and there was no sign of improvement. Almost thirty percent of the population were unemployed and their idea of making a buck was somewhat frightening. While at anchor we heard about a death and several muggings only two hundred yards from the cool, shabby bar on shore. The anchorage (which was called The Flats) was safe, but each night dinghies were vanishing at a scary rate of knots. At least four went missing in our fun-filled ten-day stay. It made you wonder how much longer before the dinghy thieves expanded their business into other malicious endeavours.

On shore, imprisoned within the compound (which had high walls with barbed wire), we were safe. Tough guys with immense attitude instead of sense walked into town, while we thought the one American dollar taxi ride was fair – why take the risk? A murder in Colon was as regular as boat maintenance.

Contrary to the plethora of advice, we learned that we could complete all the paperwork ourselves. Since a probable mugging and potential death was part and parcel of this option, and we were told that a fine of five-to-six thousand American dollars was applied if the paperwork is not completed properly, we decided to hire some help. Hiring an agent cost an extra ten percent of the total fee, with which you added the privilege of cooking a steak dinner for your mediator. The rewards of an agent were slim; they could maybe buy you one day (i.e. got you booked in earlier), but you could still be ungraciously bumped like everyone else.

We opted for the taxi driver option. This did have its pitfalls, but the drivers offered steerage through a seemingly rudderless experience. For thirty American dollars an English-speaking driver took us to each office in an air conditioned car with good locks on the doors. They helped us complete the forms that were in Spanish and explained what the beejeezus was going on.

Day one – We had to keep our patient heads screwed on tight. The Immigration office was near the laundry and showers within the grandly named compound. Spanish countries love paperwork, and we were already armed with boat papers and crew lists in triplicate. Here they stamped and signed one of the crew lists. This document was incredibly valuable, all the remaining box tickers wanted to see it. It was here that the taxi drivers started to tout for our business. Once a driver had selected us, we could sit back, (double checking that the doors were locked) and enjoy the surreal surroundings from relative safety. At customs, we completed an inordinately detailed form that covered all but our inside leg measurement. This was for each person that arrived to Panama via boat.

Next, a young officer at the marine office stamped our paperwork and signed papers with lots of scribbling; we handed over more bits of paper, and he continued scribbling. Lastly, as we started to sag at the knees with heat and a tree load of paper, we arrived at the advisors/schedulers office. Here they looked at one or two of the sheaves we possessed and arranged for the *admeasurer* to come the following day to measure the boat.

Day Two – This was where the pressure started to mount. They said that the *admeasurer* would come to our boat between 9 am and 2 pm. What they actually meant was that he would arrive at about 1 pm, leaving you in a panic to get this part done before he finished at two. You had to pay your transit fee after the *admeasurer* had given you another piece of paper, and you could only pay at a bank.

To gain a smidgen of a chance to complete the two simple tasks on the same day, we kept a sharp look out for the *admeasurer*. A boat with "pilot" written on the side cruised around the anchorage with the *admeasurer* standing on the bow in a life jacket. We engaged in ferocious waving, horn blowing, and a fair bit of shouting to make ourselves known. Other cruisers had said that if the pilot does not see you, or cannot jump on board your boat due to your sun covers being in the way, he would shrug his shoulders and tootle off home. Once we had him on board, he ran a tape measure from the bow to stern and then arranged to meet us in the bar. It was here, we found out, that you had to get to the bar early and pounce on him. If you didn't do this someone else would, and an hour or so later, you'd get your chance to complete another tonne of paperwork. For us, 2 pm had been and gone, so we had a beer or two and arranged a taxi driver to take us to the bank the following day.

Every piece of paperwork contained a little box where you had to declare your speed. Never had a little square on a bit of paper raised so much background debate. This was where true-blue, honest cruisers struggled. You *had* to lie or you didn't get to go through the canal! You *had* to put eight knots as your speed. You knew you were lying, they knew you were lying, and you all knew that everyone knew you were lying. Still, we had to write eight knots. Sitting with our friendly *admeasurer* the strain of blatant deceit took its toll, and Noel took a gamble at suggesting seven knots. It was still a lie, but a splash closer to the truth. In response, the official screwed up his eyebrows, frowned, and said, 'I'll just put eight knots anyhow!' It was all a game of ticking the right boxes and writing what they wanted to read.

Day three – We went to the bank early to avoid the heat and queues. We could pay by cash or visa. Paying by visa meant they took the fee and simply swiped the card for the buffer (the buffer being an amount to cover damages you may cause to the locks) but, didn't actually take the buffer unless you caused damage. Paying by cash meant you paid the buffer upfront and had to wait many weeks for reimbursement. After paying all this, we reached the end of the yellow brick road, allowing us to call the "wizard" after 6 pm each day to try to acquire the elusive and much sought after "go through" date.

Satisfied and a little smug that we had already organised our line-handlers in the form of family, we were a little deflated to find out we needed yet another person. My dad and Colin had flown in from the UK and Australia respectively after harassing us for a year to ensure their place on board for the great event.

Squished on board with three large men, I was a little thrown to hear I had another person to cater for. Four line-handlers were required, plus the helmsman. Finding helping hands could become tricky. In an ideal world, you line-handled for a boat and they returned the favour. However, the words 'ideal' and 'boats' just don't go in the same sentence. It fell down when the first boat reached the Pacific, and the relatively safe city of Balboa and the crew shied at the thought of returning to crime riddled Colon to return the line-handling favour.

Desirable and not so desirable backpackers milled around looking for a free ride through (although some wanted to be paid!). Taxi drivers with dollars ringing in their eyes would spiel a story how pilots had been known to leave a boat if backpackers were part of the crew. What they did not realise was that we were all backpackers of a sorts, living on our wits, just travelling with our home afloat, instead of on our backs. Employing the taxi drivers was an option, which at fifty-five American dollars per day each was exactly what they were trying to achieve. We had seen these guys in action. Even though they caused no major problems, their attention span was that of a bored gnat. The day before our departure we found Michael, a backpacker. A great find for us: he was helpful, friendly, ready to muck in, and all around good company.

You had to feed your line-handlers for the duration, give them a bed for the night (if required), and the fare back to wherever you departed from, which was usually Colon. Most cruisers asked line-handlers to bring their own bedding (where possible) to cut down on the deluge of laundry after the event.

We learned that food forethought, preparation, and paper plates would save our sanity. With six hungry crewmembers on board, timing was of the essence. Once our pilot arrived, we fed him. Having a meal prepared that simply needed re-heating for the rest of the crew was imperative. They had to wait until we had completed the first three locks to be fed – I was line-handler, cook, and washer all rolled into one. Nibble items kept vocal and tummy grumbles at bay. Heading south, like us, most boats departed in the evening, providing a comfy day-and-a-half to complete the journey. Heading north, we heard that you had to complete the entire journey in one day. This was where parts of the speed battle slotted into place and the eight knot game could be won or lost.

Dad, Noel, and I encountered our first experience of locking through on board *Theta* with our friends Barry and Judy. It was far less stressful when it was not your boat, and it was also fun if you were lucky enough to like the people you line-handled for.

Right then, we could dispel the rumour that you had to be big, strong, and tough to line-handle! For me, on our boat, being the prime caterer and finding out how to balance constantly feeding the masses, while still being part of the line-handler team was crucial for my enjoyment. We were glad that we locked through with another boat first to reduce the stress of the unknown when on *Mariah*.

We needed 4 x 36 metre lines void of knots and fraying. The lines had to be thirty millimetres in diameter with a metre long, spliced loop at one end. You could hire these from the taxi drivers for fifteen American dollars each. Some boats were asked for a fifty dollar bond, and some were not. We obviously looked a bit dodgy and warily handed over the fifty dollar deposit. For fenders you hired tyres for three dollars each; five tyres for each side, for a ten to fifteen-metre boat, was ample. Hiring the ropes and fenders was a hassle free bargain. Once we reached Balboa, the ropes were collected from shore, the deposit returned, and the tyres were collected from your boat (for an extra one dollar per tyre).

We were offered four choices of how we wanted to lock through. We could choose three. These were our preference only; our pilot had the final say on the day. (1) Rafting up with one or two other boats and tying in the middle of the lock. (2) Going alone and tying to the side of the lock, against the wall. (3) Going alone in the middle and (4) Going alongside a tug. The least favourite was against the wall. When going up, the turbulence could spin our boat, causing damage to the timber against the concrete wall. But, it all depended on what boats were locking through with you.

Between line-handling on another boat, organising our line-handlers and equipment, and ferrying water, I felt as though I was running in four directions at once and wanted to haul up the white flag. Instead, I duly called the scheduler every other day, or when instructed. Almost everybody got bumped, we heard of only one boat bumped forward by a day (only after being bumped back). You could even get bumped on the day you were going. The minimum wait was a week; there were additional options to hand over cosmic amounts of cash to speed things up, but we were more likely to pluck stars from the sky.

The compound at Colon Marina had a café/restaurant. Cheap eats were available in an air-conditioned, fly-free seated area. Burgers became a daily way to survive, grabbing the most convenient, cheap, quick meal as we galloped through the compound on our next mission. The added benefit of a hit of sodium, carbs and salt helped keep us at full speed, ensuring we fulfilled the day's projects. We gave no thought of hardening arteries and bulging fat tanks and the intolerable levels of adrenaline killing heart cells left right and centre – our laid back life had long gone over the horizon – youthful heart failure, *de rigueur*.

For ten days, we sailed along the stressful stream of organising our transit, preparing the team, and then we were finally on our way. We were told that between 5 pm and 6 pm the pilot would jump on board. We hauled up our anchor at 3 pm in preparation, and thank goodness we did. The tangle weave of our two anchor chains was incredible (we had left *Mariah* to lock through with *Theta* and had wanted the added insurance of two anchors out). It took us over two hours to sort out the mess and haul up both anchors. By then we were frustrated, tired, and irritable – and we hadn't even started!

At 5 pm, our pilot jumped on board. Thoughtfully, he had already eaten, but managed to shove a few chocolate muffins down his throat. Heading south, we puttered for about three miles while I ensured the crew/line-handlers were "nibble-satisfied." We then had to await clearance. The first three locks were in succession, and this was where the turbulence could become fierce as the water was let into the huge concrete bath. Our pilot instructed us to raft to a similar size boat and advised which boat supplied which lines. Once rafted, one boat became the main driver; the pilots provided precise and constant direction.

As we entered the first lock, we peered up at the men at the side, swinging ropes. They hurled these ropes at you with startling accuracy: one aft, one fore. On the end of the rope there was a ball of metal, called the monkey's fist. If this hits you, it hurts – take it from me. We organised our line-handlers in teams, fore and aft. Once the line was on board, we came out of cover (from the monkey's fist) and tied the ropes to the loop on our ship's lines that were on board. We were then led into the lock like a dog on a lead. On nearing position, someone somewhere shouted something and this was the signal to feed our lines out, so that the linesmen onshore could loop our lines onto their bollards. Once our lines were affixed to their bollard, it was our job to tighten/release as required. As the first three locks are in quick succession, the shore based line-handlers kept the lines and simply led us through.

The paperwork clearly stated that if we were delayed through a fault of the canal officials, they would bear the costs. But, there was a shrewdly inserted clause stating that if you could not do the declared speeds (eight knots) and caused a delay, an additional four-hundred-and-forty dollars would be chargeable. This could have been a problem if we were heading north, having to complete the whole canal in one day. Fortunately, with the grace of two days heading south, we had no need to push our engine hard.

After the third lock, we put all our faith in our pilot and he guided us to the mooring buoys. The stretch of water was unmarked, making the last part a little scary in the dark. There were two large mooring buoys to tie to. The buoys were so huge you could stand on them to tie your lines. Several boats shared the buoys. By now we were all hot and sticky and heady with the excitement of being on top of a hill in Panama! The fresh water beckoned, and even though it was 9 pm we all donned cossies and dove into the cool, refreshing water. The surplus of fresh water was such a treat after constant, careful water management on board. The following morning, while sipping our steaming cups of tea, we watched the crew of a French boat enjoy a swim. As dawn grazed the sky a small boat with a large man holding an even a larger gun headed towards the swimmers.

'I say,' someone said in their best British accent, 'they're going to shoot the French!' I couldn't help but notice the crowds gathering. The gun stayed prone, but the warning was clear to us all: you must not swim. If you do it was at your own risk.

'There are many crocodiles here,' came the stern statement. This caused more than a few shudders on board *Mariah*.

As dawn gathered momentum, we were ready to leave. Our first mistake was to untie from the mooring in readiness for our pilot. Each member of our crew received a severe reprimand for releasing our lines just moments before the pilot stepped on board. This was not a good start. After our pilot had eaten a fully cooked breakfast, had a snooze, and admitted that he had not slept the previous night, we turned our dower, scowling faces to more cheerful, welcoming smiles. Atop of the hill, before our final three locks, we enjoyed thirty miles of puttering through glistening lakes enclosed within vivid fauna and well-marked channels. Smaller boats were guided through the Banana Cut, a slightly quicker route avoiding part of the larger channel that was for the bigger ships. The last three locks were easy, gently easing us down.

As we puttered into the last lock, the monkey fist dodging was over and the inviting Pacific Ocean glimmered below. Nostalgia and emotion mixed like bubbling wakes. It had been more than five years since we had glided through this great ocean. *Mariah* hummed along with the sense of impending adventure. We were on our last leg back to Australia. Urgently, we were snapped out of our reverie; the last lock had a powerful push of water coming through and lines had to be affixed promptly, so daydreaming and reminiscing had to wait.

Finally, the mighty doors of the last lock creaked open and freed the placid boats and fidgety crew into the channel. We collected a mooring. The adrenaline come-down after completing the locks left us weary and wanting just to tie up safely. We felt the need to stop, and consume inordinate amounts of alcohol, which we did the following day.

Chattering cruisers filled the bar. A heady mix of fatigue, relief, and tangible excitement stirred through the tables. Burgers and beer were too readily available: the crew on *Mariah* clean forgot the quantity of starch we had consumed pre-canal and craved more fuel to enable us to tell others of our canal crossing and patiently listen to their experience. Audible sighs and clinking of glasses welcomed the vivid sunset across the resting boats, swinging peacefully on moorings. We sat contentedly and wondered what the hell all the fuss and worry was about.

Farewells were upon us again too quickly, and my dad and Colin flew home, leaving us to tackle the next part of our voyage: the Pacific Ocean.

22

Galapagos

Positioned in the Pacific Ocean, eight hundred nautical miles southwest of Balboa, in Panama, the Galapagos islands were a bugger to get to with cross-currents and perpetual head winds. Previous circumnavigating friends extolled fascinating Galapagos stories, but neglected to warn us of the near impossible journey. Discussing the trip with present day sailing buddies, the odd tut and many sidewards glances were thrown in our direction when we vocalised our opinion of an arduous journey ahead.

'It's only fifteen knots of head winds,' they said.

'We're going back to Panama!' Noel announced over the radio on our third day out from Panama. Try as we might, we could only make way towards Hawaii or Colombia. I suggested we head straight to French Polynesia. I didn't want to head back, besides the hurricane strength winds that were heading for Panama sort of put me off. After six hours of sailing nowhere and dozens of frustrating sail changes, we felt defeated and foolish.

'How on earth do people get there; do we have any idea what we're doing?' exclaimed Noel through gritted teeth, while I took comfort in chocolate.

With one last-ditch attempt, we sailed due west during the day and motored due south during the lesser winds at night. Eventually, we gained miles in the right direction. Our cruising buddies had plenty to say about the arduous journey into fifteen knot winds, which is twenty knots apparent.

Approaching the anchorage at Wreck Bay (aka Bahia Baquerizo Moreno) on the southwest tip of Isla San Cristóbal, in Galapagos, a huge monolith sentry stood guard, seemingly vetting all those who pass with a fixed expression of warning to respect the protected, precious land. Our night time entrance was as smooth as silken water. The dazzling shore lights that blinded our approach shattered our visions of a two-hut town. In the blanched, moonless night, Wreck Bay looked like a thriving metropolis. But, as dawn grazed the sinister darkness, the Pacific gem was unveiled. The tranquil town was devoid of harassing sales men and offensive, blaring music. It was a neat size, easy to circumnavigate on our salt dried feet. Reasonably priced laundries, mechanics, hardware, DVD/video shops, and small, practically stocked supermarkets lined the clean, dry streets.

Checking in was expensive, but easy. The Immigration office came first, with an exchange of paperwork plus fifteen American dollars per person from our wallets to theirs; then we were free to stroll five minutes down the road to the marine office. Paperwork took a few minutes longer here. But, the wad of cash we extracted from our thinning wallet gave cause for wanting a cigarette (and I don't smoke). A ten tonne boat could expect to pay about one-hundred-and-five dollars. The officials selected some boats to receive their zarpe (exit papers) when they checked in. Clearly, we looked a bit dodgy and they held ours until we graced them with our presence at a later date. Acquiring the zarpe was quick and painless.

The eight days bumping and grinding into head winds had left us feeling like we deserved a treat. *Mariah* and crew did not go to weather. Well, not without copious whinging. So, a big, fat burger to harden the arteries and coffee for topping up caffeine levels were high on our list of priorities. Indigestion became imminent on sight of our fifteen dollar bill. Our soggy, salt ridden brains finally twigged that we should have avoided the waterfront, touristy cafes and perused the back streets to sample local fare.

We stumbled upon many funky food huts, cafes, and restaurants that served the locals. Being simple folk we like a simple life and our favourite cafes and restaurants were those void of menus containing too many choices. A cool surrounding, a warm smile, and three courses, including fresh fruit drinks, all for two-to-three dollars each! Soup, fish with rice and salad, and fresh fruit dessert for a price we couldn't buy a jar of vegemite for meant daily outings for eats. We justified our good life with rationalising statements of, 'We're saving our non-perishable foods for crossing the Pacific.'

Getting ashore was novel. Our dinghy stayed prone on deck. A wave, shout, or beep to cruising taxis that buzzed around the anchorage, and fifty cents (per person) later we could step ashore (one dollar per person after dark). It was not advisable to use your own dinghy; sea lions are incredibly nosey and love checking out toys that are in the shape of dinghies. Those cruisers who tied their dinghies off the back of their sterns soon hauled them back on deck. The sea lions selected a few dinghies to play in, some to sleep in, and others to use as a toilet! Either way you certainly knew if they had paid you a visit, their eau d'fish aroma was punchy enough to curl your nose hairs.

The anchorage offered plenty of room with good holding, but had way too many tourist boats. During the season we were there, the tourist quantity was heightened as, for a temporary measure, all international flights were landing about five boat lengths from our bow – good for business on Cristóbal, not so good for us. Endless square vessels crammed with splintering benches with pale tourist bottoms parked a-top and raced past, creating disturbing wakes. Our angry waving, indicating a reduction of speed, was met with wide grinning faces and gleeful waves.

Amid the calm, serene town an industrious New Zealander had joined forces with a beautiful local lass and created an enviable couple and a good business. As Tim's first language was English, organising tailored tours was a breeze, especially for those of us who struggled with the language. Tim arranged an amazing tour, the part with the sea lions became the most magnificent event of our trip.

An adolescent laugh resonated through the smooth, grey rocks. As another bubble of giggles reached my throat and burst into the air, I realised the childish noise was coming from me.

Mimicking the sea lions, fins and arms aside, while staying still and quiet, allowed a brief trust to develop. Their sleek, glistening bodies glided slowly towards me until our noses almost touched. I stared into innocent, watery brown eyes; they stared back, deep into my eyes, which were wide and snorkel distorted. A timeless moment: the world stopped, and I became one with nature. I slowed my breathing. The liquid chocolate eyes did not reveal what was coming. Suddenly, my smooth, sneaky friend blew a burst of bubbles right into my startled face and darted off, no doubt doing a sea lion snigger.

We played this game for hours. Hypothermia started threatening my bones, but I was too distracted, tickling another slippery friend under his chin. My fingers tingled with the touch of bristly whiskers and skin that had a soft firmness, like a baby's thigh. Throughout the six years of sailing from Sydney, the sea lions at Galapagos was our most thrilling experience. Turtles, sharks, and vivid coral fish flowed to and fro in the currents, while we pointed and stared. Rough skinned iguanas sunbathed alongside a carpet of sea lions on the pristine beach; the languid lions belched loudly and chased us away when we wandered too close.

We were stocked up for the Pacific Ocean crossing, we only needed to pick up fresh items. We couldn't help ourselves, though, when we visited the supermarket and mysteriously tinned food appeared in our basket. Echoes of advice reverberated around my salt sticky head. 'Canned food goes so quickly, and it's a long way...'

'Oh, well, better get some more, just in case.'

In remote locations, it was a good idea to check the sell by dates – if the dust and cobwebs didn't give the game away, the date would. The trick to gaining the freshest fruit and vegetables available was to make a show of squeezing, smelling, and pulling faces at the products that were in need of Viagra, the odd shake of the head helped and before long the real fresh stuff would magically appear from behind the counter.

With *Mariah* almost ready to go, we did some exploring. Allow me to take you back in time to two hundred years ago. Imagine tough, stout, hairy whalers gliding into a deserted bay on their hard working vessels; imagine them rowing ashore, firmly clutching their scrawled notes in order to play postman as the stark arid landscape, the eerie mist-clad volcano, and dozens of large, inquisitive turtles welcomed them into the peaceful, uninhabited bay.

On shore, a medium sized barrel mounted on wooden struts still stands today. The whalers left letters here for their loved ones in the hope that another passing boat would one day collect the mail and send it on. Present day, this tradition was upheld by voyaging sailboats.

We arrived at Post Office Island (aka Isla Santa Maria) at Bahia Del Correo on the northwest tip at sun-down and planned an early explore. At dawn the following day, armed with water, fruit, and sun-block, we stepped ashore, ready for the walk to the "mail room." Ten strides around the corner and we were face to face with the archaic communication post, which sat in modern times. The upright barrel contained plastic bags with efficiently sorted Europe/America/rest of world post cards, all begging to be collected and mailed. Rocks, split timber, and leaves garnished the mailbox with a flourish of boat names, dates, and goodwill notes. It felt like we were partaking in a piece of history that was cloaked in human kindness. Noel and I placed our respective postcards in the barrel (one to the UK and one to Australia); we selected to mail cards to Poland and Japan. It was a great sailing tradition that allowed us to touch base and unite us with our forebears and the readings of seafarers of our youth.

But there was the snag and it was a hum-dooie. Cruisers like us, who boldly put ourselves alongside the long gone whalers, were not allowed to stop here! Only organised tours, that came expressly to see the mailbox, were permitted. During our visit we were simply lucky, most sailboats met the dour warden who turfed them out. This was irony at its best.

The third and final island we visited was moonlike Isla Isabella. The small Bay (Puerto Villamil) on the south-east corner was crowded and littered with nasty shallows. The harsh lava rock and stark surrounds were home to tubby penguins and boobies with the brightest blue feet, adding a splash of colour to the deep brown and black moonlike rock.

This was our last stop before plunging into the great Pacific Ocean with three thousand miles of a lonely expanse of water, sky, and clouds. Where after two days I'd crave a roast chicken dinner, and Noel would feel desperate to hug a tree. Memories of the unique Galapagos experience would carry us along to our next adventure.

23

Swimming with a whale

It was June 2005 and *Mariah* was bulging at the seams; we had to select which cupboards to open, depending on which tack we were on. How she stayed afloat defied logic.

'Mariah II is at 02° 16.400 south and 97° 38.300 west; all's well on board, only 2,500 miles to go.'

We spoke daily to fellow cruisers along our lonely, watery passage. From Galapagos to French Polynesia (The Marquesas group of islands) we had 2,914 nautical miles to traverse. Trade winds were in full force, currents in our favour, and despite our full load, we were are scooting along nicely.

We left the magnificent Galapagos Islands within twenty-four hours of three other boats, all larger and faster than us. Twice daily, we talked to each other on the radio, swapping positions in case the unthinkable happened. Our adventurous Turkish friend, Alim, on board *My Chance* with his beautiful wife, Kian, invented a game to make the long journey a little more interesting.

'From Galapagos to Fatu Hiva (our Marquesas island destination), *guess how long it will take you and we will see who has the closest guess when we arrive,'* announced Alim one evening. Tactics and calculations were heard buzzing over the waves that night.

'Mariah II chooses twenty days and six hours,' we predicted, but the radio stayed silent. Our friends were a little concerned that our brains were finally completely salt incrusted. We had chosen the shortest time and we were the slowest boat!

'We have chosen that time,' I revealed, 'as it means we arrive in time to celebrate our wedding anniversary.' Now that re-confirmed our daftness to the rest of the fleet.

As the days swept by surprisingly fast, we were enjoying one of our best sails. Conditions were perfect for *Mariah*, and with our routine swiftly underway, we relished the solitude.

We were completely in tune with *Mariah*, so new sounds within our home were obvious. 'Hasty Tasties' (tin cans) wriggled loose and created a drum beat with a thriving echo, stopping sleep. But it was comforting to snuggle in a comfy bunk and listen to the occasional patter of rain on deck, the ocean rushing alongside the boat, and the creaking lines.

As we ate through the miles, accompanied with the orchestral music of sailing, each day the four boats in competition disclosed their 'miles to go' on the radio. It was not many days before it was noted that *Mariah* was doing the most miles per day!

Larger sails were dug out deep from our competitors' lockers and, new sail rigs were set up, tried, and tested as the competition heated up. Astonishingly, *Mariah* continued to romp in the lead as she pushed through the ocean and spat it out behind in a white, hissing plume.

The broad shimmering band of the Pacific Ocean was saturated with rich blue, almost purple colour. Low, blue grey clouds gave way to fuzzy yellows along the horizon. The sun glided beneath the rim of the world each day, turning the sea into a thick, rich molten, reflecting the pattern from heaven. We were a minute particle upon the eternity of ocean and sky, that particle being our home and world. Birds scooped a flight path around the sails, catching air currents. We watched the moon rise lazily across the sky to her peak, lighting a silver path just for us; we marvelled in the waxing and then waning moon. Bright and bold Sirius became my neat shot of pre-dawn adrenaline, bolting me from daydreaming as it curved across the black canvas.

The largest uninhabited section of the Pacific Ocean took us exactly three weeks to cross. *Mariah's* prowess and what we had learned over our six years sailing held us all in good stead. We were a great team. Days were spent sitting comfortably at seven knots; so stable was *Mariah* that we could walk around the boat unassisted. This was our finest sail and our longest. Still, sighting the tall, green peaks of the Marquesas Islands was not only breathtaking, but a magnificent sight and a forest-green balm to our sea-blue tainted eyes.

We all arrived at different times. Alas, we missed our anniversary deadline, but only by one day. We were the first into port, but we didn't win the competition. *My Chance* staked that claim. For us, we won a better accolade – we traversed the great Pacific Ocean in the quickest time. We left the New Zealanders numb, the Americans amazed, and *My Chance* delighted for us.

With good cheer, we approached our first anchorage, The Bay of Virgins at Fatu Hiva Island; the enormous green cliffs struck high, tall, and proud into the sky where clouds tore across their peaks. The verdant valley that opened in front of us was an ideal backdrop for snarling dinosaurs. The scenery was breathtaking, but the wind too strong, funnelling through the glorious valley to hit the boats at anchor and cause sleepless nights. In a torrent of a powerful katabatic land breeze (where the wind falls down huge cliffs, gathering momentum to hit us), we anchored at the Marquesas Islands. Eager to explore but too tired after twenty-one days at sea, we both tried to sleep. The elation of completing the mammoth trip was soon wearing off when we spent the next five nights awake, keeping anchor watch within relentless howling winds.

Tears filled my eyes, and a small gasp escaped from my down-turned lips. Noel turned to me, his face full of concern. As I trolled through the many email messages, I reached the news from home. The horror of the London bombings touched our hearts. For us, the news was a week old. We had been out of touch, but that did not lessen the pain, anger, and horror. The exciting news of London hosting the 2012 Olympics was marred. It all made up to an overwhelming dose of homesickness and a longing to be with my family and helping those in need.

My mum lightened the heavy news with amusing snippets about my nieces' and nephews' antics and how they were finding their way in this beautiful, scary world. We were heading to Australia, away from my immediate family.

Noel had been away from his family for a long time, so it was time to reacquaint ourselves with our antipodean folk. It was with surprised joy we received an email from Noel's daughter, Mel.

'I'm coming to see you,' it said.

We were so excited; we had been encouraging her to visit for years.

Meanwhile, we arranged a place to meet. Once again we were planning a thousand mile trip, hoping the weather would allow us to arrive in time. Tahiti on 23 July was our rendezvous. Noel was looking forward to spending time with his daughter; I couldn't wait to share our home with another woman and friend.

Before we prepared for the exciting visit at Tahiti, we explored the island of Nuku Hiva. Anchored in Daniel's Bay, sweet scents idly drifted through the hatch into our cosy v-berth, where I was swaddled in comforting blankets listening to the rain plopping on deck. The rain disturbed the perfume of the land, and the short squall carried the sweeter smell into our watery home. It was a fresh, light scent that encouraged me to peel myself up and prepare for exploration. We left *Mariah* in her placid anchorage and headed off with cruising friends on a hike into the hills to seek out the third largest waterfall in the world.

A six-hour return trip left our limbs tired but our minds twirling with the harsh sting of cold fresh water and pummelled brains beneath the cascading waterfall. The velvet carpet of green surrounding the hidden paradise was worth the exhausting trek.

We convinced our weary limbs to haul anchor and leave that day, as we had to reach Pape'ete soon and before we did we wanted to explore the Tuamotu group of islands

As we sailed for five days through continual squalls, thoughts of plans for when we arrived back in Australia plagued our minds. We tried to stow the anxious feelings and made the effort to enjoy our trip, new places, faces, and our hard earned freedom. After all, none of us know what is lurking around the next corner during our own journey of life.

After many lengthy sails, a five-day trip was a breeze. We were well versed in the necessary preparation. We could both handle every aspect of the boat. I could reflect on how far I had come. When we purchased *Mariah*, I barely knew the front end of the boat from the back end of the boat. Now I could maintain the engine, navigate, haul and reef sails appropriately, use all the equipment on board, and handle the boat at sea and during tight manoeuvres. The daunting days of a new culture, husband, and nautical world were a long way behind me. Noel and I had become closer; we both acknowledged that during watches our lives were in each other's hands, and this helped create an extremely deep trust. We had learned that we were following and striving for the same thing on board: safety, comfort, and a good life. If we made mistakes and upset that balance, we knew well enough that it was not on purpose – we weren't sabotaging what we had. What we had was incredible: trust without limits, friendship without judgement, complete loyalty, and limitless love.

With all the ease of being seasoned sailors and travellers, we arrived at our next destination, which must have been one of the few places in the world where it was perfectly okay for men and woman of all ages to ogle wiggling, scantily clad bottoms!

The atoll named Ahe is on the northwest of the group of islands known as the Tuomotus. Ahe is a large lagoon where entering at the right time is imperative. We entered at exactly the wrong time. The entrance appeared calm and benign, but once committed to the passageway, the hidden whitecaps and tumultuous waves launched their attack. *Mariah's* Yanmar was pushed to the red line and, wide-eyed, we powered our way through. The only damage being *Mariah's* innards becoming invaded with sticky salt water and an adrenaline hit that was so hard it felt like running head first into a brick wall. With our racing hearts trying to calm, we puttered along towards the other boats and were mightily relieved to find a superb anchorage and small town just three boat lengths away.

We dragged our salty, damp bodies to shore that evening. We were tired after a lively, wet, and windy five day sail, but we wanted to experience the local festival. In the middle of the tiny town, a stage was set in the sandy streets and people gathered to watch the spectacle. Stunning, chocolate skinned girls clad in vivid sarongs, wiggled their hips at incredible speed to the rhythm of thumping drums and cheering praise.

The local dancing was punctuated with a little modern rock. The cool air, soft sand, and welcoming locals were all rich ingredients for a glorious night. Small children roamed freely, safe within the small community; a three-year-old girl captured Noel's heart. He shared his kebab and received a toothy smile. The same girl snared my heart the following morning as we quietly encroached upon the locals' Sunday morning church service. The majestic, proud women that sat behind us in their flowery Sunday best sang deep, beautiful harmonies that left us feeling enlightened and peaceful. The small neighbourhood accepted us into their community.

After four days of catching up with sleep, interspersed with fixing our worn anchor winch and attending to writing obligations, we set sail for Pape'ete in Tahiti. Noel's daughter, Mel would meet us there in four days, but first we had a two-day sail to reach our next escapade.

Captain Cook, Bligh, Robert Louis Stevenson, *Treasure Island*, and the Parry's: what's the common thread? Tahiti. In the 18th century, Cook was sent to Tahiti to study Venus, and Bligh had sailed into the striking shores. Robert Louis Stevenson's father designed the lighthouse that proudly sits on Venus Point, while Mr. Stevenson junior wrote the inspiring stories of *Treasure Island*. The Parry's? Well, the Parry's circumnavigated the island in 2005.

We arrived into Pape'ete the same day as Mel arrived via air from Ayers Rock. We were nonchalant about the timing, only because we had not considered that marvellous innovation of the date line. After negotiating low flying aircraft, we chose the most popular anchorage on the west side of the island, south of French Polynesia's Capital. The sea was as clear as spring water and welcomed us into a plethora of tightly packed boats, all owners hoping they swung in unison. Supermarkets were just a short stroll away, and the dusty, dirty city just a twenty-minute, bone-shaking bus ride.

A little tired of conversations on amps, torques, and bronze brushes, I was excited at the prospect of another woman being on board. I planned to get in depth about clothes, hair, and, well, anything but boats. Noel and Mel had a lot of time to make-up; we were both looking forward to playing host to our long awaited guest.

It wasn't until we were trawling through our emails that we came across a brief note from Mel.

'I arrive on 21 July, not 22nd!'

Four hours later, damp, dishevelled sailors and the disturbing disorder of *Mariah's* innards met Mel.

We'd been on board for over seven years; we now had the confidence to make our own obscure decisions and not follow the crowd.

'Who, in their right mind, heads east across the Pacific at this latitude?' Friends' pitiful smiles sent us off, confirming that the crew on board *Mariah* was doing "their thing" again.

With triplicate sighs of relief, we hauled anchor and watched the maelstrom of Pape'ete disappear over the smoggy horizon. Whose idea it was to circumnavigate Tahiti depended on conditions. When we hit messy, restless seas it seemed to be my decision. When we cleared the agitated water and witnessed the exquisite, barely explored shores of the south east of the island, Noel claimed the kudos.

Tucked between Nui and Iti (big part of island and little part), Port Phaeton was a peaceful sanctuary. Weaving through vibrant, intimidating coral reefs, we were thankful of the meticulous buoy system that guided us safely through. Rewards of short, sharp mountains striking through clouds, excellent protection and good holding was offered in the roomy bay. Even the muddy water and skin nipping critters didn't tarnish the cool swim I relished each day. The charming bay had a small marina with haul-out facilities and a safe dinghy landing at a locals' house; he was happy for dinghies to tether in his garden. The compact, amiable town offered supermarkets, post office, Internet, and hardware stores. The extortionate prices of Pape'ete were toned down to simply exorbitant here. Silent noise stroked *Mariah* and caressed our ears in chorus with the pure breeze that lacked the city's pungent vapour.

'This was a good idea of mine,' Noel muttered into his hard-earned sundowner.

In good old *Mariah II* fashion, we left a safe, serene harbour to quell our voyaging thirst. The target? Thirty-two miles to Baie De Tautira – the day black, the sea lumpy, and the wind particularly difficult, whacking us hard on the nose. We heard moans and whimpers from below as Mel tried to cope with the esoteric world of a live boat pummelled by grumpy seas.

'This was a dumb idea,' stated Noel, staring pointedly at me.

As the winds hugged the jagged mountains, *Mariah* became a perpetual weathercock and words such as retreat, defeat, and *blurrrrrrhhh* were heard whistling across our soggy decks. As we started to discuss our flight back, Mother Nature took pity and smoothed the waters, allowing the sails to fill with a beam-reach.

The entrance was wide and deep, permitting *Mariah* and her crew, along with the grey cloud that decided to umbrella us for the entire day, to putter slowly in without much ado. Tautira, on the northeast of Tahiti Iti, had a petite village with a well provisioned shop where prices shifted into the expensive category, instead of exorbitant. Shy locals were easy going and accommodated our shameful attempts at French. The cleanliness transported us back to Iluka in northern NSW, where freshly painted homes, quaint boulevards, and tropical flowers garnished the welcoming hamlet. Relaxing island music wafted into the shallow anchorage where we were firmly dug in. Dugout canoes were the main mode of transport, while runabouts were for fishing. Reality swam its way back into our tranquil anchorage and hunkering down in the black sand, Mel and I took advantage of running water on shore to catch up with the building laundry.

Dreams are made of tiny, soft sand islands, handsome palm trees, and crystal water. Motunono Island, ten nautical miles from Taurita, sat offshore, inviting cruisers to step onto her dazzling beach. Anchoring a short swim away, in deep water, I snorkelled to shore while Mel and Noel carried lunch and water in the dinghy. Even the two or three other groups of visitors did not upset the equilibrium of the slice of heaven. Sitting beneath idyllic shady palms, we silently absorbed the breathtaking views. The mainland stood high and proud, the green velvets of jagged peaks punctuated the rain clouds that were hurrying home. Heavy cumulonimbus clung to the zeniths and sagged in the troughs, thickening and feeding the abundant plant life. Neighbouring valleys plunged and all but called out to us, inviting for exploration. Staring at the striking panorama, I let my imagination run like a tidal stream. I studied the enchanted crests that were brushed with cloudy whispers of mystical secrets, a thousand years old. The scene was set, like the Scottish Highlands where Braveheart bounds out of the eerie mist on his bold, black stallion.

Departing from our magical lunch site, we travelled north for about six nautical miles, destination Pointe Tefauoa. A consistent reef circumnavigates Tahiti, much of it causing too many shallows to allow a completely protected run. From Motunono Island to Pointe Tefauoa, much of the journey was protected by the glorious reef, but this had its pitfalls. Reaching our proposed anchor site at four in the afternoon, we found the tiny harbour on our charts big enough for Ken and Barbie's boat, but not *Mariah*.

'Don't worry,' our illustrious leader said, 'we have a few hours. Plenty of time to find an alternative.'

For two hours, I scurried about coral chocked lagoons in the dinghy, sounding depths within possible anchor sites. Abundant anchorages of twenty-five metres were scattered along the coast, however, our anchor winch had decided to have a holiday and shallow anchorages were our arm-muscles' preference. Suddenly, the deep blue shallowed to less than a metre with vivid coral shelves; the dinghy's bottom became a little sore and the air somewhat bluer than the water. As dusk hinted at the horizon, much to Mel's horror, we discussed doing an over-nighter to Venus Point. Actually, we would have arrived around eleven at night. Mel's reluctance was backed up with mine. The dinghy survived her ungainly scrapes, but I wasn't prepared to risk the mother ship. With shortening tempers created from fear, we journeyed two miles south to reach the pass (Passe Faatautia) into the ocean. Our charts indicated a possible anchorage near the entrance, the fair weather permitting us the luxury of one last possibility of a night at anchor.

'Come on, Matilda, us girls need to do some sounding.'

Matilda had replaced our home built dinghy PJ, and she was earning her keep. The worn dinghy and my weary body cautiously puttered into the small, inviting bay near Teruaiti, and my hopes were raised as I sounded seven to twelve metres of depth. There was also enough swing room between the treacherous coral; the miserable crew on board *Mariah* morphed into happy bunnies.

After a peaceful night, we awoke to the grandeur of verdant valleys and statuesque peaks where a cascading waterfall plunged down shiny rocks like Rapunzel's lavish hair. By a shear fluke, it was Sunday, and we traipsed in the direction of the fresh falling water. Slightly smug at the deserted area and a little soggy at the sucking mud, we reached the gushing hum of the breath-snatching, cool water. Childish splashing and giggling soaked up the morning, and then our cool bodies hot-footed it back to *Mariah;* we didn't want to risk our luck in our unprotected anchorage.

As we stood on Venus Point in the footsteps of our heroes, we tried to envision what they saw. The scattered houses and thundering roads mimicked around the world, in every town near a large city would not have been here. Instead, the verdant splendour that carpets the mountains would have reached the shores, stopping short at the black beaches. The twenty-two nautical mile journey to Venus Point was hot and still. *Mariah's* Yanmar pushed her through the smooth water to the famous landmark. We heard a family's fun on the raven beaches, and in the transparent water we watched them splash about. Happy laughter, peaceful snorkelling, and safe children encompassed the sunny scene. The town was busy, small, and dirty. One of the highlights included a tourist trip to the leper colony – we decided to pass on that one. We tested the perfect water temperature many times during our three-day stay. The soft breeze cooled the boat and Venus Point sheltered us from any fetch. The searching beams of Stevenson's lighthouse accompanied the still, black nights, while Bligh and Cook's landing went unmentioned.

Time ticked on. Mel had one week left, and we wanted to spend four days at Moorea, Tahiti's neighbouring island. First, we needed gas (propane), water, and our winch repaired. A board meeting of captain, guest, and scapegoat (me!) was promptly organised with ample refreshments. As the sun tickled the horizon and offered the glorious gifts of shifting yellows and burnt orange, point one on the agenda was broached. Where to go next? A) To our original anchorage near Marina Taina, B) Moorea, or C) Try for an anchorage north of Pape'ete. We chose option C because it was somewhere different and had a short walking distance to town, which was located near the *mechanique* that had fixed the anchor winch once and should damn well do it again! Point (2) on the agenda was then tackled: red or white wine?

Five miles west, we reached the main fishing port of Tahiti. The proud, professionally maintained fishing fleet lined up against industrial wharfs and we puttered around for an hour, indecisive at where to anchor within the deep port. Near a thinning hedge on shore, a seven-metre depth was located. At the edge of the channel, we parked *Mariah* and felt rather chuffed at our pioneering discoveries. Gas refills were a short dinghy ride away (as was diesel). The *mechanique* was two boat lengths from shore and water was easily available at the small, local marina. The town was a ten-minute walk away, avoiding the bone shaking bus rides. If you ignored the layer of scum floating on the water and the perpetual chemical smell, the anchorage was perfect! Cautiously leaving one body on the boat each time we tackled jobs ashore, we were relieved to be ignored. Out of the way of the surprisingly sparse traffic, no one cared that we had anchored in the main port, and we took advantage of having all the things we required nearby.

We planned to leave the follow day for Moorea, as the winch was repaired. We vowed to remember Tahiti's magic, her enchanted valleys, her plethora of facilities, her superb anchor sites, and her kind people. But mostly, knowing that we graced the same shores of our heroes left a stimulating tingle that was sweetly shrouded with respect.

For Mel's last week on board, we explored Moorea. A safe, protected anchorage and one of the most stunning: fertile lands rendered peaceful with crystal clear water – many contented sighs wafted across the placid bay. That was until we had our second major encounter with a whale.

Facing another day in paradise, friends collected us from Mariah for a trip to splash around with the friendly stingrays. Casting off, consumed in cruisers babble, we drifted for a few minutes, all vying for our say. Until the words, 'There's a whale heading our way,' stopped the gaggle of conversations.

As the dark, sinister shadow came closer, we could clearly see the monster's tail propel his bulk through the water at an alarming speed. The three metre inflatable dinghy was overflowing with silence. The five passengers, of which I was one, sat still, stunned into silence. The thump in my chest and the squeeze I felt in my eyes as they tried to pop out stirred the silence; looking around, I noted that my companions mirrored these symptoms. The humpback whale had us in his sights, and there was nothing we could do.

The ominous silhouette moved towards us with speeding purpose. Some of us stood, some stayed frozen on bottoms. With no wave, wake, or drama the baby humpback slid beneath our grey dinghy, and there he stayed.

'He's hurt; he's a baby,' the tourist boat skipper called to us as we drifted past. We were all perplexed as to why a whale would swim into a narrow, windy channel (following the markers no less) and swim under our dinghy.

'I hope he's friendly,' I said.

The statuesque mountains paled into insignificance as we watched, helpless, while the magnificent humpback sought sanctuary beneath us.

The seventeen foot long blue/black humpback hovered sedately, seemingly content to let us drift above him. One of us reached to touch his soft, smooth skin, but did not linger. We knew we should not be this close, let alone touch him. But what could we do? We studied the tubby baby, chunks of fatty flesh hung across his solid body, possibly score marks from outboard motors, but he obviously felt safe under our shadow.

'We're drifting into shallow water, and I can't start the outboard with the whale there,' stated Thor (the elected pilot), a little too coolly for my liking.

As the men started to paddle with those ridiculous small oars that inflatable boat builders uselessly provide, we gently bumped with the whale, the shallower water brought us closer together. Our friendly giant refused to come out from his handkerchief safety cover.

'He's starting to panic,' someone called out. It may have been me.

The whale, in his comfort zone, did not notice the water lose its depth. For us, our awareness of our surroundings was reaching red alert, even through our state of awe. The athletic men struggled bravely, but they could not out row a whale! Suddenly, our gentle, giant friend flipped his hefty, proud tail and elasticised his body, arching his solid back, doing that marvellous whale dance we have all seen on TV to ease his bulk back to deeper water. The fact that he had a rubber ducky on his back with five fearful passengers hanging on for dear life, didn't seem to bother him.

'Hang on,' someone else called as panicking faces searched for the most stable part of the bucking dinghy. The comparatively small boat rose up out of the water and fell, balancing on the whale's curving back; a dip with our expensive camera became inevitable, as I tried to work out how to keep the pricey equipment above my head and dry. Sharp, unforgiving coral loomed nearer and the seriousness of the moment started banging around our heads in rhythm with the rocking dinghy. Worry lines carved patterns across the crews' tense faces.

Finally, the whale moved us all into deeper water, and I remembered to breath. We all searched for answers to what we could have done to avoid the situation. Luckily, we all survived unscathed, just losing a few thousand heartbeats each. For no rhyme or reason, the whale moved havens and wallowed under another dinghy that had helplessly stood by in the commotion.

Free of our clingy mate, we took the opportunity to race back to our mother ships and grab our snorkel gear. Noel, Thor, and I wanted to experience his company in his world; besides, we thought there must be someone we could call to get him help. Perhaps if we saw how fit he was or how hurt, it would help.

Speedily donning our masks and with our heart's thumping in our throats, we jumped into the water and slowly paddled up to the big guy. He was calm under the dinghy. His deep, chocolate, sad eyes watched us approach; we quietly allowed him to get used to us being nearby, unthreatening, before swimming closer. Gradually, I inched to his left side and just hovered in unison with his massive bulk. My wide eyes were watchful of his huge fins that kept him balanced. Tears of gratitude stung my eyes. He was simply beautiful. To me, his wounds looked superficial, like they were already healing. He was quite fat, and apart from scars, I would have said he was pretty healthy, though I am no marine vet.

We did not linger and retreated after just a few precious moments. A repeat of shallows and panicking conversation started up again, and we voiced our warnings to the other dinghy. They managed to escape, carefully turning on their outboard, so as to not cause the soft skin more damage. Cold and elated, we returned to our boats. We relished in the incredible events of the last hour, but wondered how we could help the baby find his mum.

After a hot shower and even hotter drinks, we peered outside at a small dive boat that anchored right by us. Climbing on deck to fend off and figure out just why they felt they had to be so close, we noticed the whale right by *Mariah*. On board the dive boat, a diver jumped in with the whale, grasping bulky photographic equipment. Urgently, he snapped off film and a bright flash frightened our gentle friend. He sought haven under our hull, and I hoped our small home offered the big guy a bit of protection, but another flash exploded in the water and the whale panicked. With a huge flip of his immense tail, he propelled his bulk under our bow where he promptly snagged himself between our two bridled snubbers that attached to the anchor chain. He started thrashing in his confined space, and I could almost taste his fear as he became further entangled and trapped. For about two seconds, which felt longer, I watched, horrified. He thrashed to port and without conscious thought, I took the opportunity to release the slackened starboard rope. Our giant friend swam away like a bullet. Awe and sadness sat in our boat. The gift of swimming with this glorious mammal was unforgettable. We hoped he was strong enough to survive and find his mum along the way.

The following day, as friends approached Moorea, three adult whales were spotted together with a baby. The scars matched descriptions of the whale we'd seen, so we were sure that our friend found his mum. That's our hope anyway.

We bade farewell to Mel and the small life in her tummy that would be called Matilda Jade at birth – which she had revealed to us during her stay. With a new life in our thoughts, the marvels of nature, and another parting, we left Moorea. Huahine was our next destination.

For five days, anchored within a quiet bay at Huahine, we enjoyed the solitude and caught up with paint jobs on *Mariah*. We ventured into the tiny village just twice. During our second visit, Noel's sandals that were left in the dinghy were stolen.

I was relaxed on board and by now it had been about eight years since Martin had left this world. The scars had healed; I could feel them though, and it was around this time that I had a vivid dream I would never forget. It was about Martin telling me that it was time to let him go. I had kept him too long, and it wasn't fair. I was selfish and I couldn't let him go. The second was a dream in which I felt I wasn't entirely asleep throughout its duration. I was in a small, square room. The walls and door painted beige. I was sitting on a plain, brown timber chair. It was covered with black, cracking leather, spilling crumbling foam, facing the door. Martin was in the doorway, holding the round door handle. The door was partly open, partly closed. Without saying anything, he would slowly back away, looking at me, pulling the door closed, separating us. As the door almost shut, I said, 'No, not yet. I'm not ready.' He slowly opened the door and came back into the room, partway. His hand never left the door handle. This scenario repeated several times, his lips never moved, but I could hear him say, so softly, 'It is time to let go, let me go, I want to go.' Eventually, with an empty, dull ache, I accepted and let him close the door. I found myself lying in bed crying – fully awake. The next day, I felt lighter and told Noel the whole story.

'Whether it was real or not, whether it was your body telling you to let him go – it doesn't matter,' he said gently, 'it was time to let him go completely.'

We briefly stopped at Tahaa before heading to Bora Bora. Green, lush, and exquisitely beautiful and expensive, we renamed Bora Bora 'Boring Bora' – only because we couldn't afford the costly activities on offer. Instead, we enjoyed a couple of beers at a bar named Bloody Mary's with good cruising buddies from *My Chance, Theta,* and *Adverse Conditions.* The time at the bar was not all fun and games, as we had important decisions to make, like, could we all fit into the anchorage at Aitutaki? The entrance was quite shallow, at only five feet we knew we'd just make it. *Theta* was too deep, but *My Chance* was a catamaran and *Adverse Conditions* would just follow us all in and hope for the best.

Night watches had become easy. I enjoyed the cool nights and their clarity. I could see other vessels from a long way off, their navigation lights showing their course. But there were still tough nights. We kept watch for the lottery of squalls under the cover of darkness, sometimes watching as the lightning cut the atmosphere in two. As foreboding shadows crept nearer, I could feel the taut anticipation. At times, the clouds seemed to rub out the stars. When doing sail changes at night, the fake stability of the inverted cone of deck lights provided comfort. At dawn, where any horrors would vanish, the air would become so crisp, it felt as though it would shatter with words.

Noel's briny brain had forgotten that goats smell.

'Can you kill the goat a few days earlier?' Noel asked, while I couldn't help but search the sun-dappled garden, hoping the goat was not in ear shot while we discussed its demise.

For twenty-five New Zealand dollars Noel could have a fresh skin (goat skin, that is). He planned to dry it and replace the split skin that was currently on his homemade drum. The fact that our ten metre boat would stink like a fetid abattoir and that goat hair would plague us for eternity was nothing compared to the pink fit customs would have when we sailed back into Australia.

We had made it to Aitutaki, which was described as one of the most heavenly places on Earth and considered one of the most magnificent lagoons in the world. It was comprised of a triangular shaped reef encircling a vivid clear lagoon where three volcanic islands rest within twelve coral atolls. Located directly 140 nautical miles north of Rarotonga (220 kilometres), Aitutaki is one of the southern Cook Islands visited little by sailors. Captain Bligh was the first European to discover Aitutaki in 1789 and locals hold him responsible for introducing the sweet pawpaw fruit that now grows in abundance.

The tiny bay was as calm as being moored on concrete and as beautiful as a perfect pearl. However, puttering into the bay was not for the faint-hearted. A narrow channel, buoyed with sticks on one side only, was shallow and winding. Where the sticks were leaning at an angle, we had to decide whether they had been knocked over, or more usually, it indicated to give the twig a wider berth in the slender channel! If we had a deeper draft than one-and-a-half metres, we would carve our way through the sand. Certainly over one-point-eight metres would mean a probable grounding. Mercifully, the water was clear, which made my position on the bow a whole lot easier.

The first morning within the secluded anchorage at Aitutaki, the angelic voice tickled my ears before my eyes peeled open. The soft baritone that was carried along the gentle breeze met and partnered with my intrigue and gave good reason for me to rise from my cosy pit, a challenging feat for me, most days. With a dishevelled sarong quickly wrapped around my body, I peered out from our cluttered cockpit. The angel stood on a deserted concrete peer, apparently working his smooth lungs just for us. Sadly, he spotted his mesmerised audience and my wing-less cherub strolled away and left the silent air still and my ears empty, yearning for more.

Song entered our lives daily whilst in Aitutaki. Donning our finest wear, the usual grotty cruisers smartened up for the church service. Bursting lungs, boisterous harmony, and energised eurhythmics left us breathless and wanting to applaud the show-like performance.

After our church attendance, the locals provided lunch. A little embarrassed to be guests of honour, we lingered outside the awaiting hall of food, enjoying the view.

'Did you retrieve my dinghy?' a gruff voice questioned one of our neighbouring friends, and they were perplexed.

'That was me, sir,' Noel jumped in, approaching the unsmiling local, not sure what to expect. The man thrust out his hand and Noel did all he could not to duck or jump back.

'Let me shake your hand, sir,' our new friend said. My dinghy is my livelihood, thank you so much. My son,' (said scathingly), 'did not tie the dinghy properly. I have something for you; which is your dinghy? I will leave you a gift.'

Seeking us out and shaking Noel's hand was enough thanks for us, and we carried on with our day, digging into a picnic type lunch with the locals who ensured that all visitors (all four couples on boats) were fed at least twice over before they indulged. About an hour later, as we returned to our dinghy, we found it brimming with pumpkins, several kinds of potatoes, enormous bunches of bananas, and healthy pawpaws. The booty was enjoyed by us all.

Much enjoyment was to be had at every corner. Returning home one star spangled evening, six lightly intoxicated cruisers huddled in a dinghy and, inspired by the welcoming locals, we exercised our own vocal cords. We sang a peculiar ditty, replacing Nagasaki with Aitutaki, *'Back in Aitutaki where the fellas chew tobbacy and the women wicky-wacky-woo...'*

'What do you reckon they wear under their skirts?' I whispered to my buddy, Ann from *Novia*, another sailboat that had joined us.

'I dunno,' she giggled, 'but it had better have good support!'

As the guys strutted their aggressive stuff and the girls glided gracefully to the thud of hypnotising drums I recalled our host's welcoming speech before the local dancing started.

'Kia Orana – may you live long.' She added, 'Enjoy the show and help yourselves.'

'It's only polite to do what the host asks,' I stated, grinning mischievously. The two olive skinned, strapping lads ignored the trickling sweat that coursed down their corrugated abdomens, and I tried to suppress an urge to wipe it away – at least while Noel was looking. They planted soggy kisses on my cheeks and I tried to act demure, not my age, which was too close to twice theirs.

'Thank you, you were great!' they laughed.

Partaking in the "get the blobby tourists dancing after the professional show," I paired up with a lad and copied his moves, totally forgetting that the ladies should be hip swinging with vigour. So, I wasn't sure if they found me hysterical because I danced like a man or that I just couldn't dance – maybe both. Still, the workout, fun, and laughter was well worth the comical show I gave the audience. Post performances of the professionals and the unrefined, the beautiful women and handsome men changed from their vivid dress into western shorts and t-shirts. The clothes morphed them from men to boys, their western dress was drab and a startling difference from their woven headdresses, skirts, and vastly rich costumes.

The welcome into Aitutaki surpassed any we had received throughout our journey. The elegant locals were eloquent, embracing their culture with a proud vigour. The tiny island was protected from the ugly glutton of wealth, as land could only be handed on to family.

The 'Good mornings,' from grinning grans, as they hurtled past us in their fine flowery dresses, inspired us to hire a moped and explore.

Most of the transport on the island was via a small scooter, keeping pollution, noise, and traffic to a soothing minimum. Acquiring a Cook Island bike license for ten American dollars and twenty dollars for the hire was easy. All they wanted was our first names, and we were free to rampage around the eight square kilometres island, which housed a population of just 1600. There really wasn't much to see, but the beauty of Maunga Pu, the highest point of the island, offered a fantastic three-hundred-and-sixty degree view where you could look out over the entire landscape. However, tenacious mosquitoes quickly marred the experience. Inland, small patches of houses were dotted here and there. The inhabitants were delighted when we stopped to say hello and offer candy to the shy kids. Visits were short; the battle with the fearsome mozzies was painfully lost.

'Heelllooo,' the grubby, five year old girl waved as we approached after our thirty-minute hike back from the expensive, inordinately slow Internet.

The Main Street included a couple of tiny supermarkets, together with a few basic cafes and bars. Locals serenely sped past on their thrumming two wheelers, and not one person failed to wave or nod a greeting. Our mud-smudged friend stopped practicing wiggling her tiny hips to investigate us, comparatively large, white folk. As we reached the group of kids, I raised my arms and wiggled my hips, trying to mimic her dance. The girls almost fell over, gasping and giggling at my efforts. We kept walking, but they were not prepared to let us go just yet. Spotting the new wooden drum Noel carried that we'd just purchased for a family gift, the sniggering group commandeered the drum and demanded us to dance. Noel tried the warrior dance we witnessed the previous night, their crashing knees with straw skirts made a formidable sight, but unfortunately Noel just looked like a chicken with two left legs. My wiggling was not much better and as the kids banged on the drum, they almost expired in fits of laughter.

Chores still had to be done. The tap where I gained permission to hand wash our clothes at was situated right next to a brick wall that was at the perfect height to relieve my back. The string of pine trees behind the neighbouring police station, next to the playing field, was perfect for drying. Noel filled *Mariah* with water, while I scrubbed our clothes. We hung out the washing, humming summer tunes in the warm, gentle breeze; the ambience of the island diluted the normally laborious tasks. As our colourful laundry flapped in the breeze, Noel returned with a small picnic. We sat on the soft, green grass, within the stillness of a Sunday. Our home, boat, and faithful travel companion, *Mariah* sat in sight at the end of the playing field, cooling in the breeze; we shared a quiet lunch, a calm contemplation, and maybe a short snooze.

Our arrival back to Australia was almost put on hold. Our travel bug infested bodies had come across the one place in seven years of circling the planet that we were seriously thinking of stopping at (for six months anyway). Earnest consideration to taking a break, living the Aitutakian way, and enjoying a rest, resonated through our salty minds. Already my body started to unwind. To add foundations to the idea, Noel had the offer of work. His carpentry and building skills attained him job offers all around the globe. Sense prevailed, and we decided that talking to the harbour master about hurricanes was our first step.

'We have had three hurricanes already this year and the water levels always rise up to our desks in this office.' Their office was over three metres above sea level. Noel and I backed out of the office and out of our dream. Faced with organising the boat for departure, rolling tummies in time with rolling seas and a collectively agreed "bad year" for the Pacific trades, we decided to bid farewell to Aitutaki.

As we sadly made our farewells to the locals, the goat still breathed the flowery scent that carried over the blossom-strewn garden. The skin we bought was from the island's drum maker, a second hand, clean, odourless skin, that would leave *Mariah* before we arrived in Australia. The goat's time, though, was short; a feast was planned... *Kia manuia* (may good fortune shine on you).

From Aitutaki, we had a short, smooth sail to Palmerston Island, where locals spoiled the cruising visitors in exchange for gifts. The anchorage was rolling within the swells of the mighty Pacific Ocean, and we stayed just a few days before heading to Niue.

Four or five day sails were now considered short hops. Like a well-oiled engine, Noel and I smoothly completed the tasks for setting sail, and our shifts ran like clockwork. As *Mariah* sailed herself towards our next destination, I started to wonder what would happen back in civilisation. In the meantime, Niue and a new set of experiences loomed over the horizon.

'If I don't go right now, I'm not going to do it,' my voice betrayed an ungainly combination of conviction and caution. I hoped the rest of the crowd couldn't hear it. They all moved aside to let me go, revealing through actions that they could hear the fear as much as I could taste it.

We were fifteen metres underground in a silent, echoing cave. Only the solemn plop of icy, fresh water could be heard, woven between our awed whispers. I took two big breaths, the chill of the encompassing sapphire water temporarily forgotten. Two metres down, with lungs bursting only moments after a big breath, I turned underwater to head through to the next cave. My thrashing arms and legs fought for propulsion, and I felt stuck in a current that did not exist. I saw the torch light from our guide in the next submerged cave and headed toward the surface, seeking much needed oxygen. I was that close to being able to breathe again. I knew I could make it. Suddenly, a firm hand reached down and pushed my head back under. I was coming up too early; my soft head was on course for sharp, jagged rock. Fighting to withhold my panic, I swam farther along and the hand released me. I broke back into my world, gasping in the sweet smell of air. In reality, I had been under water a few seconds and swam a few metres. 'That was pretty easy,' I grinned.

The unofficial tour of underwater caves was discreet and unsanctioned. If we had injured ourselves the responsibility would be at our door only. The sign to the entrance of the sunken paradise made it perfectly clear. Willy Kalah, our guide, took us on the tour for free; he owned a bar and hoped that we would pay him a visit – a good deal.

The alien surroundings and phallic like rock glistened with their golds and yellows brightened by our torch beams. The thriving green foliage around the startling blue pools of clear water were extraordinary. 'Wow,' 'oooh,' and 'arrhhh,' became the group's vocabulary between grunting from climbing up and down sheer faces of slippery rock with only a fraying rope to assist.

Later, at Willy's bar, he absorbed our weary minds in the tale of how his great grandfather was a pioneer in the island's banana export and import. The Kalah's have their roots deeply entrenched in the tiny island, completing work that present day cruisers are glad for. Centuries ago, the Kalah's had a hand in blasting through the rocks to enable supply ships to make their deliveries by a dock and enable today's travellers to make an easy landfall and haul their dinghies to a safe place.

Niue is a country in its own right. The small island sits like the gem set in a gold of ocean. Situated approximately 230 nautical miles directly east of Tonga and 672 nautical miles east of Suva in Fiji, Niue created a welcome rest while sailing between Palmerston Island and Tonga. Niue is one of the last jewels in the ornamental circumnavigation ring.

We met some interesting characters whilst here. The tears that pricked Mr. Premier's eyes were not from the whispering smoke of his cigarette, but rather his emotions. His eyes shone as he frankly described losing his wife. He lost her first when she was alive. He felt that he had neglected her, as he worked endless hours fulfilling his task of leader of Niue. He lost her again when she sadly left this world.

A mountain of a man sat beside him. His bodyguard seemed to have an easy time and enjoyed the myriad of conversations. As Mr. Premier sat with a few of us cruisers, sipping his cool beer in companionable chat, we could feel his excitement and love for his country. His honesty, friendliness, and down-to-earth spirit was refreshing and offers of residency were made with sincerity.

Twenty mooring buoys were on offer for visiting boats, a bargain at five American dollars per day. Anchoring was difficult within deep, coral strewn waters. With boats coming and going, most days there were one or two available moorings. Getting ashore was exciting. The sheer cliff face and rolling seas did not allow beach landings. An unprotected concrete jetty with a small crane was the only way to make landfall. Hoicking yourself and all your gear from dinghy to the slippery concrete steps was like riding a galloping horse while trying to stand up. Timing was critical: ride the swells and understand the movement before making your move. One unlucky blighter stayed in the dinghy while the crane was lowered towards them, having the lifting straps ready to start with was imperative. The person in the dinghy secured the hook, and the crane operator (whoever was standing nearest) could lift the dinghy. The person in the boat had a tough time in the rolling swells of the Pacific and then performed a balancing act as the dinghy was lifted up. A trolley was provided and we all lined our dinghies up neatly, it was like the car park at a supermarket. After just a few shaky starts, we all became dab hands at the process.

Alofi, Niue's main town, was small, friendly, and funky. The quiet streets carried the good-humoured laughter of local lads shooting pool. Shady trees stood proud outside the popular Internet cafe, under which a cruiser or two sat exchanging information as only water gypsies do. Watering holes perched on the headland, where we could peer thirty metres down over our silent boats, creating enticing dreams that we were fulfilling. Towards the end of the town, square blocks of concrete foundations sat in vivid gardens, where, once upon a time houses stood. In 2004, a violent hurricane kicked up waves high enough to reach over the massive rock structure and wash the buildings away. The hospital, lives, and dreams were carried away that year. The town was rebuilding, but it was a long way from flourishing. Flights to Niue were extraordinarily expensive, much desired tourist trade seemed too far out of reach.

Having a taste of mopeds in Aitutaki, we were eager to hire bikes and explore this tiny country to see what other gems this jewel had to offer. A small group was organised and three couples hired small, lightweight motorbikes (125cc).

James and Ann on board *Novia* (meaning sweetheart) were a typical British couple with an extra dose of daring. James had always wanted to ride a bike, but never had. Noel offered a five-minute verbal instruction, forgetting to point out the rear brake. The end of the instruction was finished with a flap of his hand saying, 'It's easy, you'll be right, mate.'

What James didn't realise was that Noel had been riding bikes all his life. James jumped on, started up, amazingly got the wheels turning first go, and flew straight into a bush. We were all more than slightly relieved he veered right into bushes, instead of left off the cliff face!

James came back on foot, with a few bloody scratches on his cheek. Ann was speechless and none of us knew what to say between belly cramping giggles.

'Ahem,' started James, 'ready, Ann?'

All heads turned to Ann with wide eyes.

'Yup,' she smiled, jumped on board, and off they went!

Two days later, at a local fete, James was teaching a fellow cruiser how to ride. The stoic, single mindedness and blind bravado of the British lives on.

The empty roads were perfect for novices and old hands alike. Like sailboats, the motorbikes allowed thoughts and ideas to enter our minds and spill out before they took hold.

The island's sixty-seven kilometre road worms through pockets of communities nearing extinction; vacant houses, bolted church doors, and limp business signs smothered the odd occupied home, where residents tried to shut out the failing town with pretty curtains and freshly painted front doors. Each town felt desolate, confirmed by the stray hungry dogs, bored grubby kids, and obvious lack of money.

On the positive side, hidden down unbeaten trails, Niue hid striking sights. Volcanic moonlike rock topped with skin tearing shards lined the path that weaved between the heavy jungles. Enormous ugly spiders hung in the trees, the females clearly carrying young. Breaking through the foliage, the pacified Pacific Ocean greeted us, and we watched the strength of the waves pummel the land. Enterprising locals had built ladders and steps to allow the adventurous to do their thing. Securely tied to a ten metre sheer drop was a strong wooden ladder. At the foot was an enclosed beach that, after traversing huge boulders, led to a secret garden. If a mermaid had stepped from the water and offered us a rainbow, it wouldn't have been a shock. In the peaceful silence, vivid climbing greens clung along the sheer rock faces, and startling blue clear pools urged us in for a cool swim.

Alas, the time ticked on and, again, and we had to say farewell. The too familiar hand that squeezed our hearts was back, to remind us of our lot – our life that was full of farewells. Next stop was Tonga, where our trusty home and transport, *Mariah II* had spent summers many years ago.

It was funny, as we got closer to home, with more miles and experience under our belts, the more fearful the journey became. Everything had gone so well so far; surely it was time for a drama?

As we dropped the mooring and watched Niue shrink in the distance, we knew we'd never return to this unique country and we felt privileged to have had the opportunity to experience this solitary little world.

The drama we thought we were due for arrived in the form of windy and his mates. Basically, it blew like shit all the way to Va'vau in Tonga. *Mariah* swept up and down the building seas while Noel and I clung on. There was no fear, no shouting, no stress. We knew *Mariah* so well that we knew she'd cope with the seas. We knew we would cope too. We also knew it would finally stop, at some point. Life was so different now on board. The romping wind and waves were uncomfortable and tiring, but that was all. A strong, proven boat and strong proven crew kept our shoulders relaxed and at ease. I felt like I could do this forever. The sailing had completely ceased being any sort of drama. It was the next chapter in our lives that would become the drama – the transition back onto land.

24

Absent from society, but not for long

Our stay in Tonga was a restful one; we had no need or desire to participate in tours. Noel and I were content enough to just enjoy the soft scenery and giggling kids splashing on shore. The kind welcome from the locals was enough to help us experience their way of life. After a few days rest we weighed anchor, bound for Fiji.

Once upon a time, we had left Coffs Harbour in NSW bound for Fiji, and a storm had blown us back as we could no longer fight the malevolent ocean. We had re-grouped and decided to follow the trade winds. Seven years later, we finally made it to Fiji, heading in the right direction, some 30,000 nautical miles later.

The Royal Suva Yacht Club was an island bar with chipped wood, plastic tablecloths, cheap beer, and reasonable food. Together with our friends on board *Iron Mistress* (Robert and Elyse), *My Chance* (Alim and Kian), and *Adverse Conditions* (Nana and Spencer), we all dressed up in our finery and enjoyed one of our last "on the road" meals together. We all planned to meet in New Caledonia and from there we would be parting to go our separate ways. Suddenly, it was ending.

Before we left the Fiji anchorage we witnessed a large waterspout not far from the anchorage. We watched intently, realising how lucky we had been on our voyage. There had been no real damage to *Mariah* or to us. In a way, this made us more nervous, as something was bound to happen now.

In Noumea, New Caledonia, we were all in a marina. With great French food, gleaming and expensive bars, we indulged in a little luxury before heading home. It seemed a poignant time, a parting of friends. We would head south, while most of the other boats were heading north in Australia or down to New Zealand.

The separation from our buddies was tougher than I imagined. We had not spent a great deal of time together, zigzagging between anchorages – sometime we met up, sometimes we didn't. But the ease of our friendships, the lack of expectations, and the fun times we had all shared gave a sense of belonging. Good friends and fun folk made our journey the incredible experience it was. We would miss them.

Australia had a horrid reputation of being one of the worst places in the world to check in to. It really wasn't if you followed their rules. Their rules were strict, but not hard to adhere by, and they were there for a reason.

We had an amazing sail into Bundaberg QLD. Within near perfect conditions, *Mariah* blasted her way back into Australian waters. Three days out, on flat seas, I was sitting in the cockpit naked (it was hot). Suddenly, I could hear an engine. I quickly tied on my sarong. There wasn't one boat in sight, so I looked up. The Australian Customs plane came so close that they could read *Mariah's* name off our bow!

'*Mariah II*, this is Australian Customs, how many people do you have on board?'

'Good afternoon! Two people on board.'

'Very good. Do you have any plants or animals?'

'No,' I replied. I always feel guilty with officials, even though I had never done anything wrong. However, I had read and re-read the rules and requirements for checking in, and I knew we were good. With a few more questions, they wished us well and flew off, flying over us every day until we reached port.

The unique colours of the Australian sky were drawing us home. As the sun sloped off behind the horizon, it painted the sky Aussie golds, which were woven with tinges of low pearly clouds.

For a few glorious moments, the sea was warmed by the reflection of yellow. We were absent from society, but not for long.

25

"I hate it"

On 11 November 2005, we completed our circumnavigation. Checking in was a breeze. With our paperwork in order, we were soon free to experience Bundaberg and make plans. 'If we don't leave soon, I'm flying to England!'

Queensland was hot; I had trouble coping in the heat. As soon as I stepped from the shower, I was a bundle of sweat.

'Why are you getting so hot and bothered?' a neighbouring cruiser had said to me.

It wasn't until later that they revealed they had air-conditioning!

The trip had been successful. But, we still had to coastal hop south, and it was now that things started to get tense.

We didn't really know where we'd end up. We had family in southern NSW, so that was a good start. Mel was due to have her baby any day, so Wollongong was our first stop.

After Noel cheerily became a grandad, we sought the next safe harbour south, which was Greenwell Point. A small, quaint town that would open up seemingly impossible doors and steer us to further adventures that we hadn't even dare dream of. But first we had to deal with the transition of being "home."

'I hate it; I just want to leave,' I said.

Just one month back and my skin already crawled with an erratic, insatiable, itch. I felt heavy. I just didn't fit, and I was already fed up with trying.

For the first month back, I was numb. Family issues had to be dealt with. Noel's mum had moved into a home; this was an incredibly emotional time. Her house had to be cleared. Sixty-seven years worth of stuff had to be moved – what was the point? Memories? We all have memories. Should we keep the boxes of photos? What's the point, they would only sit in another person's attic, collecting dust and the perplexed questions of, 'I wonder who that is?'

Noel and I planned to collect nothing further.

'You can't get away from bureaucracy,' a friend wrote in an email back to me after I had been whinging about the crummy life back in Australia. I disagreed. Yes, we had had to check into countries. But that was it. The freedom I had held had been lost. I didn't really understand why. We were still on the boat; we were not working for someone else. Our time was our own – but was it?

Family were nearby, and we were obliged to become involved. We wanted to, of course; we wanted to see them and catch up, so that wasn't the problem. We both have wonderful families that had supported us fabulously. So what was going on? What was this chain I felt squeezing around my neck, the despair, the slight depressed feeling?

It was dealing with land people and what that meant: phones for a start ('What? You *haven't* got a mobile?'), taxes, supermarkets, curtains, divorce, carpets, arguments, garages, TV.

TV! Yikes, I hated it. The sadness overwhelmed me – murder, sexual assault, torture, war, floods, hurricanes, riots, politicians, lies, death, and destruction. We hadn't watched TV for years; we rarely tuned into the news or purchased a newspaper. The head-in-the-sand theory had been a blessed relief from the woes of the world and some of the hideous people that inhabited it. But now it came back to us in full force, *everyone* watched the news and we couldn't escape it. I felt like crying every time I heard it. I wanted to be an ostrich again. I wanted to get back to my simple way of life.

Within the first couple of weeks of our return, we discussed the purchase of a phone and a car. I refused to get a phone and did my best to avoid buying a car. I just didn't want any of that stuff.

A month later it became worse: family issues across the globe dragged us down. We were stuck in a lovely port, but were at the whim of the wind, which was blowing against us – we felt trapped. We were rudderless within a storm of transition.

We had to decide which foot to put forward, the left or right. We had to become proactive and do something for us; which was funny, as we'd been doing something for us for the past nine years! Perhaps enjoying life had made us selfish.

We started to think logically. We had years of sea-time under our belts, so we decided to put that to good use. We tried to research what courses were available, but it was January and everyone was on holiday. Our life was in limbo.

We did start to settle in, but continued to feel out of sync and kilter, even with new friends. I had to turn things around in my head. I had to see that this wasn't the end of the adventure; it was the beginning of a new chapter.

Finally, we got back onto the right track. I started to enjoy the fact that we weren't moving all the time. I liked knowing where the shops were. Focussing on the positives helped and, really, what had we to complain about? We were healthy, happy, and had time to plan more escapades.

We enrolled in a full time, six week, six days' a week maritime course. During which, I did so well, I was asked to teach the following class!

We sold our house in England and purchased a little cottage in Greenwell Point, NSW. We sold *Mariah*. We never thought we would, but we started to enjoy land-life: a bathroom, a full- length mirror, grass, and 'good mornings' from friendly town folk.

We joined the Marine Rescue, and with further training we became skippers. I was their first woman skipper. I had some issues with some of the crewmembers, but I was much stronger than they realised. I'd been dealing with testosterone-fuelled comments on boats for years; it was water off a duck's back. The guys that chose to come out with me on the boats I valued immensely.

I could now recall conversations with people on board *Mariah* that had suggested Noel should be the one to bring us in to ports, saying, in other words, they did not think I was up to it. When this had happened, I remembered shedding some private tears. People I deeply respected had judged me. I had felt my confidence drain away; I had wanted to give up, the fight felt too hard. Now I realised that these people had helped me. I had proven my abilities; I had worked my way through the doubts.

I am a fighter, and with my experience on *Mariah*, I had completed successful rescues in violent weather. I was now able to pass on my knowledge to students, witnessing them blossom in exciting maritime careers. I had learned enough to help others. I was a professional, and when Noel and I went on to study for our Master IV course (qualifying us to skipper vessels up to eighty metres), I was chuffed to receive many compliments from my tutors about my work. During our boat practicals, guess who did the best boat handling of the day?

I had become a fully trained commercial skipper. I was a qualified Marine Engine Driver. In fact, I did so well in our class (twelve men and one woman – me), I received joint top-of-the-class award.

It was then I was asked to teach maritime classes. I learned a lot more from students willing to share their knowledge. Of course, I had those students who couldn't be taught by a woman. But they were few and far between. I learned something from every person on those courses and not just about boats.

I had also witnessed the students develop faith in me. Once I had proven myself to them, I gained a remarkable amount of respect that made my teaching experience something I would return to time and again.

Back on land, we read about how dangerous things were while cruising – in Borneo you could no longer play with the orangutans, crocodiles prevented swimming in Panama, cruisers could not go through the canal without an expensive agent. I wondered how true it all was. From experience, I figured it was exaggerated semi-truths. I had learned not to let other people's enjoyment of creating fear affect me.

I had learned a hell of a lot. Leading a water gypsy's life for almost nine years changed me in many ways. I have become more open minded. I practice forgiveness, remembering that I never really knew what is going on in other people's lives; a curt remark on a first meeting may not be rudeness, it maybe shyness or fear.

I have learned to think more of myself, my abilities, my body, and my personalities (yes, there are a few). I've learned to trust myself. I've unbound my emotional corset. I am getting to know *me*.

On the flip side, in other ways I have become bigoted, frustrated, and sometimes I have short-sighted, frighteningly fierce opinions that I cannot seem to control at times; my views on kindness, evil, mistreatment, and fairness. I thought I would be stronger, but at times I think I'm weaker. Any kind of sadness, whatever shape or form in this world, cripples me emotionally.

As for Noel and I, we are unlike most couples we meet. There is a deep unwavering respect. Our loyalty to each other sometimes overwhelms me. Our trust is remarkable; we've been responsible for each other's lives. That does something to you, it really does. We may not be doe-eyed at each other all the time, but the bond between us is mind-blowing.

I am older, wiser; I've been introduced to middle-age (isn't *that* a bundle of fun), but I'm proud of my grey hairs. I have earned every single one of them.

Perhaps it is not about finding where you fit, but with whom you fit with. Well, that certainly applies to us. It has been fifteen years since I started this book. Noel and I have been married more than sixteen years now. We sailed the world, as you now know. But since then we have become qualified mariners, we purchased another sail boat in San Francisco, and spent two years bringing her home and importing her into Australia.

We bought and sold a house in Australia. We trekked part of the Bicentennial National Trail in Australia with five horses, a tent, and just the two of us for an incredible, eye-opening nine weeks.

I found a depth of fulfilment I didn't know existed. I've found that I can choose happiness.

Some time in Europe with my immediate family is our next plan and maybe a canal boat.

The ups and downs of the journey are worth it. Life is for living, being brave, and taking chances. We've had our hearts broken with farewells, we've been excited beyond belief, but we still haven't found "home." Maybe we will wander all our lives; it's just in our makeup. The point is, home is with each other, wherever that is on our planet.

Life at sea is a love-hate relationship, a roller coaster. The journey becomes etched on your skin. We learned something new each day, about sailing and ourselves. Sailing the oceans isn't easy, but offers magnificent rewards with perseverance. We whinged about the effort, but secretly we were glad, because if it was easy, everyone would be doing it.

Now, it's a song, a drumbeat, a waft of salt air, or heady diesel fumes that activates our memories and transports us back to those days on *Mariah*; the chug of a marine engine is enough to spark the tiniest sense of sea-sickness, that bout of anxiousness prior to a voyage – that unmatched excitement.

This kind of journey was an experience as a whole, not just hops from one place to the next – it was the preparation, research, learning, trying new things, romance, escapade, the rich harvest of adventures together.

And, yes, it is about the good yarn at the end of it all.

Time Line

1998
8 August 1998 – became the proud owners of *Mariah II*
17 August – Brisbane
6 November – Moreton Bay
1 December – Brisbane and 'Jack's becoming quite the apprentice, changing filters and oil, soldering wires, helping me fit "Wander."'

1999
25 January – Coxswain's course
19 June – left Coffs Harbour, NSW, for first attempt to Fiji
1 August – 'doubt we will traverse an ocean' – back in Mooloolaba

2000
10 Aug 2000 – new engine, water tanks fuel tanks and headed north to Darwin
6 September – Darwin
14 September – left Darwin, Australia (two days after I received my Australian residency!)
17 September – Ashmore reef – finally free!
20 September – received our first ever Weatherfax!
24 September – arrived into Bali harbour
10 October – Kangean Island 14 October – Borneo
23 October – Crossed equator for the first time 31 October – Nongsa Point marina
9 November – departed Lumut 14 November – Langkawi
9 December – Ko Rok Nok
12 December – arrived Phi Phi Don
19 December – Yacht Haven, Phuket

2001

18 January – left Thailand

19 January – traversed the Nicobars and lightning storm

24 January – Noel wrote in the log, 'hey, we're in 3,800 metres of water! – feel better?!'

27 January – Sri Lanka

14 February – St. Valentine's Day, arrived at Maldives

24 February – Noel wrote in the log, 'someone has stolen the moon.' 3 March – arrived in Oman

21 March – arrived Eritrea (Massawa)

4 April – scampered into Marsa Halaib – strong winds

10 April – left Marsa Halaib

11 April – Ras Banias, another hidey hole (bilge/water/vomit) 12 April – *Solmates* arrived and did their unique flour delivery! 14 April – left Ras Banias, stopped at Fury Bay

15 April – arrived Lui Lu – safe haven in strong winds

19 April – anchored at Marsa Imbarak taking shelter 21 April – El Quesire anchorage – taking shelter

22 April – Safaga at last

30 April – arrived Suez into sand storm

5 May – on second leg of canal and out to the Med 7 May – Larnaca Cyprus

1 June – left Cyprus

3 June – now on a course for Rhode Island (Lindos)

12 June – Kaio, Greece, small beautiful harbour

14 June – left Kaio en route to Kalamata to meet my sisters

27 June – left Kalamata Marina

28 June – I found the Snickers bars and kept eating them! (Noel hides my chocolate).

30 June – arrived in Bangara, end of Messina straits 1 July – left Bangara

2 July – arrived Lipari (marina for shower treat)
5 July – arrived at Olbia, North West Sardinia
11 July – Cala de Volpe
13 July – Ajaccio in Corsica (France whoo hoo)
23 July – arrived Golfe de Fos – start the French canals
October finished French canals

Remainder of **2001** and all **2002** we stayed in England recouping the coffers.

2003
10 June – left Shenley
12 July – Falmouth harbour
4 August – Bay of Biscay
6 August – Muros, Spain
20 August – Leixious Portugal
23 August – anchored at Barra de Aveiro, thick fog followed us in
1 September – my new niece is born, Samantha Louise Lawrence
2 September – arrived Lisbon marina
9 September – anchored Caiscais (pronounced Cashkysh)
5 October – Sines (our tenant in our UK house gives notice)
8 October – arrived Casablanca
10 October – left Casablanca – note in log: 'lots of boats tonight, I especially like the ones that feel it necessary to turn off their navigation lights as they approach us!'
12 October – arrived Agadir
15 October – Port Naos, Lanzarote, met *Frodo* here
17 October – Rubicon Marina, Mum and Dad holiday with us
2 November – my new nephew is born, Efezino Owhe
20 November – Grand Canaries – Noel's brother Den passes away
27 November – hit a whale

1 December – Isle de Sal in the Cape Verdes. Noel's sister-in-law, Joy, passes away.
10 December – left Cape Verdes for Barbados
27 December – landfall Barbados after 17 days! Arrival into Speightstown
30 December – moved to Bridgetown anchorage after having to move in middle of night (boat on rocks!)

2004
29 January – farewell to Barbados and *Frodo*
30 January – St Lucia
12 February – Rodney Bay
19 February – left Martinique
21 February – anchored in beautiful port of Portsmouth, Dominica
28 February – en route to Guadaloupe – only 20 miles away 6 March – leaving Guadaloupe for Puerto Rico
Passed Monseratt, volcano spitting ash
10 March – anchored at San Juan
13 April – anchored at Mayaguana Bahamas, awaiting front to pass
20 April – left Mayaguana (didn't check in)
24 April – arrived at Lake Worth, Palm Beach, Florida and nearly sunk the boat!
30 April – Mum and Dad spent time with us
Completed The Great Loop well into 2004

During the rest of **2004** (from October) we were in Alabama and did the trip to the UK to sort out our house.

2005
5 March – what a year! – leaving Demopolis Alabama
6 March – rang 'Tash (*Frodo*) in Holland, they've had twin girls (Debby and Kim)

17 March – short run to Tampa
26 March – Florida Keys
27 March – Dry Tortugas
30 March - Cuba, Havana
6 April – anchored in San Pedro Bay, South Cuba, awaiting better weather
9 April – Caymens at last (birds visited, died!) Find Dad
16 April – Jamaica, anchored for one night – Dad a real trooper
21 April – San Blas
24 April – Colon Panama, greeted by Barry & Judy on *Theta* with a heavenly breakfast
28 April – all aboard *Theta* as line-handlers and practice run through the canal
4 May – Colin arriving into Panama to do transit with us on *Mariah*
13 May – leaving Balboa
21 May – crossed the equator for the second time
22 May – Galapagos
28 June -Fatu Hiva
11 June – Daniels Bay
15 July – Tuamotos
21 July – Pape'ete Tahiti, Melanie spent four weeks on board with us
6 September – Aitutaki
14 September – Palmerston Island
22 September – Niue
27 September – Tonga
21 October – left Fiji for New Caledonia (arrived at Fiji between 11/10 and 20/10 – this part of log book damaged!)
28 October – Noumea marina
11 November – arrived in Bundaberg QLD and completed our circumnavigation

2006
January 26th – Matilda Jade was born, Noel's a Grandad!
January – moored at Greenwell Point, NSW
October – sailed south to Moruya to attend Master 5 course
December – bought house in Greenwell Point

2007 – sad time, as we sold *Mariah* and a happy time, as we started a new chapter.

Map of our route

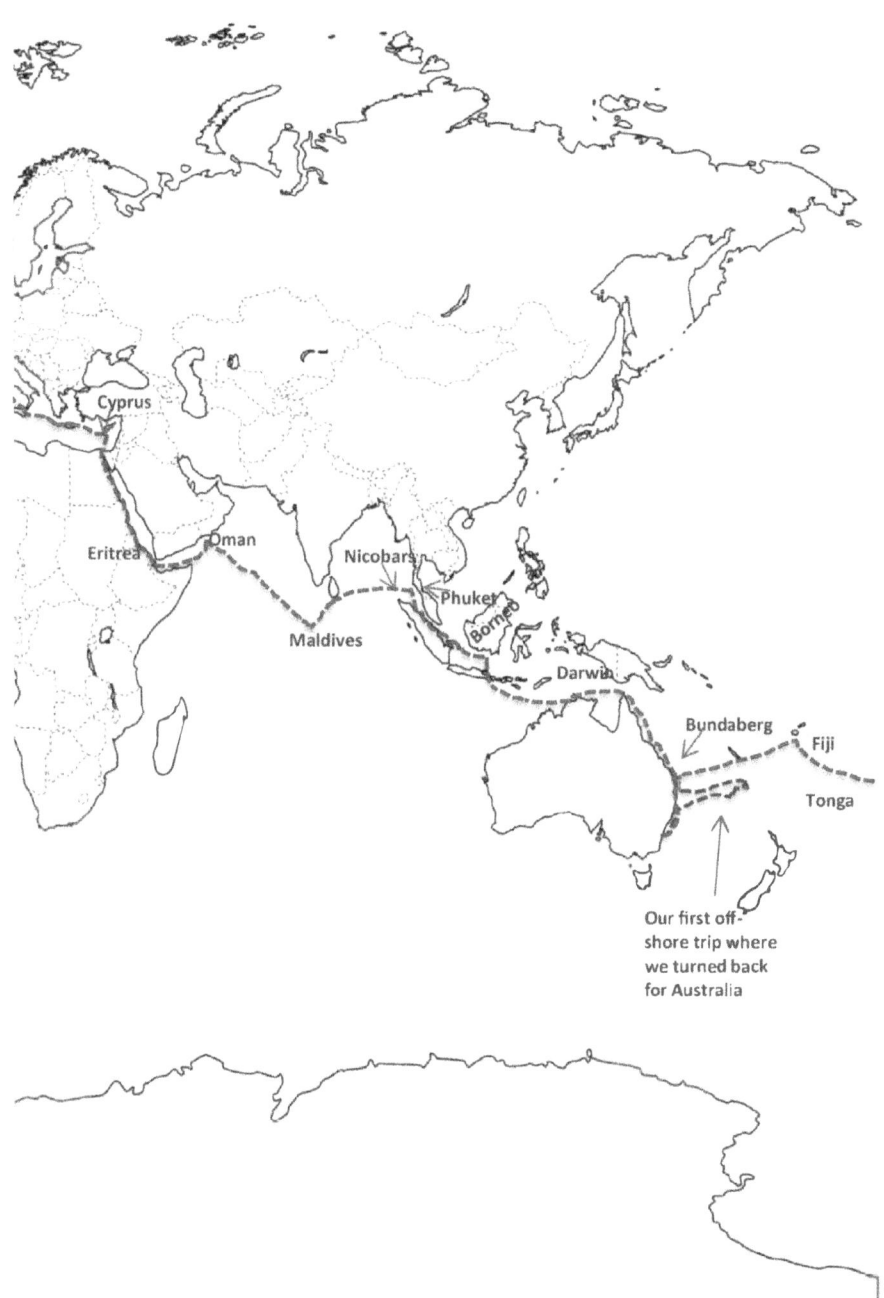

Glossary of Nautical Terms

Apparent wind: The wind as it is experienced on board a moving sailing vessel, as a result of the combined effects of the true wind and the boat's speed.

Backing sails: Pushing out a sail so that the wind fills it from the opposite side. It is used to slow a boat. In effect, it is stalling the sail by putting the wind at its 'back'. The sail is no longer drawing the boat along, but rather acting as a brake.

Beam: Widest part of boat.

Bowsprit: A spar running out from a ship's bow, to which the forestays are fastened.

Broaching: When a sailing vessel loses control and is forced sideways to the wind and waves. This can become very dangerous in heavy seas as the boat will often heel heavily, leading to capsize. The change in direction is called *broaching-to*.

Canoe Stern or Double-ender: Describing a vessel with no transom at the stern, both the bow and stern come to a point.

Collision Regulations or Col Regs or Rules of the Road: International regulations for preventing collisions at sea.

Cush drive: Part of an engine drive-train that is designed to reduce stress from engine torque damaging other components during gear or throttle changes.

Cutter Rigged Sloop: One masted sailboat, similar to a Bermuda sloop, i.e. forestay meeting the backstay at the top of the mast. A cutter rig has the addition of an inner forestay. The inner forestay can carry the staysail or storm jib. Both our boats had this type of rig with furlers on the forestay and slab reefing on the main.

Displacement: In maritime the displacement (mass) of a floating boat equals, exactly, the mass of the water it displaces. Remember Archimedes principle? - *any 'body' partially or completely submerged in a fluid is buoyed up by a force equal to the weight of the fluid displaced by the body.* Another way to say it is; a floating object displaces a volume of water, equal to the mass of the object. As an example, when you get into a bath of water, the water rises a certain amount. Weigh that amount of water (the amount it has risen by) and that would be your displacement.

Draft: Maximum depth of vessel in the water.

Drogue: A conical or funnel-shaped device with open ends, towed behind a boat to reduce speed and/or improve stability. We used a Sea Squid. We named it Mr Squiddly!

Faraday Cage: An earthed metal screen surrounding a piece of equipment to exclude electrostatic and electromagnetic influences. A metal oven can work as a great place to safeguard the GPS in an electric storm.

Foot (of sail): The foot of a sail is its lowest edge, bound by the clew and the tack (the clew is the aft corner, and the tack is the forward corner).

Fuel cock: A valve that is used to control the flow of diesel.

Genoa: A type of large jib-sail (pronounced like the city, or as *jenny*). The term *genoa* is often used interchangeably with *jib*, but technically there is a clear delineation. A jib is only as large as the fore-triangle, which is the triangular area formed by the mast, deck or bowsprit, and forestay. A genoa is larger, with the leech going past the mast and overlapping the mainsail. To maximize sail area the foot of the sail is generally parallel and very close to the deck when close hauled. Genoas are categorized by the percentage of overlap.

Gunwales: The upper edge or planking of the side of a boat or ship.

Gypsy (on anchor windlass/winch): A notched wheel that engages the links of a chain.

HF: See Radios (below).

Hove to: Heaving-to or to hove-to involves backing your jib, releasing your mainsail and pushing and holding the tiller away. This causes conflicting forces on the boat. The backed jib is trying to push the bow away from the wind and the rudder is turning the boat into the wind. The flapping mainsail and the backed jib prevent air flow over the sail and therefore stops the driving motion. Heaving-to is a sailing tactic that gives you time to stop and rest, wait for daylight for a safe entry into a new port, and when the conditions are rough.

Jib: A triangular staysail set ahead of the foremost mast of a sailing boat. Its tack is fixed to the bowsprit, to the bow, or to the deck. The clew does not extend aft past the mast.

Jib sheeted amidships: The jib sail was hauled in to the middle of the boat, using both sheets.

Jibe or Gybe: A sailing manoeuvre whereby a sailing vessel that is reaching downwind turns its stern through the wind, so that the wind direction changes from one side of the boat to the other.

Leech (of sail): The aft edge of the sail, between the head and the clew.

Low or low pressure system: A low pressure area, or a low for short, is a region where the atmospheric pressure is lower than that of a surrounding area. A low pressure system develops when warm and moist air rises from the Earth's surface. Air near the centre of this mass is usually unstable. As the warm and humid air rises, it can become unstable enough to produce rain, storms and strong winds.

Luff (of sail): The forward, or leading edge, of the sail, between the head and the tack.

Main or mainsail or mains'l: Usually the most important sail, raised on the aft side of the main (or only) mast of a sailing vessel.

On the hard: Where a boat has been hauled out of the water and is placed in a yard.

On the quarter: If the wind is on the boat's quarter, it is said to be on a direction of forty-five degrees or less from the stern of the boat. (Not directly behind and not on the beam (side) of the boat, but in-between).

Painter: Is a rope that is attached to the bow of a dinghy, or other small boat, and used for tying up or towing.

Pick: Another name for an anchor.

Pole out: See Spinnaker Pole.

Radios: Marine Radios: VHF (very high frequency), short range. Maximum range is usually when aerials are in line of sight. HF (high frequency) -long range radio, works by a radio wave signal that is transmitted, it then bounces off the ionosphere, and reflects down to another point on earth (the ionosphere consists of layers of ionized gas situated a few hundred miles above earth). This means that the range of the HF radio could be thousands of miles, with good equipment, set-up, conditions and propagation (behaviour of radio waves). (HF can be referred to as SSB, which means Single Side Band).

RIB: Rigid Inflatable Boat.

Rounding up: Rounding up is when your sailboat, against your will, automatically turns up into the wind. Rounding up is caused by many factors. One is too much wind and force aloft which tends to heel the boat over, when you have too much mainsail set. Another is the centre of pressure of wind on the sails moves far aft which then pushes the aft of the boat downwind and thus the front of the boat up wind. It is prevented by reducing sail and/or easing sheets.

Scheds/Nets: Radio Scheds and radio Nets are 'Schedules' and 'Networks'. This just means that they are a planned meeting of people on the radio at a set time and frequency.

Seacock: A valve sealing off an opening through a ship's hull below or near to the waterline (e.g. one connecting a ship's galley sink to the sea).

Sextant: An instrument with a graduated arc of one-hundred-and-twenty degrees and a sighting mechanism, used for measuring the angular distances between objects and especially for taking altitudes in navigation.

Sheets: In sailing, a sheet is a line (rope, cable or chain) used to control the movable corner(s) (clews) of a sail.

Snubbers: Used to prevent transferring the shock load from the anchor chain to the boat.

Speed – over the ground and through the water: Speed over the ground is true speed, a GPS provides speed over the ground. Speed through the water is how fast you are moving through the water.

Spinnaker Pole/Whisker Pole: A spinnaker pole is a spar used on sailboats to help support and control a variety of headsails, particularly the spinnaker.

Spinnaker sail: A special type of sail that is designed specifically for sailing off the wind from a reaching course to downwind. The spinnaker fills with wind and balloons out in front of the boat when it is deployed, called *flying*. It is constructed of very lightweight fabric, and is often brightly coloured. The use of this sail is usually limited to apparent winds under 12-15 knots.

Staysail or stays'l: A fore-and-aft rigged jib sail whose luff can be affixed to an inner forestay (aft of the forestay), running forward from a mast to the deck. Triangular staysails set forward of the foremost mast are called jibs, headsails, or foresails. The innermost such sail on a cutter, schooner, and many other rigs having two or more foresails is referred to simply as *the staysail*, while the others are referred to as jibs or flying jibs. The inner jib of a yacht with two jibs is called the staysail, and the outer (foremost) the jib. This combination of two jibs is called a cutter rig. There are differences between European and American terminology, however, a sailboat with one mast rigged with two jibs and a mainsail is called a cutter.

Storm jib (or any storm sail): A sail of smaller size and stronger material than the corresponding one used in ordinary weather.

Tacking: A sailing manoeuvre by which a sailing vessel turns its bow through the wind, placing the apparent wind on the opposite bow.

Traffic Separation Zone or Scheme: An area in the sea where navigation of ships is highly regulated. It is meant to create lanes in the water, and ships in a specific lane are all going in (roughly) the same direction.

Transom: Flat stern of the ship, at ninety degrees to the fore and aft line.

VHF: See Radios (above).

Victualling: To take on or obtain victuals (victuals: food, supplies, provisions).

Wake (of vessel): A vessel's wake is the region of recirculating flow immediately behind it, caused by the flow of surrounding water around the boat.

Water line: The level normally reached by the water on the side of a ship.

Wind Vane: Wind vane self-steering gear is an entirely mechanical device which senses the apparent wind direction and holds the vessel on a course relative to it. The power to steer is provided by the force of moving water over the water vane part of the wind vane apparatus.

Windward: Facing the wind.

Yankee: A Yankee is a high clewed headsail and is a very common sail on an off-shore yacht. Having the clew set high allows the waves to wash past the foot of the sail without adding extra stress loads on the sail. This sail can be used for reaching and upwind sailing.

From the Author

Thanks for purchasing and reading *Of Foreign Build* - I hope you enjoyed it. A lot of people don't realise that the best way to help an author is to leave a review – if you did enjoy my story, please return to the site you bought it from and leave a review. It doesn't need to be long, a few words as to why you enjoyed the book is fine, and so very much appreciated.

I love hearing from readers and other authors alike, so if you'd like to stay in touch and be the first to find out about forthcoming books and our travels/escapades, why not drop by and visit me at:

    www.jackieparry.com
    www.noelandjackiesjourneys.com
    FB: Noel and Jackie's Journeys
    FB: SisterShip Training
    www.sistershiptraining.com
    www.sailingeden.com

Acknowledgements

A huge thank you to the following people for their feedback and support during the writing process for Of Foreign Build: Rachel Amphlett, Anne Norris, Nick Furmidge and Carole Erdman Grant.

To Danielle Rose – your professionalism, advice and support helped shape my book into what it should be, thank you.

To my family and friends – thanks for all your support in whatever form you've provided it. I love writing and appreciate everyone allowing me the time I need to do so.

To everyone who's been following me on Twitter and Facebook, etc., I sincerely thank you too. Your positive messages and reviews mean more to me than you'll ever know.

Our Other Adventures

This Is It: 2 Hemispheres, 2 People, and 1 Boat

Reviews:
"It made me laugh out loud, it also made me cry; it had me perching on the edge of my seat."

"This story is raw, emotional, and dangerous!"

"I couldn't put it down!"

A Standard Journey: 5 Horses, 2 People, and 1 Tent

Reviews:
"Special and unique."

"A hauntingly beautiful book."

"Will stick with readers for a long time."

Cruisers' AA (Reference Book)

Reviews:
"Probably the most comprehensive reference book designed for preparation for a cruising life."
"A remarkable reference, there is a depth of information that beggars the imagination."
"This is a new and fascinating insight on how to go cruising."

www.ingramcontent.com/pod-product-compliance
Lightning Source LLC
Chambersburg PA
CBHW062055290426
44110CB00022B/2605